Intimate Activism

Intimate Activism

≡

The Struggle for Sexual Rights

in Postrevolutionary Nicaragua

CYMENE HOWE

DUKE UNIVERSITY PRESS

DURHAM AND LONDON   2013

Printed in the United States of America on acid-free paper ∞
Typeset in Whitman by Tseng Information Systems, Inc.

Library of Congress Cataloging-in-Publication Data
Howe, Cymene.
Intimate activism : the struggle for sexual rights in
postrevolutionary Nicaragua / Cymene Howe.
pages cm
Includes bibliographical references and index.
ISBN 978-0-8223-5437-6 (cloth : alk. paper)
ISBN 978-0-8223-5450-5 (pbk. : alk. paper)
1. Gay liberation movement—Nicaragua. 2. Sexual rights—
Nicaragua. 3. Lesbian activists—Nicaragua. 4. Nicaragua—
Politics and government—1990– I. Title.
HQ76.8.N5H69 2013
306.76′6097285—dc23
2013011688

CONTENTS

≡

ACKNOWLEDGMENTS

=

Sitting down to write these acknowledgments is an exercise in
nostalgic reckoning, through many years, places, experiences,
and relationships. While this book is now complete, it is hard
to know precisely where it began. I am sure it had something
to do with growing up with "two grandmas" on my mom's side
of the family and never really thinking there was anything out
of the ordinary about that. I am sure that my first trip to Nicaragua as a punky backpacker was influential, too. I was im-
pressed with how loquacious and proud Nicaraguans were,
especially when they were reflecting on their revolutionary experiences—and rightly so. I am sure that this book had some
start in the fact that I was exposed to feminist teachers from
high school on and that I was able to read Judith Butler's *Gender Trouble*, when it first came out, at Berkeley as an under-
graduate. This is all to say that it may be impossible to know
where a project like this one, which spans so much of my life
in so many dimensions, began. It has involved a lot of sweat
and a lot of screen time. And in the end—and this is a truism,
to be sure—I could not have done it without you all.

In the town of San Marcos, in Nicaragua's western highlands, I spent many days and nights talking with Chefo, who
shared his experiences, both good and bad, as a *cochón* ("fag").
Chefo made sexuality and gender constructions far more real,
and far more complex, than they ever were in the pages of academic life or in my experiences in the United States. I thank
him. The stories he told me in the early 1990s were foundational to the work I have done in Nicaragua over the years. I
am glad that he and I got to share a bottle of Flor de Caña and
dance together again, just a few years ago. San Marcos was a

wonderful place for me, and the generosity of Alba Luz, Carolina, Inti, and Maria Berta made it so.

In Managua, I had the honor of being able to work with many committed advocates for sexual and gender rights. They generously gave me their time, explaining the intricacies and intimacies of life in Nicaragua and the life of the *lucha* as well. Without their dedication and without their investment in our conversations, this research and this text surely never would have come into being. While I will maintain the confidentiality that we agreed to at the time these conversations took place, I suspect that all of you will know who you are, even if only by your given names. For all of the information, and all of the good times, I thank Ada Luz, Agner, Amy, Evelyn, Ana C., Ana P., Ana Q., Bismark, Brigitte, Carolina, Christian, Clara, Elena, Elieth, Erick, Fernando, Geraldine, Hazel, Helen D., Helena R., Ileana, Isabel, Julia, Kefrén, Maira, Maria Lidia, Marlene, Mary, Mavíla, Mikel, Patricia, Rita, Roger, Rosario, Rubén, Sheyla, and Victoria. I extend my very deep appreciation to Martita, whose presence throughout my fieldwork, and beyond, has been inspiring. While conducting my research over the course of three years, I lived with two different families who, again, were kind and patient and, luckily for me, wonderful people to talk to and hang out with. So I thank Norma and Noreli, and I thank Doña Xilo and the whole family.

A considerable amount of appreciation goes to my friends and mentors at the University of New Mexico, who spent countless hours with me, in and out of class, helping me to think through this project. Without the intellectual generosity and supportive friendship of Les Field in particular, I certainly would not have become the anthropologist I am today; I hope I have even a fraction of the commitment and compassion that he does. Elizabeth Hutchison, Louise Lamphere, Roger Lancaster, Carole Nagengast, Sylvia Rodriguez, and Marta Weigel were also caring and productively critical companions and guides in my graduate school sojourn. Someone once told me that choosing one's dissertation committee is like getting to select your academic parents; if in some karmic way that is in fact true, then I am most pleased with my choice of kin. In addition to being inspirational sexuality scholars, Martin Manalansan and Ellen Lewin have been truly phenomenal with their feedback and, not incidentally, encouragement on this project. At various junctures along the way, all of the following friends and colleagues have given me valuable responses to this work, as well as intellectual support and companionship. I thank them all: Florence Babb, Jodi Barnes, Andrew Bickford, Evelyn Blackwood, Katherine Bliss, Yarimar Bonilla, Dominic Boyer, Hector Carrillo, Jane Fajans, James Faubion, Melissa Fisher, Katherine Frank, William French, Nia Georges, Victoria González-Rivera, Rosemary Hennessey, Gilbert Herdt, Nell Haynes, Sarah Horton, William Leap, Paul Liffman, Lois Lorentzen, Jeffrey Mantz, Michelle Marzullo, Linda Mayo, Lavinia Nicolae, Ratheesh Radhikrishna, Margaret Randall, Brian Riedel, Susan Terrio, Niels Teunis, Deborah Tolman, Terry Turner, Jennifer Tyburczy, Marike van Gijsel, David Vine, and Thomas Walker. The participants in the Mellon Faculty Seminar at Cornell University (2005–2006, 2006–2007), as well as all of the participants in the Sexuality Studies Working Group at Rice University, have my appreciation for their commentaries and enthusiasm. The many students with whom I have had the pleasure of working over the past few years also deserve accolades for the ways in which they have shaped this book through their excellent questions and clarifications. They have pushed me to create a lucid text out of what is, for me, an immensely compelling story that my Nicaraguan interlocutors have lived.

Financial support, as we all know, is absolutely crucial to fieldwork and to our ability to carry out research and write. I am grateful to the Fulbright Foundation, the National Women's Studies Association, and the Mellon Foundation for their remunerative support of this project. The institutions at which I have worked over the past handful of years also have contributed to field excursions and supported my ability to develop this project and the book itself; thanks are due to American University, Cornell University, Rice University, San Francisco State University, and the University of New Mexico. This manuscript has seen a lot of locales, and I believe little epistemic bits of Washington, D.C., San Francisco, Ithaca, Albuquerque, and Houston, and of course Managua, are woven into the text itself.

Anonymous reviewers at *Cultural Anthropology*, *City and Society*, GLQ, the *Journal of Latin American and Caribbean Anthropology*, and Duke University Press have provided productive and engaged comments on this text as it has developed and matured. I appreciate their time, intelligence, and close readings of the manuscript in various stages. Sue Deeks provided excellent, detailed copyediting on the manuscript, and Liz Smith, Sara Leone, Naomi Linzer and Amy Buchanan also have my deepest appreciation for the work they have done bringing this book to press. Ken

Wissoker definitely deserves recognition and then some for guiding this project to completion. His support and cheerful e-mails have meant a lot.

My utmost thanks go to my mom and dad for their overall support of me as a fledgling being and of course their willingness to hear yet one more report about Nicaraguan sexual rights activists. Barbara and John Boyer have also been an important source of support and encouragement to me; it is good to have writers in the family, if only to know that there is always a sympathetic wordsmith nearby. Melissa Abrams, Brenda Maiale, and Rocky Patten should also count themselves among the most appreciated friends, correspondents, and people mentioned here.

Finally, I reserve one last thank you — one that is not really captured by the concept of an "acknowledgment." And that is for the love of my life. You know who you are.

＝

The Struggle

Nicaragua is a place where people like to talk, even about things one is not really supposed to talk about. Because the subject of homosexuality has been not only taboo but illegal to "promote" or "propagandize" for most of the past two decades, Nicaraguans have needed more than a little courage to speak about sexuality, rights, and social change. Marta, who has spent long years in the struggle for sexual rights, was my closest friend in Nicaragua. We often shared our opinions about the differences between lesbian and gay rights movements in Nicaragua and el Norte (the United States). But our conversations were also peppered with more quotidian topics: Marta's concerns about her mother's health, stories about former girlfriends, or speculations about the plot twists in Nicaragua's first social-justice soap opera. Marta and I spent many hours at Galería Praxis, an art gallery and café in the middle of Managua. Galería Praxis was a place that evoked many of the significant political trajectories that have affected Nicaragua over the past three decades. The café has hosted celebrations for Orgullo Lésbico-Gay (Lesbian and Gay Pride), and its moniker, "Praxis," conjures Marx's humanist call to combine theory with practice, a reminder of Nicaragua's Sandinista Revolution and the politics of liberation that have been fundamental to contemporary sexual rights activism. But Marta and I also liked Praxis simply because it served excellent *tostones* (fried plantains), just salty enough to make us really appreciate our cold orange Fantas. Sheltered from the late afternoon sun by the broad leaves of banana trees, Marta explained to me one day that she believed that Nicaraguans were changing the way they thought about homosexuality:

> They're beginning to understand same-sex sexuality in different terms. . . . The people are becoming more educated. It used to be, even just a couple of years ago, that you would see in the newspapers some report that "this and that *fulano* [what's-his-name], a *cochón* [fag], robbed someone . . . or some *cochona* [dyke] got drunk and beat up her woman." But this is changing, and you don't see the news reports using those old-fashioned and negative terms. Now the reporters don't put that kind of thing in there, the sexuality of the person. This has been changing little by little because of the campaign for Sexuality Free from Prejudice and maybe, in some smaller ways, because of the lessons and conversations we have been having in our lesbian discussion group.

Marta was quick to admit that the changes have been incremental and processual. But she also believed these particular shifts in awareness and representation were occurring in part because of her commitment and that of other sexual rights activists. Marta's thoughts call attention to several key aspects of the social and political dimensions that are critical to the work of sexual rights activists. She highlights the ways in which ideas about sexuality are being transformed by the media; how everyday conversations about, and perceptions of, sexual identity are shifting; and, finally, the important role sexual rights activists see themselves playing as mediators who will help to establish a better future for sexually marginalized people in Nicaragua.

For as long as most Nicaraguans can remember, there have been *cochones* and *cochonas*. More recently, however, newer categories have become pervasive in the sexual lexicon of Nicaragua: *homosexuales* (or *gays*) and *lesbianas*. Many factors have led to this emergence, including international lesbian and gay rights movements, globally broadcast television programs and films, increased flows of digital information, and people's migratory paths between the global North and Nicaragua. Nicaraguan advocates for sexual rights have also played an instrumental role in how same-sex sexuality is coming to be understood in both public culture and private interactions. In this book I follow the work of Nicaraguan sexual rights activists who, I argue, have served as key mediators in the transformation of ideas about, and experiences of, same-sex sexuality. Activists' interventions have grown out of a political and intellectual commitment to combine human rights, identity politics, and global discourses with the quotidian realities of sexuality that are specific to Nicaragua. In an era in which political practices—from communitarian impulses to liberal rights—move rapidly across borders, understanding activists as a class of mediators who actively craft and situate political ideals allows us to understand not only activists' values and the settings of their struggles but also the points of "friction" (Tsing 2004) at which globally disseminated rights and concepts of sexuality become reformulated in local contexts.

Nicaragua's Sandinista Revolution (1979–90) was one of very few successful social revolutions in Latin America. It brought together strands of Marxism, nationalism, and liberation theology to overturn the country's long-standing dictatorial regime. Because of the Sandinista experiment, Nicaragua was an iconic example of a "third world" country that dared to challenge U.S. hegemony in the final chilly years of the Cold War. What is perhaps less well known is that in 1992, during the U.S.-supported administration of President Violeta Barrios de Chamorro, Nicaragua instituted Article 204, the most repressive antisodomy law in the Americas. Article 204 mandated up to three years imprisonment for "anyone who induces, promotes, propagandizes or practices in scandalous form sexual intercourse between persons of the same sex." It targeted not only men but also women. It was a law that threatened to incarcerate, potentially, anyone who wrote about, spoke about, or putatively propagandized the subject of homosexuality in any way. By the time the Sandinistas returned to power in 2006, Nicaragua was the only country in Latin America that criminalized same-sex sexual relations between consenting adults, male or female. Then, in 2007, in what a prominent Nicaraguan national newspaper called "a surprise decision," the antisodomy law was repealed. Why Nicaragua "surprisingly" moved from an oppressive antisodomy regime to greater tolerance for same-sex sexuality remains, officially, an open question.[1] This book is an attempt to provide a partial answer by considering the work of Nicaraguan sexual rights advocates whose campaigns were largely spurred by the antisodomy law, but whose activism has attempted to change not only policy but also culture. From my point of view, activists deserve credit and congratulations for the work they have done to overturn the antisodomy law. However, this book is not simply a celebratory reflection on a hard-won victory.

Rather than a retrospective of a successful social movement, this book is an ethnography of activism. It considers the intellectual and performative practices of advocates to better understand how they are attempting to transform culture through political means, from the inside, out. Sexual rights activists see themselves as participants in what they call *una lucha* (a struggle) to transform *la vida cotidiana* (daily life). The lucha for sexual rights, I argue, illustrates a pivotal moment in a continuum from revolution to rights as many activists who were revolutionaries, or who were influenced by the revolution's spirit, are now committed to more identity-based human rights projects. Their struggle for sexual rights illustrates some of the ways in which political objectives have changed from a revolutionary impulse to overturn the state to a set of political values aimed at protecting individuals from the state, and from national upheaval to a politics of personal transformation and securing rights.

As Nicaraguan activists have attempted to transform the moral terrain at home, many of them have looked beyond the country's borders to engage in a now global conversation about sexual rights.[2] Like many political actors, Nicaraguan activists are influenced by concepts of sexual subjectivity, ideals of romantic love, and international lesbian and gay rights movements. These political models, inherited from Enlightenment ideals of rational mutual understanding, are symptomatic of what Elizabeth Povinelli (2004: 6) has called the "liberal diaspora."[3] A liberal logic of rights and movements has been persuasive in Nicaragua's postrevolutionary, neoliberal economic climate and has, in part, set the stage for cultural and political reconfigurations of sexuality. However, activists have not been bound by these logics. Instead, they have translated aspects of the country's revolutionary ethos into terms commensurate with the contemporary politics of sexual rights, often reconfiguring trans-local political practices so they resonate more profoundly with local political histories and priorities. The Nicaraguan struggle for sexual rights is, I believe, distinct from many other sexual equality movements around the world not only because activists have had to confront a formidable antisodomy law, but also because activists themselves come armed with organizing experiences learned, and earned, during the revolutionary process. Just as the Sandinista Revolution was a mixture of political, social, and religious principles, sexual rights activists have developed a similar kind of bricolage, creatively appropriating and engaging a hybrid set of political approaches.

Nicaraguan sexual rights activists articulate their politics in multiple ways as they attempt to engage with the public and create a public sphere that recognizes and appreciates the values of sexual rights. Lesbian and gay discussion groups, public protests and street demonstrations, and social-justice radio and television programming are important arenas for advocacy, each representing a different dimension and scale of engagement. These are key *sites* of activists' interventions. However, equally important is the work that advocates do to create a *subject* for sexual rights. Whether on the street or on the airwaves, activists must calibrate their politics for their audience, the people of Nicaragua, as well as for each other. The debates that take place behind the scenes as activists prepare for public events and produce media materials, for instance, are not only illustrative of content, messaging, and strategizing; they also demonstrate how ideological negotiations inflect and inform the work that activists do. Conversations about how, or whether, to use particular political tropes — including *declaración* (outness), identity, sexual "options" or "orientations," "pride," or "sexuality free from prejudice" — become an experimental terrain for advocates to refashion and reposition transnational political values and notions of subjectivity. Translating the terms associated with sexuality, and the uneven ways they index identity and behavior, is not simply a linguistic exercise but also a conceptual one.[4] These mediations, perhaps unsurprisingly, often have a gendered dimension. The contingencies of machismo, changing perceptions of women's sexual agency, and the social inequalities between women and men all indicate, in profound ways, how sexual subjectivity cannot be divorced from gender.

Although this book describes sexual rights activism on behalf of both women and men in Nicaragua, I focus somewhat more attention on *derechos lesbianos* (lesbian rights). In one sense, my subjectivity and the many years I spent in the "dyke scene" in California guided this decision.[5] As a (bisexual) woman, I also probably had more access to the social world of lesbian politics than I would have had as a man (or, conversely, as a woman attempting to access the intimate domains of men's same-sex sexuality in Nicaragua). However, there is a more primary, political, and "Nica" reason behind my focus on derechos lesbianos. While Nicaraguans have long been aware of la cochona, women's same-sex sexuality has never had the same degree of recognition as men's same-sex sexuality. La cochona has never been as visible as el cochón in Nicaraguan public culture. When sexual rights activists lobby for derechos lesbianos, they are therefore not only calling attention to a relatively new sexual subject in Nicaragua, the lesbian, but they are also highlighting the existence of women's same-sex sexuality as such.

The sexual rights advocates whose work and aspirations are reflected here are a diverse group; some are grassroots activists, and others are employed by nongovernmental organizations (NGOs), health clinics, or other social service agencies.[6] During my field research, I spent time with street protestors and feminist thinkers, university students and HIV-prevention educators, spectators of queer cinema and radio show hosts, discussion group participants and pride party attendees, soap opera screenwriters and attorneys who were well versed in the vicissitudes of human rights, sexual identity, and Nicaraguan law. Many sexual rights advocates were long-time Sandinista *militantes*, and others were neoliberal converts. Most were Nicaraguan, but a handful were foreign nationals and expatriates, some of whom had lived in Nicaragua since the revolutionary era.[7] I also spent much of my time in Nicaragua with people who were known around the neighborhood as a cochón or a cochona and who increasingly were referring to themselves as *gay* (or *homosexual*) and lesbiana.[8] Participating in meetings of the Women's Network against Violence, helping to plan the weeklong Sexuality Free from Prejudice (SFFP) events, joining lesbian discussion groups, attending HIV/AIDS-prevention events, and helping to create a database of Latin American gay and lesbian organizations all inform my understanding of sexual rights advocacy in Nicaragua. My networks and contacts expanded and deepened over time through overlapping personal and professional connections, or what social scientists like to call "snowball" sampling, although snowballs seem a strange methodological metaphor in the tropical swelter of Managua.

There were days when I shared *pinolillo*, a traditional drink made of corn and cacao, with my Nicaraguan friends and coworkers; but my conversations most often occurred over well-sugared lukewarm coffee. I was also more likely to hear the best anecdotes and the bawdier details after the bottle of Flor de Caña rum had gone around the table a couple of times and the Shakira song had subsided on the speakers at the *disco gay*. In the relatively small world of activist networks, NGOs, social service agencies, and health centers in Managua, an interloping *gringa* is not unheard of.[9] The country has a long history of *internacionalistas*, both those who came during the revolutionary period and those who continue to arrive in support of development projects around the country.[10] My initial experiences in Nicaragua, living in a small town in the western highlands in the early 1990s, inspired my interest in sexual rights activism in the country. However, most of what I describe in this book derives from daily conversations and interactions with people during sixteen months of field research in 1999, 2000, and 2001, followed by several trips back since then, including as an international elections observer in 2006 when the Sandinistas returned to power. During the time that this field research took place, it was illegal to promote, propagandize, or practice homosexuality in Nicaragua. However, this is precisely what many activists were doing. To ensure complete confidentiality, I have used pseudonyms for all of the individuals whose stories and words are included here.[11] While Article 204 is no longer in effect and I do not expect any of the people represented in this book to be legally or personally endangered in the present, I have chosen to err on the side of caution for the sake of my friends and interlocutors. Maintaining this confidentiality is a long-standing anthropological convention, but it is also one that, in this case, seems especially warranted.

Thick Experience, Social Theories, and la Vida Cotidiana

Nicaraguan activists have what Clifford Geertz (1973) might have called "thick experience" with revolution, social change, and transnational political paradigms. The Sandinista revolutionary state was a polymorphous blend of political priorities and initiatives, ranging from land reform and workers' cooperatives to literacy brigades and the prohibition of exploitative images of women. It was during the revolutionary era that Nicaraguan women became more fully politicized and North American and European allies traveled to the country in solidarity with the revolutionary project. The Sandinista state achieved some of its egalitarian goals. But the revolution was truncated and foiled by the U.S. covert war against the country, as well as by internal mismanagement and an increasingly neoliberal economic climate.[12] What followed was a series of socially conservative regimes and structural adjustment policies that relegated Nicaragua to the United Nations' list of the world's most highly indebted poor countries. By the late 1990s and early 2000s, Nicaragua was regularly receiving more development aid per capita than any other country in the Americas. As one Nicaraguan diplomat put it in our conversation, "Our country is forced to go begging to the World Bank and the International Monetary Fund." Once a globally recognized symbol of revolution and resistance, Nicaragua had taken on a new "identity" as the second poorest country in the Western Hemisphere. Stranded on the margins of the global economy, Nicaraguan activists have had to craft their advocacy campaigns with limited resources, at best.

In response to deepening social conservatism and structural adjustment policies that made the Nicaraguan state much less able, and seemingly less willing, to provide even a modicum of social welfare, many social justice activists established new political venues in civil society. Gender and sexual rights activists founded an influential women's movement, the Movimiento Autónomo de Mujeres (Autonomous Women's Movement), national networks for violence prevention, grassroots initiatives for sexual rights, and organizations dedicated to HIV/AIDS prevention and education. In the early 1990s, the country underwent what Nicaraguans call *el boom* of NGOs, which became increasingly responsible for clinical services such as reproductive and sexual health and assumed many political tasks, including lobbying for human rights and social justice agendas (Molyneux 2003; Paley 2002, 2008). The politics of social transformation became, to a degree, institutionalized in NGOs, many of which have been dependent on the good graces of foreign governments, foundations, and nonprofit organizations for their funding. In this economically precarious situation, activists are acutely aware that their projects are vulnerable to the capriciousness of foreign capital. At the same time, they are also adamant that their projects remain their own; many advocates are vocal about the fact that their foreign support comes "with no strings attached." The fact that some activists' projects are funded and deemed worthy while other projects are not, however, suggests that financial strings are inherent in a context in which economic dependence is the starting point for political projects.

Opposing the antisodomy law has been an ongoing battle for many activists, but sexual rights advocates also see themselves as struggling against what they call *fundamentalismo cristiano* (Christian fundamentalism). Fundamentalismo cristiano appears in anti-abortion campaigns by religious institutions, biased sexual education in schools, "fiscal terrorism" against women's organizations,[13] and attacks on the leadership of health clinics and progressive NGOs. The majority of Nicaraguans identify as Catholic, and the church has an enormous amount of influence in Nicaraguan politics and public opinion. Public commentaries by representatives of the Catholic church are regularly featured in the national newspapers, and Nicaraguan Catholic clergy historically have functioned as key arbiters in national politics.[14] Evangelical denominations, which have grown across the country, also leverage ideological and moral influence in the country. Church doctrine that designates homosexuality sinful, and the widely held opinion among Nicaraguans that homosexuality is a sickness, have both proved to be difficult obstacles in activists' work.

Antisodomy laws and powerful church lobbies do not, however, tell the whole story of sexuality in contemporary Nicaragua. The weekly magazine *Salud y Sexualidad* (Health and Sexuality), a colorful insert in the national newspaper *El Nuevo Diario* (New Daily), often runs features on sexuality, including same-sex sexuality, making these topics a regular part of quotidian dialogues.[15] Political scandals, such as the accusations of incest and rape leveled against (former and current) President Daniel Ortega by his adopted stepdaughter, offer salient, if salacious, moments for the body politic to reflect on sexuality as a social and political phenomenon. Popular television shows featuring gay characters, such as *Betty la Fea* (*Ugly Betty*), have opened new spaces to discuss sexuality, if in stereotyped forms. Increasing access to the Internet has meant that (primarily urban) Nicaraguans can find material about sexual behavior, health, and rights from around the world. Changes such as these have allowed some Nicaraguans to claim lesbian, gay, or homosexual identities in very public, vocal, and visible ways. Others have depended on tacit recognition, claiming instead, "I am neither in the closet nor on the balcony" (Babb 2003, 2009). There are still others who are *cuidadosa* (careful, mindful) and perhaps even suspicious of sexual-identity categories and the meanings they are believed to embody. This book closely considers these dynamics, assessing the ways in which the ongoing work of sexual rights activists has transformed how Nicaraguans talk about and perhaps, think about sexuality.

From Revolution to Rights

When I first lived in Nicaragua in the early 1990s, I knew I had just missed the revolution, as people were quick to lament. However, the ease with which just about anyone on the street discussed the finer points of heralded communist tracts such as Karl Marx's *The Eighteenth Brumaire* or

Antonio Gramsci's *Prison Notebooks* made it seem as though the revolution was not that far gone. By the time I returned to do fieldwork in the late 1990s and early 2000s, the intellectual heroes of aspiring communists were much less a part of the public repertoire. When political theory did arise, it was no longer people in the street who did most of the talking. Instead, an educated, progressive, and often middle-class cohort of political actors was engaged in these conversations, and the theory I was beginning to hear was Foucault's. Ernesto, a member of the Men's Network against Violence, put it this way one afternoon, "You see, Cymene, it is like Foucault says: power moves in incremental ways, moves in language, and it is all about discourse." Times had changed and they had stayed the same: Nicaragua was still a country actively engaged with social theory, but the theoretical repertoire had changed, as had the subject of political struggles.[16]

The ways in which Nicaragua has moved from Marx and Foucault to liberal paradigms and human rights illustrate not only how the country as a whole has engaged with political theorizing and practice, but also how advocates themselves—their interventions and their thinking—have been influenced by them. Partially due to the relatively short time horizon between the Sandinista Revolution and other struggles for equality in Nicaragua, individual advocates have, for example, been revolutionaries in the late 1970s, Sandinista supporters in the 1980s, feminist leaders in the 1990s, and sexual rights proponents in the early part of the twenty-first century. Activists who have opposed socially conservative values and the coercive force of the antisodomy law find resonance in Gramsci's proposition that power is enacted through dominant culture, normative hegemonies, and state coercion. Advocates who have focused their attention on sexual subjectivity find themselves engaged with what Foucault understood as a proliferation of sexual discourses and diffuse operations of power. Therefore, it is not that Gramsci and Marx are no longer useful in a Foucauldian Nicaragua; indeed, many activists describe their current work as a continuum in which the political expertise they gained during the revolution is coupled with recent lessons learned on the geopolitical world stage. However, if Marx and Gramsci influenced an earlier revolutionary impulse, and Foucault partly conditioned Nicaragua's postrevolutionary era, human rights have become, as one activist pithily put it, *de moda* (in style).[17]

Human rights arrived in Nicaragua through the usual channels: international organizations, development projects, and Nicaraguan advocates' participation in transnational politics. Since the early 1990s, human rights discourses have become de rigueur in funding proposals to organizations in the global North, and they have become an integral part of activists' knowledge regimes. At face value, human rights appear to be a relatively straightforward proposition: a formula for equality based on what Hannah Arendt (1958: 299) called "the assumed existence of a human being as such." However, following a longer tradition in Western political philosophy from Aristotle on, human rights have also been a provocation, questioning what it means to be human and ultimately how humanity can achieve a "common standard of decency" (Nagengast and Turner 1997: 269).[18] Human rights and, in turn, sexual rights are not a transparent set of practices; they are a social and historical process rather than an innate set of values (Žižek 2005). For many activists in Nicaragua, human rights offer a space to collectively safeguard people's lives and dignity and to call attention to how, as Judith Butler (2004: 32) has put it, "certain lives are vulnerable and worthy of protection, [and] certain deaths are grievable and worthy of public recognition." As advocates lobby for policy change, they are aiming to legitimate sexual rights as a political project. At the same time, as activists designate sexual difference "worthy of protection," they are also participating in a deeper set of philosophical queries about the qualities of freedom.

As in many places around the world where liberalism and rights-based values are increasingly hegemonic, human rights approaches have multiplied in Nicaragua as the "concept of choice" (Boellstorff 2003a: 24). However, human rights have not entirely replaced other political frameworks. In their work to construct a hybrid politics of sexual rights, activists explicitly incorporate the political values of liberalism, rights, and identity. But in the interest of tactical expediency, they also actively edit, alter, or dismiss elements of these political approaches.[19] The concept of Sexuality Free from Prejudice, for instance, insists that when laws such as Article 204 are in place, everyone's sexuality—not just that of lesbians and gays—is at risk. Imagining the possibility of a sexual worldview that is "free from prejudice" also parallels Sandinismo's communitarian impulse to transform all of society, not just individuals' subjectivity. Campaigns such as "We Are Different, We Are Equal" draw on multiculturalist notions of protecting and promoting difference and tolerance. Rhetorical approaches that emphasize a biological rationale for sexuality, rather than simply questioning social norms, find their roots in developmental narratives and a biopolitical body of knowledge. As with many contemporary political projects, particularly in the developing world, Nicaraguan activists must mediate between ideological paradigms, financial contingencies, and local political histories and priorities (Hale 2006; Speed 2007). These efforts have resulted in a multidimensional and continually negotiated set of principles that combine liberal strands of politics—such as human rights, multiculturalism, and development—with the country's Marxian history.

From Movements to Struggles

In the second half of June one will find rainbow flags fluttering over many of Managua's main thoroughfares. During the time of my fieldwork I found banners proclaiming "Los Derechos de Homosexuales y Lesbianas Son Derechos Humanos" (The Rights of Homosexuals and Lesbians Are Human Rights) posted at intersections next to posters peppered with pink triangles. These were, I thought, sure signs of a vibrant lesbian and gay movement. I was therefore a little surprised, I have to admit, when in my early conversations with Nicaraguan sexual rights activists I was told, "No hay un movimiento gay aquí" (There is not a gay movement here). As someone who had been involved in lesbian and gay political movements in the United States—helping to organize the annual Dyke March in San Francisco, for example—I was baffled that Nicaraguan activists were so quick to reject the existence of a movement that seemed so apparent. I offered a little convivial protest: "But you have a whole week of 'sexuality free from prejudice' events here in Nicaragua, whereas in the United States, we have only one weekend for Lesbian and Gay Pride. And you have lesbian and gay publications like *Fuera del Closet* (Out of the Closet) and lots of NGOs that do work on sexual health and rights. And . . ." My interlocutors patiently assured me, "Yes, we have all of that. . . . But it's not a 'movement.'" "What we have," they said, echoing the language of Latin American leftists, "is a lucha (struggle)." My friends explained that, for them, there were qualitative differences between a "movement" and a "struggle." They elaborated that some challenges, such as overcoming machismo, were based more in culture than in policy. The social conditions that sustained machismo and *heterosexismo* at times seemed intractable, requiring the laborious and fine-grained daily remediation of struggle. And then there was the question of size. In a country in which mass-mobilization led to national up-heaval and an overthrow of the state, the term "movement" has a particu-larly massive quality. While many individual activists, coalitions, groups, networks, and organizations had been promoting sexual rights in Nica-ragua, by local standards of scope and scale, these interventions did not quite reach the magnitude of a movement. The lesbian and gay movement I thought I first saw on the streets of Managua was not, then, precisely a "movement." Neither was it exactly "lesbian" and "gay."

Promoting tolerance for those marked as sexually "other," including lesbianas, *gays*, and homosexuales, has been a fundamental element of sexual rights activists' work. But theirs is not simply a lesbian and gay rights movement. Nicaragua's history of sexuality differs, rather substan-tially, from many North American and European contexts in which many lesbian and gay rights movements have their roots. The terms "lesbian," "gay," and "homosexual" do not always capture the complexities of desire, behavior, and naming practices that are found in Nicaragua. When they use these terms, activists intend them to be very flexible categories, and they are cognizant of both the opportunities and limitations of identity. Moreover, many activists have chosen to think of their constituency in national terms rather than limit their advocacy work to those who define themselves, or are defined by others, as "gay" or "homosexual" or "lesbian." Therefore, rather than describing activists' interventions as another les-bian and gay rights movement, I believe that activists' work is more appro-priately described as a struggle for sexual rights. "Sexual rights" highlights sexuality as a political *object* and joins it to rights as a political *method*, without delineating a particular identity category.

Gay and lesbian movements, identity politics, LGBTQ pride, and "out" sexual politics have found much traction in places such as North America and Europe.[20] But sexual rights activists in Nicaragua, as elsewhere, must consider how well these approaches coincide with the needs, desires, and practices found in the global South. The new social movements of the 1960s and '70s were an effort to establish new categories of rights and to address the inequalities faced by women, indigenous people, and lesbians and gays, among others.[21] However, the very concept of a movement, as Kay Warren (1998: 209) puts it, relies on a "Western grammar" that articu-lates a relatively coherent and unified set of purposes. This particular logic of movements, as Nicaraguan activists themselves aver, does not quite capture the tenor of their politics. Indeed, sexual rights advocacy projects in Nicaragua do not precisely follow the contours of a new social movement; their interventions are less "new," less "social," and less of a "movement" than they may at first appear. Instead, they reflect older forms of political praxis creatively recombined with human rights, identity politics, and media interventions.

Because they were often seen to be oriented toward individual subjectivity and self-fulfillment, new social movements supposedly were a radical departure from the "old left" politics of class-consciousness.[22] However, the dividing line between "new" and "old" social movements and political initiatives is not always so stark. Les W. Field (1998, 1999) has demonstrated, for example, that socioeconomic and identity-based politics—particularly in regard to women and ethnic minorities—were never entirely separate projects in Nicaragua (see also Hale 1996). As I will describe further in chapter 2, Nicaragua's Marxian legacy, of the old social movement ilk, continues to inform new struggles for sexual rights. Many prominent sexual rights activists have managed to parlay their revolutionary *militancia* into present-day influence. Younger generations of activists are, like their Sandinista predecessors, acutely aware of how Nicaragua's difficult socioeconomic conditions affect people's ability to claim an identity or participate in the struggle for sexual rights. A linear narrative of "old" versus "new" approaches to advocacy, therefore, risks obscuring more than it reveals: activists are multiply situated in time, as are their political goals.

The goal of changing social policy and overturning the antisodomy law has been critical for many sexual rights advocates. But equally, if not more, important is the transformation of "culture." Activists often speak about Nicaraguan culture as a system of shared meanings—knowledge, symbols, and practices that render an internal logic. While not necessarily homogenous, from their point of view, culture reflects a historical patrimony and a set of values that are recognizable as *puro Nicaragüense* (purely, truly Nicaraguan). Culture is an entity that activists work for and from, meaning that political and cultural aims often overlap and combine and, in many cases, become "inextricable" (Fox and Starn 1997: 3; Keck and Sikkink 1998). As activists envision culture as a precondition for politics, their advocacy interventions are often less social than they are cultural—representing a more pluricentric political universe.

The Subject of Sexual Rights and Holding Hands across the Border

"Is it true," Maria Elena asked me one day, "that girlfriends really can hold hands on the street in the North? Or is that just a myth that we hear from Nicas who have been to the United States? Is it really just something that only happens in the movies?" In trying to respond to Maria Elena's question, I realized that my answer required some qualification. I wanted her to know that, yes, in some places in the United States, this is indeed possible—but not everywhere. I explained that in San Francisco, a place well known for queer culture, I had no concerns about holding hands with my girlfriend, especially in neighborhoods like the Castro or in the Mission District. Beyond the possibility of public displays of affection, however, Maria Elena's question reflected a larger supposition that I heard many times in Nicaragua, if in different words and with different levels of doubt or certainty. It went something like this: "In the North, you are much more developed with your sexual rights" or "Gays and lesbians have many more freedom in the United States. It is a much more tolerant and open place." I usually agreed that in the North, there are many legal protections, such as civil unions (and in some places, marriage equality),[23] antidiscrimination laws, and penalties for hate crimes. However, I also felt that it was important to point out that the United States is not a gay utopia. For one, it is not without homophobia. Gay bashing and a belief that "homosexual panic" can drive one to commit hate crimes persist and, in the worst cases, have ended in murder. In contrast, historically, Nicaragua has not had a clear history of "organized, lethal violence nor panicked attacks" against those who are, or are believed to be, homosexual (Lancaster 1992: 247).[24] Historically, Nicaragua's gender and sexual system, unlike the United States, has not fostered the social conditions that would lead to gay bashing or hate crimes.[25] Most of the lesbian and gay Nicaraguans with whom I spoke, did not emphasize experiences of violence; instead, intimidation, humiliation, bullying, and blackmail have been the weapons of choice against cochones and cochonas although this too appears to be changing. The Nicaraguan government did institute and uphold a particularly draconian antisodomy law, indicating that the country has hardly been hospitable to sexual difference. However, few people were prosecuted under the law.[26] Contradictions abound. In Nicaragua, as in the North, what counts as "developed" sexual rights is a complicated question involving legal prohibitions, cultural precedent, and distinct

The Struggle

—

15

ways of viewing same-sex sexuality. The proposition that industrialized countries have achieved perfect equity for sexual "minorities" is incorrect, and it fits all too neatly into dubious narratives of Western superiority and Northern progress, modernity, and egalitarianism. These sorts of questions about how to effectively institute sexual rights and how to gauge their success, however, are both provocation and motivation for Nicaraguan sexual rights activists. They are also questions that, in all of their complexity, are foundational to much of the thinking in this book.[27]

Grappling with how to conceptualize, define, and animate "sexuality" as a political device is foundational to the intellectual and political mediations of Nicaraguan activists. However, ascribing fixity to sexual terms is a notoriously slippery proposition. Sexuality is a vast category that has been used to give name and voice to desires and practices, to codify political solidarity, and to define subjectivity and identity. As lesbian and gay rights movements have emerged around the world, sexuality has come to have a certain global political currency, or a "new primacy" (Weeks 1999: 35).[28] However, the politics of sexuality is not without controversy in Nicaragua and elsewhere; it is a topic that stirs moral sentiments. Although sexuality has been, and continues to be, a semiotic location to create solidarities, it is also a category that can be used to scrutinize subjects, often under the auspices of health, psychiatry, and law (see, e.g., Foucault 1979; Halperin 2002; Mosse 1985). The so-called culture wars, which at times have appeared global in scope, often deploy sexuality as the heavy artillery for generating moral panics and accusations of unchecked libertinage or cultural imperialism (Duggan 2004; Gitlin 1995; Herat 2009; Massad 2002, 2008). The proliferation of sexual discourses can have disciplinary repercussions, at times turning desire into diagnosis — or, as in Nicaragua, criminality. As Nicaraguan activists attempt to establish a politics of sexual rights, they take certain calculated risks. By lobbying for a set of rights associated with sexuality, they challenge some socially conservative values, but they also open the door to backlash and accusations of moral impropriety. Managing these sorts of contingencies, both positive and negative, is central to activists' work on the conceptual borders of sexual rights.

The rise of sexual rights movements in many places around the world sometimes makes it appear as though there is a singular, identifiable, and universally understood "subject" of sexual rights. However, same-sex desire, or practice, does not necessarily lead to a shared sense of community or an unassailable appreciation of personal identity. The adoption of particular terms (such as "gay," "lesbian," or "queer") quickly uncovers the difficulty of ascribing universal meaning to unique social, historical, and political circumstances.[29] As Evelyn Blackwood (2005: 44) has described it, "One cannot talk about heterosexuality or homosexuality or any sexuality without recognizing how it is interpreted, constructed, hedged about, and defined differently across genders, ethnicities and classes." For some Nicaraguan activists, an important part of the lucha for sexual rights involves fostering a shared sense of identity among women and men who are, or would be, involved in same-sex relationships. This proposition is sometimes effective; at other times, it is less so. As many advocates have found, there are polymorphous ways to define—or to choose *not* to define—one's sexuality. In discussion groups, for example, Nicaraguan activist-facilitators encounter cochonas who are suspicious of "lesbian" identity paradigms. Hosting lesbian discussion groups rather than cochona discussion groups is, in the end, an ideological decision linked to liberal value systems. It reflects a desire on the part of activists to place same-sex sexuality under very particular signs of identity that are, not inconsequentially, internationally legible.

Of Fags and Men; or, Finding the Women in Long-Sleeve Shirts

Nicaragua was once described as a place where there is "homosexuality without a gay world" (Adam 1993): a place without gay ghettos but, more important, a place where men could have sex with other men and never be dubbed a homosexual or a fag. As long as a man maintained his "macho" assertive, insertive, and *activo* role in a sexual encounter with another man, he would not be considered gay. His *pasivo* male partner, however, would suffer the stigma of being marked as sexually deviant. Only he would wear the mantle of *cochón*, *maricón* (fag), or *loca* (crazy, queen, queer). An *hombre hombre* (manly man, real man)—or what Nicaraguans sometimes colloquially term the *cochonero* (lit., one who 'drives' or directs the cochón)—could enjoy the sexual "conquest" of cochones as long as he continued to privilege sex with women and never let his masculinity flag (Lancaster 1992: 241–44). Cochones have been marked by their faulty masculinity, their failed performance of machismo,[30] and their (putatively passive) role in sexual encounters; the cochón, in other words, is indexed not by his (male) object of sexual desire but by the nature of his desire and the feminized sexual role he occupies. This paradigm of male homosexuality—what some scholars have called the "Mediterranean model"—

stands in some distinction to the egalitarian model that predominates in many places in the global North.[31] In the egalitarian model, one's choice of a same-sex object is the defining criterion of one's homosexual status. Both partners are viewed as equally homosexual and equally stigmatized, no matter what their sexual role.[32]

The ways that status and stigma, honor and dishonor are apportioned in these models are distinct (Lancaster 1987). However, models, in the end, are simply templates that are prone to fissures.[33] Martin Manalansan (1997) has shown us, for example, that particular values of modernity and development become embedded in models of gay and lesbian identity that assume a trajectory of progress from gender, role-based, "traditional" sexual behaviors to egalitarian, "modern," same-sex relationships. Sexual citizenship in the global South may not follow the contours of putatively "proper" gay and lesbian identities that have become hegemonic in much of the global North, including identities that are idealized as egalitarian and out. But neither does this mean that notions of the sexual self that have their genesis in the global South are evolutionarily backward or "underdeveloped" (Boellstorff 2005). Hector Carrillo (2002) documents, for example, that Mexican men's same-sex sexual activities can be comprehended and categorized following older models of gender roles and, contemporaneously, linked to gay or homosexual identity. Rather than (so-called) modern identities' replacing (so-called) traditional formulations of same-sex sexual activities, these are synthetic, locally contextualized ways to conceive of sexual identity and practice. Although particular "sexual scripts" (Gagnon 2004) may condition and contextualize behavior and desire,[34] the ways in which sexuality is practiced and experienced is not easily codified by a singular definition. What constitutes "homosexuality" for an individual or within a particular community, in a given place and time, is perhaps infinitely mutable. Sexuality has many histories, none of them in the absolute singular, universal, or constant.

While it is likely that there have always been women in Nicaragua who have had affective and sexual relationships with other women, like much of the West historically (Hall 1990 [1928]; Lorde 1984; Rich 1980), women's same-sex sexuality has not had much public visibility in Nicaragua. Roger Lancaster, an anthropologist working in Nicaragua in the late 1980s and early 1990s, claimed for example, that there is "little popular interest in categorizing or regulating female same-sex relations and little exists in the popular lexicon [of Nicaragua] to account for it" (Lancaster

1992: 271). Although women's same-sex sexuality may not have the same degree of recognition in the popular imagination as the cochón,[35] I have never encountered a Nicaraguan who was unfamiliar with the term and the personage embodied by the "cochona."[36] Cochonas, Nicaraguans will explain (invoking stereotypes to do so), are easily identified by their *hombruna* (mannish) behavior and the long-sleeve men's shirts they are said to favor.[37] Cochonas' partners and girlfriends were often described to me as *femenina* or *muy mujer* (very womanish): women who followed the rules of feminine comportment. Subscribing to Nicaraguan gender norms and, supposedly, taking a pasiva sexual role, femeninas could be in relationships with other women yet never be seen as lesbians.[38] Femeninas—like their macho analogue, the cochonero—typically have not attracted either stigma or mockery. In my experiences, they also never garnered the same kind of attention or notice on the street that gender-transgressive cochonas did.[39] When activists work to establish lesbian identity among both cochonas and femeninas, therefore, it is not simply that a new, positive term ("lesbiana") is being affixed to an older and more familiar personage (the cochona). Rather, a more expansive sexual category is being created that is populated not only with "dykes" but also with their muy mujer partners and lovers. In other words, femenina women who would not have been considered gay in the past, now are.

Like so many other lesbian rights movements and communities in the global South, Nicaraguan women's same-sex sexuality and struggles for sexual rights have been absent in much of the social science scholarship.[40] As Norma Mogrovejo (1999: 207), a Peruvian feminist sociologist, has put it, uncovering "the history of the lesbian movement in Latin America is not only a historical, anthropological, sociological or political task, it is also an archaeological task."[41] Although the omission of women's same-sex sexuality is beginning to be remedied in some academic circles, there is more to be done (Boellstorff 2007; Weston 1993).[42] While the erasure of women's same-sex sexuality is one compelling reason I focus attention on derechos lesbianos, there are two, more locally salient reasons to do so. First, women's same-sex sexuality and lesbian rights have had a very controversial presence in Nicaraguan gender politics and women's rights organizing, from Sandinismo to the present.[43] The question of where lesbians "fit" into the country's political schema is an ongoing one. Second, the antisodomy penalties Nicaragua instituted in 1992 were unusual in their gendered scope. The law effectively criminalized women's same-sex encounters, not only those of men—as is often the case with antisodomy laws. In a punitive way, the law signaled some form of "egalitarian" criminal liability that put women's same-sex sexuality at risk in ways that it had not been before. Activism on behalf of lesbian rights, then, constitutes a rather dramatic intervention. It demands acknowledging the ways in which women's same-sex sexuality has been less visible in public culture and, at the same time, politically volatile within women's rights advocacy. Orienting sexual rights toward lesbianas establishes a more immediately visible category of identity. As rights claims are made on behalf of la lesbiana rather than la cochona—or for los homosexuales or los gays rather than los cochones—sexual rights become a location not only to establish ideals of equality but also to reimagine the categories themselves (Valentine 2004). How sexual rights advocates in Nicaragua have undertaken these mediations of knowledge and political practice—from intimate pedagogies and epistemological engineering to the mass-mediation of sexual subjectivity—is the subject of the chapters that follow.

How the Book Unfolds

I begin the story of sexual rights activism in Nicaragua with history because it is through successive political regimes that activists have honed their particular approaches to sexual rights advocacy. In chapter 1, "A History of Sexuality," I describe the different ways that sexuality has emerged as a political category in Nicaragua, from the Somoza dictatorship through the Sandinista years and into the neoliberal era of the twenty-first century. The ethos of the Sandinista Revolution, advocacy by Nicaraguan feminists and women's rights proponents, and U.S. political and economic interventions have all played important roles in how activists have articulated the contemporary politics of sexual rights. From the Marxism, nationalism, and liberation theology of the revolutionary period to the human rights politics of the present, I describe the ways in which sexuality has been used to legitimate particular moral paradigms and political projects and, in turn, how these have coincided with other movements and political priorities.

In chapter 2, "Intimate Pedagogies," I analyze a series of lesbian discussion groups hosted by different NGOs and grassroots advocates in both urban and rural settings. I describe the interactions and pedagogical dynamics that occur in discussion groups and demonstrate how activists and participants are involved in co-constructing an intimate dimension of sexual rights advocacy. As they articulate concepts such as lesbian "consciousness," *orientación sexual*, and *opción sexual*, the discussion groups' leaders hope to draw from global registers of rights and identity. But they are also attentive to the realities of participants' lives. In these *talleres* (workshops), activists and participants strive to develop "lesbian" as a designation that can, and does, stand for many things. Activists who act as discussion group leaders are usually less focused on crafting a particular model of lesbian identity than they are committed to cultivating participants' desire to understand, to question, and, above all, to name their sexuality as such. Activists' intimate pedagogical work and their efforts to train participants in a repertoire of sexual identities, I argue, involves a particular education of desire: to become *bien educada* (well mannered, well educated) in the subject of sexuality.

As activists endeavor to change the way Nicaraguans understand sexuality, they must negotiate thorny questions about how to best present the public face of sexual rights. In chapter 3, "Pride and Prejudice," I analyze several events, including press conferences, expert presentations, meetings, and celebrations. Negotiating how the lucha will be represented is an important dimension of activists' mediations, particularly in events such as these, which are explicitly intended to influence the larger Nicaraguan population. It is this very publicness that compels advocates to assiduously craft particular ways of representing sexuality and subjectivity, for as the lucha "comes out," the stakes rise. In their ongoing debates about lesbian and gay pride and sexuality free from prejudice, and in their attention to the politics of *declaración* and drag, I have found that activists are engaged in epistemological negotiations, attempting to intellectually engineer the public face of sexual rights.

In chapter 4, "Mediating Sexual Subjectivities," I discuss how sexual rights activists have used television, radio, and print to construct and convey the values of sexual rights through public culture. The representation of lesbian and gay characters in mass-media forums is an important venue for activists to perform particular ideals of sexuality and, in turn, tolerance. The social justice *telenovela* (soap opera) *Sexto Sentido* was produced by a Nicaraguan feminist NGO and scripted, shot, and screened with an explicitly political purpose: to "normalize" lesbians and gay men. Activists who have produced radio programming that addresses sexuality and stigma, such as the radio show *Sin Máscaras* (Without Masks), like the activist producers of the *telenovela*, have aimed for broad public appeal and interactions with their audience. They have invited listeners to produce queries and engagements with the subject of sexuality. Nicaragua's first and only lesbian magazine, *Humanas* ([Female] Humans), was developed by a group of activists in an effort to critique the country's antisodomy law and create greater visibility for lesbians and lesbian rights. Although the print run was small, the magazine was dense with semiotic and political significance. In each of these mass-mediated approaches to advocacy, sexual rights activists have been aware of the need to protect both their audience and their authors from potential persecution or prosecution. Their media productions therefore illustrate how sexual rights become visible and embodied through the disembodying practices of anonymity on the airwaves and in print. In each of these media interventions, I argue, activists have sought to create a dialogic relationship and a reciprocal exchange of information between themselves and their audience. In doing so, sexual rights advocates have attempted to incorporate the democratic and non-hierarchical principles that are central to their political mission.

"Getting the Word Out," the concluding chapter, provides an update to the work of Nicaraguan sexual rights advocates, assessing their accomplishments and unfulfilled goals, as well as the ways in which their struggle continues. Reflecting on an asylum trial for a Nicaraguan gay man for which I served as an expert witness, I pose the difficult question of how to qualify success in the domain of sexual rights. I also return to a central proposition that has motivated this book: how ethnographies of activism can help us to better understand the politics of the twenty-first century. Activist "cultures," are not, I suggest, dissimilar to the "cultures" of ethnographic research that anthropologists have developed. Each of them depends on close and collaborative conversations, grappling with the social issues of the time, and a commitment to engaging a broader public. The study of activism is, however, complicated by the fact that analysis and critique must be weighed against the desire among many anthropologists, myself included, to advocate for the social justice agendas of the people with whom we work. Despite the difficult union between analysis and advocacy, I believe that it is valuable to be in close conversation with activists. Their work signals many of the social dynamics of the contemporary moment, including the frictions and conjunctions that are inherent when global paradigms become reimagined in local contexts.

CHAPTER ONE

A History of Sexuality

How to Overturn Things

The heat of the afternoon seemed to be retreating as Miguel and I finished off our last gulp of sugary coffee. In the working-class neighborhood of Managua where Miguel lived, the woman in charge of the *fritanga* (outdoor eatery) down the street was heating the grill for *pollo asado* while one of her daughters arranged little plastic chairs around tables in the street for the night's dining. As the usual evening rituals unfolded, Miguel began to narrate how he had become involved in the *lucha* for sexual rights and how this articulated with his participation in the revolutionary project. After years of commitment to the Sandinista cause and of performing his duties as a loyal soldier, Miguel was summarily dismissed from the Sandinista army. Although the Contra war demanded massive troop deployments and the continuation of an unpopular military draft, Miguel's superiors were dismayed by his behaving "like a *cochón*." According to Miguel, the officers thought he was "too broken-wristed"—or, in North American terms, too effeminate for military service. They were worried about his

FIGURE 1.1 Miguel holding a photograph of himself when he was enlisted in the Sandinista Army. He was later dismissed for being "too broken-wristed" for military service. He went on to become one of the founders of the sexual rights struggle in Nicaragua and continued to support the Sandinista cause.

impact on the other men in his unit and therefore asked him to resign his post. Even after he was castigated and discharged, Miguel continued to actively support Nicaragua's revolutionary party, the Frente Sandinista de Liberación Nacional (FSLN). He also became one of the earliest and most *declarado* (declared, out) advocates for what he called *derechos homosexuales* (homosexual rights). Miguel understood his revolutionary commitments, whether Sandinista or within the struggle for sexual rights, as intimately linked processes. Indeed, he drew very explicit parallels between these two political projects. "What the battle against the dictatorship and the revolutionary struggle taught us here in Nicaragua," he explained, "was how to overturn things."

The history that led Nicaragua from decades of dictatorship to the Sandinista revolution and finally to the lucha for sexual rights is marked by a series of "overturnings." Peasant revolutionaries at the beginning of the century, Marxist university students in the 1960s, feminists in the 1990s, and sexual rights advocates in the contemporary era have all faced both tensions and triumphs in their political struggles. In this chapter, I describe how sexuality as a concept has been used to legitimate different kinds of moral paradigms and political projects in Nicaragua, from the era of Somocismo (1937–79) through the Sandinista revolutionary period (1979–90) and into the neoliberal climate of the early twenty-first century. Contemporary sexual rights activism, I argue, has been fundamentally shaped by three overlapping and sometimes competing phenomena: the Sandinista revolutionary project; Nicaraguan feminism and gender advocacy; and U.S. economic, political, and military intervention. The various ways in which sexual rights advocates have grappled with these political dynamics illustrate how activists engage with their country's past, and present, place in the world. As political histories are remembered and reconstructed in particular ways, significant political events and eras can provide opportunities for advocates to situate sexual rights as ethical projects. Activists' work in the contemporary moment is necessarily informed by the politics of the past, and a vital aspect of activists' interventions is to evaluate, mediate, and craft the chronoscape of Nicaragua's political history.

In different ways, and to different degrees, revolution, feminism, and the specter of imperialism all have contributed to the shape of sexual rights in Nicaragua. It would be impossible, for example, to narrate a political history of Nicaragua without accounting for the massive influence of U.S. intrusions in the country from the colonial era to the present. Just as U.S. intervention spurred many revolutionaries to action, the legacy of imperialism continues to motivate sexual rights activists, in the wake of revolution, to emphasize their national heritage of social transformation. Political exchanges between the global North and Nicaragua do explain, in part, how liberal discourses have made their way into sexual rights struggles in Nicaragua. However, at the same time, the legacy of U.S. imperialism compels Nicaraguan activists to be wary of Northern political forms, including liberal individualism and identity politics. Partly in response to this history of intervention, activists have been cautious about adopting the sexual identities, categories, and political strategies that are often associated with the United States.

The fall of the dictatorship and the ensuing Sandinista project provided practical experience for a generation of sexual rights activists. But it also—and, perhaps, more importantly—furnished a political model that combined diverse ideological forms, blending them into a relatively unified vision for social transformation. Even as contemporary activists engage with politically liberal notions of sexual subjectivity and human rights, they draw from a national political history based on communitarian ideals and a hybrid approach to social justice. Sexual rights advocates have also been very aware of the ways in which Sandinismo failed to provide for a full range of rights, particularly for women and sexual minorities. During the Sandinista era, political participation among Nicaraguan women increased dramatically. As the Nicaraguan feminist intellectual Sofia Montenegro put it, women became "protagonists in their own history" (quoted in Field 1999: 132), and greater numbers of women became more explicitly engaged with national politics.[1] Although some women had been politically active before the revolution,[2] the new opportunities afforded by the Sandinista era allowed women to more fully negotiate the political and bureaucratic nuances of the Nicaraguan state. As they sought to remediate the particular forms of discrimination that women faced—including legal barriers and structural inequalities, as well as those seen to be cultural, such as the abuses of machismo—many Nicaraguan women gained skills that would prove invaluable in their work with international allies and development agencies in the decades to come. Feminism and women's politicization were critical to the development of lesbian and gay politics in Nicaragua. For many activists, gender politics and sexual rights are intimately related projects, both personally and politically. The overlapping agendas of gender and sexual rights, as well as the tensions between them, inform contemporary activist interventions in ways that are both explicitly articulated and implicitly understood. Just as the history of Nicaragua must be viewed in light of imperial impositions, so, too, are the politics of gender and sexuality deeply intertwined projects in the nation's history.

From Imperial Outpost to Revolutionary Beacon: Sandino, Somocismo, and Sexuality

Many Nicaraguans are fond of an expression that I would often hear them say in wise resignation: "Here in Nicaragua, we are so far from God and so close to the United States."[3] In other words, God may be preoccupied with many things, but Uncle Sam seems ever vigilant, keeping Nicaragua carefully trained within the crosshairs of U.S. military power. From outright interventions—such as installing dictators sympathetic to U.S. interests or U.S. officials' making "voting recommendations" to the Nicaraguan electorate—the relationship between the United States and Nicaragua has been one of very uneven power dynamics. Indeed, the fledgling

FIGURE 1.2 Augusto César Sandino continues to be memorialized throughout Nicaragua as an iconic figure of anti-imperialism and Nicaraguan patrimony. Here his likeness is painted on the wall of a house in San Marcos, Carazo, during the elections in 2006. The FSLN flag is painted to his right; the portrait itself was in blue and white, the colors of the Nicaraguan flag.

state of Nicaragua was marred from the beginning by U.S. intervention. Within a few years of the country's independence (1838), William Walker, a U.S. national, trekked to Nicaragua where he managed to establish political leverage by taking advantage of a long-standing political rivalry between the conservatives and the liberals.[4] Walker, a "white supremacist," seized control of the country, declared himself President of the Republic, instituted slavery, and proclaimed English the country's official language (Field 1999: 789). Walker's foray was short-lived; he was ousted and then executed less than two years into his reign. His brief political coup, however, was a harbinger of future U.S. political, economic, and military interventions. While Nicaragua is a country that has endured myriad impositions, it is also true that Nicaraguans have responded, often very profoundly, to assaults on their sovereignty.

An enduring icon of Nicaragua's anti-imperialist spirit is embodied in the national hero, Augusto César Sandino (Ramírez 1981; Ramírez and Conrad 1990). Sandino, from whom the Sandinistas took their name,

FIGURE 1.3 Sandino was famous for his oversized hat. In contemporary Nicaragua, the hat, in different media, is the most ubiquitous representation of Sandino's legacy. Here someone has created a piece of public art from scrap metal and a tree trunk and placed it in a park in Managua. Most street drawings of Sandino's hat are, like this sculpture, simply an infinity sign topped with a half-circle.

continues to be memorialized throughout Nicaragua. Representations of his oversize hat are still spray-painted on walls and sidewalks and scratched into trees and wooden benches. Sandino honed his legendary anti-imperialism in battles against the U.S. Marines who, in an effort to protect U.S. political and financial interests, occupied Nicaragua from 1912 to 1933. Sandino rallied his peasant army in the 1920s, calling for an end to U.S. occupation. He famously declared, "The liberty and sovereignty of a people are not matters for discussion. They are to be defended with arms" (quoted in Collinson 1990: 4). The guerrilla war that Sandino orchestrated forced the Marines to withdraw, and his victory against such a daunting enemy rejuvenated Nicaraguan national pride. Sandino also became internationally acclaimed for his anti-imperialism and his adherence to an idiosyncratic Marxism that rejected communist orthodoxy and was uncompromisingly nationalist. Sandino's successful confrontation of U.S. military power made him a hero throughout much of Latin America in his time and, indeed, for decades to come. His accomplishments, as well as his mythos, served as inspiration for the Cuban Revolution in the mid-twentieth century, and his name continues to resonate, for example, in the political rhetoric of Hugo Chávez's Bolivarian Revolution. Sandino's effort to upset the instruments of U.S. power, though legendary, was short-lived; soon after his victory against the Marines he was assassinated in 1934 by the U.S.-trained Guardia Nacional (National Guard).

Following Sandino's rebellion, the United States managed to maintain its grip on Nicaragua by cultivating a cozy relationship with the Somoza family, who would rule the country for more than four decades (1937–79) through a series of dynastic dictatorships.[5] There was little question that support and advice from successive U.S. administrations guided the Somoza dictatorships. Franklin Delano Roosevelt, for example, rather famously said of the eldest Somoza, "He may be a son of a bitch, but he's our son of a bitch." U.S. military personnel were responsible for training the feared National Guard, Nicaraguan nationals who served the Somoza regime through repressive policing and the disappearing of dissidents. Over time, the Somoza family's control over the country evolved into Somocismo, a political institution that was characterized by liberal economic policies, political repression, nepotism, and the extraction of both labor and resources. Although U.S. interests are no longer managed through the dictatorial state, the ongoing political and economic influence of the United States evokes shades of Somocismo for many Nicaraguans. Reflecting on the economic difficulties wrought by neoliberalism and structural adjustment policies in the 1990s and voting suggestions made publically by U.S. officials in the 2001 and 2006 elections in Nicaragua's national newspapers, for example, several Nicaraguans pointedly noted to me, "Here we are again, living in a Somocista state." History has not been forgotten, especially when it comes to U.S. power.

Somocismo codified a particular form of rule, and repression, allowing for certain kinds of foreign intervention, investment, and extraction. As the dictator of a nominally democratic state, Somoza promoted a populist agenda predicated on nepotism and favors to the faithful. Some women who demonstrated their loyalty to the regime benefited from employment and political favors doled out by Somoza. As Victoria González-Rivera (2010, 2011) has demonstrated, women's political participation in the national project has a long and complex history. The first wave of Nicaraguan feminism, which began in the nineteenth century, lobbied for women's suffrage and access to education. However, early feminist politics would be appropriated over time by the partisan and non-feminist projects of Somocismo. Successive regimes managed a state that consisted, in part, of client-citizens. Within this framework of clientelistic populism, socially conservative, economically elite women, as well as middle-class and working-class Nicaraguans who adhered to Somocismo, were able to acquire benefits from the state (Kettering 1988). Somocismo's populism was, like other Latin American states at the time, "selectively inclusive" of women and tended to reflect "corporatist favoritism" (Molyneux 2000: 56). Through employment opportunities, goods, and other forms of material support, a segment of Nicaragua's female population became invested in Somocismo, and women came to form part of the symbolic portrait promoted by the Somozas (González-Rivera 2010, 2011). It was a point of pride, for example—and one that followed the politically liberal logic of Somocismo—that women achieved the right to vote in 1955 during the first phase of the nominally democratic Somoza dynasty. Despite these concessions, however, the majority of Nicaraguan women lived at the bottom of a hierarchical, corrupt, and exploitative system that was managed through dictatorial rule. Their status, both economically and socially, placed them beneath their husbands, many of whom were vulnerable to the vicissitudes of abusive labor conditions and political repression. Most Nicaraguan women had few political and economic tools that would enable them to overcome their marginalized position. Overall, the consolidation of power in the hands of the Somozas, for both women and men, was fraught. It was, according to Jeffrey Gould (1990: 45), both "a contradictory acceptance and simultaneous rejection of the dominant exploitative system." The specific forms of marginalization that women endured and, more specifically, the way that women's sexuality was exploited figured heavily in the portrayal of a sadistic Somocismo and became a central political trope during the revolutionary era.

Sexual commerce certainly existed in Nicaragua long before the Somozas came to power. However, the dictatorship was—and in many ways continues to be—profoundly linked to prostitution in the minds of many Nicaraguans. Prostitution became illegal in the 1880s (an act of vagrancy) but was legalized from the late 1920s to the mid-1950s. The elder Somoza declared prostitution illegal in 1955 (the same year women's suffrage was established) and brothel managers, male and female, risked prison sentences for facilitating sexual labor. However, in reality, the legal maneuver to criminalize prostitution was a ruse. By this time, the Somoza regime and the National Guard were in full control of the prostitution industry in Nicaragua (González-Rivera 2011: 143) and only those who refused to pay the appropriate *mordidas* (bribes) and protection payments were truly at risk for prosecution. As one legal scholar put it, "From a legal perspective prostitution [was] prohibited; from a sanitary perspective, there [was] no control of prostitution, and from a policing point of view, there [was] no prosecution of prostitution" (E. Mendieta, quoted in González-Rivera 2011: 144). The state's role in the sex industry was widely known among Nicaraguans and it was evident that the National Guard and senior officials were benefiting financially, and otherwise, from what many Nicaraguans understood as the sexual exploitation of women who had few other resources or options. Perhaps more nefariously, it was widely rumored that the Somozas tolerated prostitution within their ranks. Many accusations circulated about prominent Somoza women, claiming they were prostitutes or had been instrumental in the exploitation of young women by entreating them to enter into the sex trade.[6]

In addition to their rather explicit profiteering from prostitution, the Somoza dynasty faced further accusations of moral and sexual impropriety. The regime was known to use sexual torture against dissidents, male and female, to elicit information from political prisoners and punish political adversaries. These brutal techniques to extract information, sometimes carried out by members of the Somoza family (Heyck 1990: 64–67), were relatively well known among the Nicaraguan population. But it was not until a series of high-profile rape cases that the Somoza regime encountered more massive public reaction and outcry. Two prominent revolutionaries and a female volunteer with the U.S. Peace Corps were raped by the National Guard for ostensibly political reasons and their stories were circulated in international channels (Hoyt 1996: 62; Randall 1981). However, the collective rape of almost twenty peasant women in the town of El Cua in 1968 likely remains the most salient reminder of sexual violence under Somocismo. The National Guard, in an effort to silence and punish women opposed to the Somoza regime, orchestrated the rape to demonstrate what political dissent might auger. The infamous sexual violence represented by the attacks in El Cua, even for many Somocista stalwarts and supporters, was the final straw. Indeed, the legacy of El Cua even almost a half-century later lives on in the collective public imaginary; most adult Nicaraguans know, by heart, the song composed by Carlos Mejia Godoy about the incident.[7] The Nicaraguan author Viktor Morales Henríquez posited that it was sexual corruption that allowed the first Somoza dictatorship to seize control of the country. Over time it would be that same sexual impropriety that would undermine any moral authority the regime had accumulated. As Morales Henríquez saw it, it was "plunder, sex and death" that sustained the Somoza dynasty (Morales Henríquez 1980: 45). The political rapes carried out by the National Guard in El Cua, coupled with the systematic abuses and exploitation of women who worked in the nation's state-run brothels, later proved to be precisely the image of moral and sexual depravity that would animate many Sandinista policies to "clean up" the country. Sexuality, as one might predict, became a key site for programs of moral hygiene.

How the long Somoza years affected men and women who were marked as *cochones* or *cochonas* is less clear than in the case of women, sex workers, and some of the higher-profile incidents of sexual violence. Accounts about how Nicaraguan sexual minorities were treated during the Somoza era differ; they speak of both repression and tolerance. It is commonly believed that the Somoza administrations openly tolerated male prostitution on the streets of Managua and that lesbians and gay men were allowed to join the ranks of the Liberal Party, as long as they remained well closeted. According to several sexual rights advocates, some members of the National Guard were known to frequent the public gathering places of cochones in search of sexual encounters. A well-known nightclub in Managua, Swan Lake — or, as it was colloquially and somewhat derogatorily known, el Charco de los Patos (the Duck Puddle)[8] — was a place where both heterosexual and homosexual women and men could interact, dance, and drink together.[9] Older Nicaraguan lesbians and gay men still remember the nightclub as a place of relative tolerance. It was also one that was effectively under the protection of the ruling regime and the National Guard. Although it was located in a modest building in an impoverished neighborhood in Managua, the Swan Lake nightclub was known as a place where certain members of the Somoza family and sectors of the Nicaraguan elite would carouse. The club itself is rumored to have been owned, or co-owned, by Bernabé Somoza, the son of Luis Somoza Debayle. Several people with whom I spoke in the early 1990s claimed that the senior Somoza was also known to have invited select cochones to his lavish parties. Others, however, reported a very different story. Rafael, a long-time sexual rights activist, claimed that "Somoza and la Guardia were the worst. . . . They had it out for us, for the cochones. Always!"

Women who had erotic and affective relationships with other women were said to have been welcome at venues such as Swan Lake and closeted lesbian women were, putatively, able to participate in the Somocista project as long as discretion was maintained. However, their stories and experiences rarely figure in the history of sexuality and Somocismo. There is one startling exception to Somoza-era erasures of "lesbians" (or, more accurately, women who had affective and erotic relationships with other women). Carmen Aguirre was a dedicated supporter of Somoza to the very end and someone who was both famous and infamous as La Caimana (the alligator woman).[10] Carmen (also known as "Carmelo" or "Carlos") owned a hugely successful fireworks business that, according to her widow, Hilda Scott, was launched with three *córdobas* (about fifty cents) lent by the senior Somoza himself. Aguirre achieved true fame when he appeared in the prominent liberal daily *La Prensa* sporting a moustache and a full suit and tie, his preferred mode of public presentation. Aguirre also openly declared her love for Scott, whom she married in a public ceremony, a bold act in Nicaragua in the 1960s. Together, they raised six adopted children. Aguirre's success in business allowed him to provide patronage to local folkloric events and dances; thus, he reflected the ethos of patron–client relations that ruled Nicaragua at the time. In one interview, Scott recounted that although Aguirre had suffered for her sexual alterity (and had been married off at thirteen to a man), she refused to endure intolerance on the street. Aguirre "react[ed] violently" to insults, according to Scott, and was victorious in several brawls with men that began with provocations about her gender and sexual preferences. She was, as Scott described it, a *machista*. While La Caimana's mythos is remarkable—and continues to be a topic of conversation in contemporary Nicaragua—his experiences were singular. Most women who had romances with other women, as most of my interlocutors reported, did so in clandestine ways and were unable to live public lives as lesbians. Most of their histories, unlike La Caimana's, have been lost (cf. Bolt González 1996a, 1996b; van Gijsel 2003).

Government-supported brothels and the relative tolerance that may have been given to some homosexual men and women indicate that sexuality was publicly visible, as a cultural phenomenon, during Somocismo. At best, men's homosexual encounters were ignored, tolerated, or allowed to continue within defined settings. At worst, sexual minorities as a class were singled out for abuse. The relationships that individuals had with powerful Somocistas or the National Guard seem to have deeply affected the treatment that particular cochones and cochonas received. Overall, the patterns of sexual tolerance, or lack of it, followed the same clientelist logic that shaped the country's political climate on a national scale. The specter of sexual licentiousness and morally corrupt practices that, among other things, had come to be associated with Somocismo would later become an important trope in Sandinista campaigns to discredit the dictatorial regime. First, however, there was a revolution to be had.

A Decade of Red and Black: Women, Feminism, and Sexual Rights in the Revolutionary Era

In 1979, after almost twenty years in the making, the FSLN marched triumphantly into Managua.[11] During his retreat from the capital city, "Tachito," the last of the Somoza family dictators, robbed the Treasury and heavily bombed the country before fleeing to the United States. To achieve this hard won victory the FSLN had combined lessons from the Cuban Revolution and the liberation theology of Vatican II, to craft a unique political model. The Sandinista vision diverged from classical Marxism's opposition to capitalism and was instead situated in opposition to Somocismo, imperialism, and the country's marginal position in the capitalist world system (Field 1999: 96–97). As one prominent Sandinista put it, the revolution was founded on a commitment to "Nationalism, Christian Values, Democracy, and Social Justice" (Miguel d'Escoto, quoted in Rosset and Vandermeer 1986: 441).[12] The early architects of the Sandinista project were students of Marxism who had become disenchanted with the Nicaraguan Socialist Party. Instead, they sought a more radical and nationalist challenge to the dictatorship. Carlos Fonseca, one of the founders of the FSLN, played a key role in crafting the revolutionary agenda and mission. Taking Sandino's earlier calls to action in the 1920s and '30s, Fonseca reworked and distilled Sandino's intellectual and ideological framework for a new generation of revolutionaries in the 1960s and '70s. The revolution was successful in large part because of the FSLN's ability to convene a remarkably diverse resistance to the dictatorship that included people from many socioeconomic classes, religious convictions, and regional affiliations.[13] Not all Nicaraguans supported the revolution, to be sure, but there was an extraordinary amount of popular support behind the insurrection, its communitarian ideals, and the prospect of national transformation. Importantly, from its very beginnings, the Sandinista Revolution was a composite political project, in terms of both its protagonists and the political goals that inspired them.

Exposing the moral corruption of Somocismo was high on the Sandinista agenda, and sexuality became a central political trope in these campaigns. Vilifying the dictatorship was not difficult to do. The Somoza regime had a sordid record of violations against the Nicaraguan people including well-known acts of political repression, rape, and torture. Beyond these obvious abuses, the Sandinistas also focused attention on the putatively moral transgressions of homosexuality and prostitution to signal the depravity of Somocismo in very specific, sexual terms. The Somozas and the National Guard had profited from women's prostitution, and it was not coincidental that Somoza-era brothels were some of the first buildings to be destroyed by the Sandinista state. As one of the founders of the FSLN put it, "Prostitution is a war of prejudice, discrimination . . . a war in which capitalism tries to turn women into trash, buying and selling them like merchandise, like a luxury item or cheap vegetable, depending on the quality of the merchandise" (Tomás Borge, quoted in Collinson 1990: 69). Reeducation and job training programs were established to provide skills for former female sex workers and as a way to incorporate them into the revolutionary project. In response to the perceived lasciviousness of Somoza-era capitalism, the Sandinistas also banned the use of women's bodies in advertising (Padilla et al. 1987). Banning these images was, arguably, a feminist act. However, the ideology motivating the legislation was more anticapitalist and anti-Somocista in its intent, critiquing the injurious nature of capitalist exploitation rather than signaling the unequal gender relations that also contributed to sex workers' marginality and denigration. Finally, and again invoking Somoza-era prostitution, the Sandinista government in the early 1980s prioritized closing gay bars and cordoning off streets in Managua where homosexual men gathered. In all, these efforts were more focused on eradicating the legacy of Somocismo and the exploitative conditions of capitalism than they were feminist commentaries. Rectifying the sins of sexuality was understood as a partial antidote to the multiple forms of putative deviance that characterized both the dictatorship and the corrupting forces of capitalism. Sexuality provided essential political leverage in the early years of Sandinismo.

For many Sandinista supporters with whom I have spoken, Somocismo was a time of "sexual chaos." Whether Nicaragua's sexual landscape — including prostitution or the public presence of cochones — was more or less chaotic during Somocismo or Sandinismo is debatable. What is clear is that the rhetoric of the time, and the policies that followed, aimed to link Somocismo with sexual impropriety and abuse. The claim that sex work and homosexuality were at odds with the revolutionary spirit — and, indeed, antithetical to its future — echoes orthodox versions of Marxism in both the nineteenth century and the twentieth. For many Marxist projects, sexual behavior that was not reproductive in nature was highly suspect. Whether because they were homoerotic couplings or because they were commodified in sex work, these relationships ultimately failed to (re)produce more new Marxists. Sex with prostitutes or sex between men was easily cast as a dalliance that detracted from the revolutionary endeavor, a decadent indulgence that reeked of bourgeois entitlement rather than the ideals associated with the revolution's "new man." In the case of prostitution, sexual energy was squandered, but perhaps more important, capitalist exploitation and the commodification of human bodies were vividly apparent. The fact that the Sandinistas chose to politically prioritize sexuality very early in the revolutionary effort suggests that sex was important to the Sandinistas. The policies they instituted were intended to counter exploitation with liberation and moral corruption with ethical propriety. The discourses and politics surrounding sex were a way to translate the intimacy of private domains into the political register of moral authority.

Although its shortcomings were many, the revolutionary project was intended to alleviate the inequalities that had long epitomized the country's history. Particularly in its early years, the Sandinista state was widely recognized for its social programs that sought to provide more equitable distribution of power and wealth to disenfranchised sectors of the population, including rural peasants, the urban poor, women, and workers. Many commentators have argued that Sandinista Nicaragua instituted the most democratic distribution of land in Latin America (Hoyt 2004: 17). The FSLN's Agrarian Reform and Cooperative Laws (1981) were the first in Latin America to recognize women's right to equal wages. Rural infrastructure in Nicaragua was invigorated with new housing, health posts, public transportation, schools, electricity, safe drinking water, vaccination campaigns, and a distribution network for basic food. Young urban women and men, often university students, were mobilized en masse to participate in literacy and health brigades in the countryside where they were to both teach and learn from *campesinos* (farmers, country folk). In some regions, women's illiteracy under the Somoza regimes had been as high as 100 percent. After mobilizing the literacy *brigadistas*, the Sandinistas brought the national illiteracy rate from 50 percent to 13 percent within just a few years (Randall 1994: 12). The Sandinista state also expanded preventive medicine to international acclaim. Three months of maternity leave and legal rights for "illegitimate" children challenged entrenched values regarding marital norms and constructions of the family (Collinson 1990; Molyneux 1985b). Commentators, Nicaraguan and otherwise, have debated the ultimate effectiveness of these programs. From their inception they were hobbled by limited resources and later were diminished by wartime privations. It is impossible to know how these programs might have ultimately flourished or failed, however, because the revolutionary project was a target of U.S. aggression from the start.

The Sandinista revolution took place at a time when Cold War tensions were high. Claiming that a communist threat was growing in what Washington dubbed America's "back yard," the U.S. administration and Central Intelligence Agency (CIA) mounted a covert war against Sandinista Nicaragua. Under the auspices of preventing "Marxist-Leninist dictatorships," U.S. military advisers began training the Frente Democrática Nicaragüense, better known as the Contras. The Contras were paramilitary fighters who were trained with the objective of unseating the Sandinistas and fomenting civil strife. The strategists managing the Contra campaign used armed guerrilla warfare and explosives in an attempt to defeat the Sandinista military forces. But a companion strategy also sought to destabilize the revolutionary government with attacks against so-called soft targets such as schools, health centers, and agricultural cooperatives sponsored by the FSLN. U.S. financial support for the counterinsurgency campaign was surreptitiously funneled to the Contras, paid for by the illegal sale of arms to Iran. As the magnitude of the U.S. government's illegal financial and military machinations became uncovered, "Iran–Contra" evolved into one of the largest political and military scandals in U.S. history.

Attacks in the form of military actions were central aspects of U.S. intervention, but propaganda campaigns were also instrumental in attempts to discredit the revolutionary regime. The Reagan administration, for example, vociferously denounced the human rights abuses that occurred when the Sandinistas displaced indigenous people on the country's Atlantic Coast (Bourgois 1981; Vilas 1989).[14] This accusation was meant to highlight the Sandinistas' failings and distract international attention from the more pervasive abuses that the U.S. government was supporting in Nicaragua and other parts of Latin America at the time.[15] A full-scale embargo initiated by the United States, coupled with a Sandinista conscription policy mandating military service for Nicaraguan men, eventually eroded the FSLN's base of support. The Contra war cost Nicaragua more than thirty thousand lives and slowly but surely bankrupted the economy. Militarily and symbolically, U.S. imperialism had come to cast a long shadow on Nicaragua, one that continues to have vestiges in the politics of the present.

During the Sandinista years, many iconic images of resistance and revolution depicted women in battle fatigues, sometimes with babies strapped to their backs or "una AK-47" slung over their shoulder. Working as combatants, field commanders, messengers, and keepers of safe houses, women made up approximately 30 percent of the insurrectionary forces.[16] Reflecting on the role of women in the revolutionary effort, one Sandinista woman said, "We never entered into a lot of theoretical discussions about women's liberation. . . . In fact we never said that we were equal—we simply demonstrated it in the battlefields, on the barricades and in the mountains" (quoted in Collinson 1990: 140). León was the first city to be fully liberated during the revolutionary insurrection, captured by a female *comandante*, Dora María Téllez. Women's involvement in the revolutionary effort at various levels was critical to the ultimate success of the Sandinista project. However, despite the heroics of the revolution's heroines, no woman was ever to be a part of the nine-man national directorate that ruled Sandinista Nicaragua. At the highest levels of decision making, women's roles were limited. Nonetheless, throughout the 1980s, formal participation by women in national political institutions was higher than it had ever been. Politically active groups of women were invited to comment on drafts of the country's new constitution. On International Women's Day in 1987, proponents of women's rights presented the "Proclama," which boldly denounced machismo as a hindrance to Nicaragua's social development and defined it as a sociocultural condition that required reform. The "Proclama" was a major policy victory at the time. It also served as a prelude to what many Nicaraguans understood to be cultural barriers to women's equality that became important arenas for political organizing in the 1990s and 2000s.

The Sandinista state developed formal political projects intended to incorporate women, but in many cases their purpose was to ensure women's continued involvement in the revolutionary project rather than to innovate new approaches to gender politics (Molyneux 1985a, 1985b). The FSLN formed the Asociación de Mujeres Nicaragüenses, Luisa Amanda Espinosa (AMNLAE), early in the revolutionary process to serve as an umbrella organization that would address issues such as family planning, domestic violence, and rape. While the Sandinista state had charted a set of expectations about AMNLAE's function, women within the organization were involved in a series of questions about the mission of the association. Would it be an instrument of the Sandinista party or a women's organization that might challenge the party hierarchies? Women's participation in AMNLAE, and the political experience they gained through their interactions with the Sandinista state and each other, effectively made political subjects out of women who were once defined as objects of policy.[17] The debates among the women of AMNLAE about the proper role of the organization within the country's political structure also set the stage for negotiating two particularly controversial gender issues: lesbian rights and abortion.

Although controversy about abortion and lesbianism would continue for many years—indeed, it continues into the present—AMNLAE's treatment of these issues offers an insight into the political challenges around sexuality and reproductive choice (Wessel 1991). Some members of AMNLAE hoped to address lesbian rights and abortion as part of the association's political mission. Others believed that these issues were too controversial both for the Sandinista state and for Nicaraguan society more generally. Elective abortion was illegal in Nicaragua prior to Sandinista control. However, a provision called "therapeutic abortion" allowed the procedure under special circumstances, including when the woman's life was endangered by the pregnancy or when the pregnancy had been caused by incest or rape. Since therapeutic abortion was available only in very limited circumstances and with the approval of at least three physicians, access to hygienic and safe abortions was very limited for most Nicaraguan women. Although illegal, botched abortions were among the leading causes of death among women of reproductive age in Nicaragua, the Sandinistas never legalized elective abortion (Collinson 1990: 118–19). The heavy casualties of the Contra war also buoyed a pro-natalist stance that encouraged women to have more children to repopulate the country (Kampwirth 2010: 164–65). In part, the FSLN and AMNLAE were wary of addressing any change to abortion law for fear of alienating the politically and morally influential Catholic church. For similar reasons, lesbian rights were seen by some members of AMNLAE as politically taboo. In the late 1980s, the director of AMNLAE publicly confirmed that lesbian rights were outside the organization's mandate, declaring that "lesbians march under their own banner" (quoted in Collinson 1990: 25). Although she later recanted her statement, her comment signaled that AMNLAE — at least at the leadership level — hoped to distance itself from the contentious topics of lesbianism and sexual rights.[18] What the director's comment and its retraction also indicate are the complex ways in which the history of sexuality and gender activism in Nicaragua cannot be easily divorced, ideologically or strategically, from the efforts to establish a more egalitarian society for both women and sexual minorities.

The political ethos of Sandinismo aimed to dissolve oppression of all kinds, including, presumably, those that were predicated on gender and sexuality. However, this was more difficult in practice than in theory. The relationship between Sandinismo and women's rights during the 1980s was a complicated negotiation between two apparently contradictory positions. The revolutionary state was committed to a particular form of communitarian politics,[19] and while Sandinismo did raise the profile of women as political actors, Sandinismo was not a feminist project per se. As with many Marxist projects, the inequalities that women faced were subordinated to the larger goal of ameliorating socioeconomic inequalities for a broader constituency in the name of *el pueblo* (the people). Some male leaders in the FSLN did acknowledge that the oppression of women was qualitatively distinct from class struggle. They recognized that women, even among the elite, endured specific forms of exploitation and marginalization that men did not. However, the official party line of the FSLN held that gender inequalities ought to be addressed within a political-economic framework. As an FSLN directive put it, "The emancipation of women as the outcome of a struggle against men . . . is divisive and distracts the people from their fundamental tasks . . . to lead the ideological, political and socioeconomic battles [to eliminate] all forms of oppression and discrimination."[20] As with many Eastern European forms of socialism, the "woman question" was difficult to reconcile within a set of revolutionary priorities that were grounded in the logics of socioeconomic class (Gal and Kligman 2000). Although the Sandinistas never fully incorporated a feminist orientation into their ideological framework, the revolution did provide several possibilities for women's participation in the country's future. However imperfectly, the Sandinista experiment expanded women's role in the arena of public struggle even if women's roles as mothers and victims of sexual commodification and machismo drove much of the FSLN's treatment of gender (see, e.g., Chuchryk 1991;

González-Rivera 2011; Randall 1994; Saporta Sternbach et al. 1992). Had gender-based concerns been more integral to the revolutionary process, the politics of gender equality and sexual rights might have been debated sooner and more profoundly.

Like feminism, sexual rights were not seen by the FSLN as a legitimate goal for revolutionary transformation. However, the Sandinistas' willingness to engage in some debate about gender offered a first step toward the organized work of self-identified *lesbianas*, *gays*, and *homosexuales*. The ability to discuss machismo, violence against women, and women's exclusion from positions of power in the Sandinista party opened the door to new ways of thinking about discrimination. The incorporation of women into the political process and debates about women's roles were signs of a growing public consciousness: inequalities based on sexual and gender difference were becoming politicized. For these reasons, many Nicaraguans, as well as scholars, credit the revolutionary period with giving sexual minorities more "room to maneuver" (Thayer 1997: 401). Nicaraguans marked by their sexual difference, historically categorized as cochones or cochonas, were, in a limited way, becoming associated with the new terms "*homosexual*," "*gay*," and "*lesbiana*." These initial lexical shifts began to emerge in earnest in the 1980s, circulated among a largely urban, educated, and politically engaged sector of the population.[21] However, sexuality as a political issue and sexual identity as a social category were beginning to become known by more and more of the Nicaraguan population.

The Nicaraguan Gay Movement, the Sandinistas, and *el SIDA*

The ideological and military demands of the Sandinista state were multiple, complex, and, more often than not, deeply ambivalent in regard to sexual rights. Sandinista Nicaragua did not systematically repress sexual minorities as a matter of policy. However, as was clear with Miguel's dismissal from his post in the Sandinista army, there were acts of discrimination against individual lesbians and gay men. Some prominent Sandinista spokespeople were also openly dismissive of gay and lesbian rights and, at times, vocal in disparaging same-sex sexuality. Individuals who were thought to be lesbian or gay, for example, were sometimes prevented from joining the Sandinista party (Babb 2001: 231). Beyond these instances of intolerance, the Sandinista state had to contend with elements of Marxist ideology that equated homosexuality with sexual decadence and capitalist corruption. The integration of sexual rights into the Sandinista project was made more difficult by the fact that homosexuality was often associated with the United States and Europe, locations in the global North that were, at times, believed to be morally suspect. Therefore, in the simplest terms, homosexuality was bourgeois decadence and an imperialist importation all at once. However, what also became clear through the Sandinista experiment is that neither of these reductionist positions would hold; the politics of sexuality and sexual rights were far more complex and dynamic.

The Nicaraguan Gay Movement was short-lived but ambitious. Founded in the mid-1980s and composed of *internacionalistas* and Nicaraguans who self-identified as homosexuales, gays, or lesbianas, the group began to meet in an effort to establish a place for sexual rights within the revolutionary trajectory. By 1986, as many as sixty people were gathering for clandestine meetings at which members discussed some of the challenges they faced as sexual minorities (Babb 2001; Randall 1993). However, the Sandinista state prohibited organizing outside formal political structures, and by March 1987, the movement had been secretly infiltrated by Sandinista State Security. Some thirty participants were brought in for questioning and fingerprinting, and some were arrested. Everyone charged by State Security was released the same day, suggesting that the government was not prioritizing severe punishment and repression but instead was sending a stern warning about political activity and sexual identity. Former members of the Nicaraguan Gay Movement with whom I have spoken have different interpretations of their treatment by Sandinista State Security. During one conversation, for instance, Humberto explained that participants were "treated badly." Some members said that they were "interrogated" and told that their gatherings were "counterrevolutionary" or a "political deviation." But other participants in the Nicaraguan Gay Movement were surprised at how well they were treated during questioning; no one was held for more than a few hours. Some of those questioned even claimed that Sandinista State Security was embarrassed about its decision to infiltrate the group (Babb 2001: 231). The silencing of the movement was seen as an overreaction to a relatively small coterie of participants who had not yet established an influential political voice. Furthermore, and ironically, most of the members of the Nicaraguan Gay Movement had been, and continued to be, supporters of the revolutionary project. Many were members of the Sandinista Party (Randall 1993:

912). In the end, members of the group chose to protect the revolutionary state by vowing not to speak of the group's infiltration and coerced closure. They did so largely because they supported the revolutionary cause and did not want to endanger its success. Members of the movement also agreed not to speak with the international media, because this would reflect badly on the revolution and provide fodder for critics of the Sandinista state, including the U.S. government.

The decision to break up the meetings of the Nicaraguan Gay Movement was made in a difficult context: Nicaragua was at war, security precautions were at their height, and there were ongoing efforts to topple the revolutionary regime. State Security agents warned members of the Nicaraguan Gay Movement that "in a state of siege this kind of group cannot exist" (Amy Bank, quoted in Randall 1993: 913). The Sandinistas had already faced international criticism for their treatment of minorities (the indigenous populations of the Atlantic coast region), and evidence of further suppression might have added more fuel to the fire of Cold War rhetoric. However, some influential individuals within the Sandinista power structure were also suspicious about the loyalty of sexual minorities. As one member of the Nicaraguan Gay Movement put it, "They said that bisexuals and homosexuals could easily be bought by the enemy, utilized in ways that could hurt the revolution" (Hazel Fonseca, quoted in Randall 1993: 916). The Nicaraguan Gay Movement's meetings may have been halted because of wartime precautions and the government's fear of further international criticism. However, the fact that the Nicaraguan Gay Movement was seen by many Sandinistas as antithetical to the ideals of the revolutionary project certainly played a role in the movement's being dismantled.

During the revolutionary era, homosexuality was at times configured as a Northern import—something associated with North America and Europe—and therefore an affront to "traditional" Nicaraguan values.[22] Organizing politically around the issue of sexual identity, like the "woman question," challenged the Marxian orientation of the revolutionary project. For some members of the Sandinista ruling elite, homosexuality was a bourgeois perversion that was incommensurable with the ideal of what was called the "new man." The revolution's new man was one who exercised self-sacrifice, educated himself in the tenets of revolutionary consciousness, and did not engage in the sexual degradation of women (González-Rivera 2011: 16). He was a man who was expected to forgo the putative perversions wrought by capitalism and the previous social orders. The transgressive sexuality of effeminate men who had sex with men and of women involved in same-sex relationships were envisioned by some Sandinistas as forms of self-indulgence that needed to be curtailed. Those who wished to organize a political voice around a singular social identity or issue—whether in terms of gender or sexuality—seemed to pose a threat to the communitarian spirit of the revolution.

The politics of sexuality continued to be stifled and largely operated underground in the mid-1980s. However, soon after the controversial yet relatively quiet infiltration of the country's first gay organization, the Sandinistas did forge their first working relationship with sexual health advocates, some of whom would go on to become powerful proponents of sexual rights. In 1988, responding to a potential increase in HIV infection, the Sandinista state devised a collaborative project with advocates and sexual health workers. The Sandinista Minister of Health, Dora María Téllez (the comandante made famous during the insurrection), devised a remarkably forward-thinking program to combat the spread of HIV/AIDS.[23] Téllez invited lesbians and homosexual men to collaborate with the Ministry of Health on a new sex-education outreach project that would work to inform vulnerable sectors of the population about HIV infection and prevention. The Collective of Popular Educators Concerned with HIV/AIDS (CEP-SIDA) recruited two hundred people to conduct community health education and outreach. They distributed pamphlets, condoms, and advice to men who had sex with men, as well as to female sex workers.[24] Nonetheless, sexuality continued to be, and AIDS was becoming, a sensitive issue. In fact, Téllez's first task on behalf of CEP-SIDA was to convince the revolutionary government that outreach workers should not be harassed by the police or other officials. Health *brigadistas* from the United States and Europe arrived in Nicaragua to collaborate with local activists in CEP-SIDA. These solidarity brigades provided material support (such as condoms and popular education materials) for the grassroots campaigns that were already under way in cruising areas frequented by men in search of sex with other men and among female sex workers (Randall 1994).[25] At the same time, the participation of Northern allies in these campaigns lent further evidence to suspicions that homosexuality, sexual disease, and, perhaps, degeneracy originated in the North. The co-development of CEP-SIDA by grassroots advocates and the Sandinista government did not result in unqualified Sandinista support for sexual rights, but it was a significant policy shift. It marked the first large-scale and "out" relationship among Nicaraguan sexual health activists, their allies in the United States and Europe, and the revolutionary government.

Over the course of the 1980s, the Sandinistas' treatment of sexuality moved from a policy of infiltration to one of limited cooperation. Policies to alleviate the discrimination faced by sexual minorities on the street, in the workplace, and in the home were never a part of the Sandinista agenda. The suppression of the Nicaraguan Gay Movement also indicated that the revolutionary regime was suspicious of sexual rights as a political project. However, Sandinista Nicaragua did not practice the heavy-handed persecution, detention, and quarantine of (suspected or known) homosexuals, as was the case in Cuba.[26] Early Sandinista programs to clear out homosexual men's gathering places signaled that sexuality continued to be a morally and politically volatile issue. And yet the revolutionary regime did manage to foster a political climate that created a greater degree of visibility for Nicaraguan lesbians and homosexual men. One of the first public displays of Nicaraguan gay pride, for instance, appeared in 1989, at the tenth anniversary celebration of the revolution, when a group of approximately thirty lesbian and gay Nicaraguans marched to Managua's Plaza of the Revolution wearing black T-shirts emblazoned with pink triangles (Randall 1994: 281).

Many Nicaraguans in the 1980s who were beginning to identify themselves as lesbian, gay, or homosexual were, like their neighbors in the *barrio*, schooled in Sandinismo; their approaches to activism would come to reflect this. Many sexual rights advocates were interested in revolutionizing how society itself conceived of sexuality. As Millie Thayer put it, "These were demands not just for space in society, but for a thorough transformation of the society in which lesbians [and gay men] wanted to be included" (1997: 393). Sexual rights activists were intent on spreading their message to the larger Nicaraguan population, not only to those who already saw themselves as members of a sexual minority. Activists also began to construct a political project in which tolerance and respect for difference would be embraced by all Nicaraguans, not only gays and lesbians. Foundational to these sorts of advocacy strategies was the belief that social transformation would not be achieved through enclave politics. True transformation, the real *revuelta* (uprising), demanded that society, in its entirety, be changed.[27] This political orientation, one that envisions the nation as the proper object of social transformation, continues to reverberate in the present in interventions such as the Sexualidad Libre de Prejuicios (Sexuality Free from Prejudice) events held in a number of Nicaraguan cities every June.

Sexual rights activism began to take shape in Nicaragua in part because Sandinismo offered opportunities to question the status quo. Yet both gender politics and sexual rights were, officially, suspected of being possible deviations from the true revolutionary path. The combination of these political openings and, ironically, closures ultimately offered a template for future struggles. For activists whose political skills were honed during this time, the communitarian ethos of revolution was a constant provocation; it inspired them to imagine social transformation in national dimensions and, at the same time, highlighted the arenas of discrimination that were unresolved by the revolutionary project. Indeed, some activists who would become involved in and committed to sexual rights were compelled by the Sandinista state's refusal to do so. Several Nicaraguans who identified themselves as lesbian or gay told me that they became reinvested in sexual rights activism precisely because they had been prohibited from doing so, openly, during the Sandinistas' reign. Like many feminists in the wake of the revolutionary period, proponents of sexual rights were able voice their experiences of persecution more publicly and devote their activist energy to concerns about sexual equality when the revolution came to an end. The demise of the revolutionary regime in 1990 signaled the close of a particular ideological epoch, but it also inaugurated an era of greater global networks for advocates, the growth of Nicaraguan NGOs, and increased civil society activism. By this time, too, closet doors were opening around the world, and Nicaraguan activists were beginning to see themselves as part of a growing global movement for sexual rights (see also Adam et al. 1999; Altman 2001; de la Dehesa 2010; Donham 1998; Parker 1999; Warner 1999).

Neoliberalism, Post-Sandinismo and the NGO "Boom": 1990–2001

Sandinismo created political prospects and opportunities that were impossible in previous times. But the ideals and policies of the decade-long Sandinista experiment were quickly dissolved by succeeding regimes and replaced with more socially conservative agendas. Partly in response to new forms of conservatism, a new generation of sexual politics—both rights-based and reactionary—arose over the next two decades. The electoral defeat of the Sandinistas was the end of the revolution and, for some, "a triumph for U.S. policy" (Prevost and Vanden 1997: 3). Before the national elections in 1990, when the Sandinistas were voted out of office, the Contra war was escalated and tens of millions of dollars were funneled from the United States, through the CIA and the National Endowment for Democracy, to support the Unified National Opposition (UNO) party that was challenging the Sandinistas (Walker and Armory 2000: 77).[28] Violeta Barrios Chamorro, UNO's presidential candidate, won by a significant margin. She would become the first elected female head of state in the Americas and the only woman ever to have unseated an incumbent president. Chamorro's platform, one largely based on "mothering" the nation and moving the country toward reconciliation, was not, however, a feminist victory (Kampwirth 1996b).[29] Services that were especially critical for women, such as child care and health programs, were decimated by structural adjustment policies. In this more socially conservative climate, activists found themselves united and, in many ways, revitalized in their struggles against a common enemy. As Dora Maria Téllez put it, "On the one hand, feminist movements everywhere [in the world] are gaining in strength. In Nicaragua, the fact that there's been a depolarization, politically speaking, has also opened up a space for this sort of struggle. And I think there's something else, which may be the most interesting reason of all: this government and the political Right in general, have pushed a very conservative line on women" (quoted in Randall 1994: 259). For many activists, crossing this "very conservative line" became a political priority. Women's rights became a critical arena of contestation. At the same time, sexuality continued to provoke something akin to a moral crisis, and conservative calls for the criminalization of homosexuality became institutionalized.

Once Chamorro's administration was securely in place, the Nicaraguan National Assembly voted to approve a set of revisions to the country's penal code. Article 204, the "antisodomy" provision in the penal code, was made far more severe. The more virulent text now pronounced, "Anyone who induces, promotes, propagandizes, or practices in scandalous form sexual intercourse between persons of the same sex commits the crime of sodomy and shall incur one to three years of imprisonment."[30] Nicaragua's more virulent antisodomy law implicated not only men who had sex with men (the common province of antisodomy legislation) but also women. The broad language of the legislation, indicting "anyone who induces, promotes, [or] propagandizes (same-sex intercourse)," also threatened organizations, therapists, social workers, or journalists who might be regarded as promoting same-sex sexuality in some form. The sheer scope of the law's prosecutorial reach had a chilling effect, even if NGO employees, journalists, and social service providers were never actually arrested. At a time that the vast majority of Latin American countries had no anti-sodomy laws or specific legal prohibitions against same-sex sexual interactions between consenting adults, Nicaragua's decision to institute such legislation appeared acutely retrograde (Corrales and Pecheny 2010). Notably, the Sandinista members of the National Assembly voted against the revisions to Article 204, unanimously.[31]

While it is impossible to ascertain all of the contingencies that led legislators to increase the scope of the antisodomy law, their actions were certainly related to the wider political dynamics of the time. Civil society was booming, and nongovernmental entities, often funded by foreign governments and institutions, were gaining influence in Nicaraguan politics and garnering greater recognition among the population. Nicaraguan lawmakers may have been concerned about ebbing state power, worried about the influence of nongovernmental actors, and hoping to bolster the sovereignty of their own legal purview. Whatever the influence of NGOs, the effects of profound neoliberal economic policies were being felt; there was greater corporate and foreign influence in the country and, hence, a greater affront to state power. Influential transnational anti-abortion campaigns and the growing prominence of Christian fundamentalism all conditioned the political context in which National Assembly members cast their votes. But perhaps above all was the perception that by moving the country to the right, in a more socially conservative direction, non-Sandinista lawmakers might be able to provide an antidote to the progressive gains made during the revolutionary era.

For sexual rights advocates and others, the legislative decision to enhance the antisodomy law was not only an attack on sexual minorities, but also a violation of privacy and an attack on individual rights, both of which are enshrined in the Nicaraguan constitution. Their comments on the legislation illustrate how advocates were beginning both to voice a collective response and to draw on notions of national patrimony and human rights in their political discourse. Their statement proclaimed, "The lesbian and homosexual collectives have rejected Article 204 as unconstitutional and a violation of our human and civil rights. . . . The Nicaraguan Constitution protects all citizens from discrimination or persecution based on race, ideology, religion or sex, and this latter point includes sexual preference. . . . The ambiguous language of the article could be used against two same-sex people living together, were this deemed 'scandalous' or to persecute journalists writing about homosexuals said to be 'promoting' homosexuality. The public does not support Article 204. . . . It threatens everyone's right to keep the government out of the bedroom."[32] In response to Article 204, sexual rights advocates created an educational campaign about sexual preference, distributed flyers, and collected more than four thousand signatures to support a presidential veto of the legislation (Bolt González 1996a: 128). Following the implementation of Article 204, twenty-five organizations gathered for a series of events to campaign for Sexuality Free from Prejudice. Activists also produced a highly critical analysis and response to Article 204 and held protests at the National Assembly. An appeal was made to the Supreme Court claiming that Article 204 violated the right to privacy, freedom of expression, and nondiscrimination before the law and therefore that it contravened international standards for human rights. Those who opposed Article 204 found allies in organizations such as Amnesty International and the International Gay and Lesbian Human Rights Commission (IGLHRC), both of which condemned the legislation as violating the human rights of all Nicaraguans. As a spokesperson for IGLHRC explained, "While other countries are making progress on human rights issues, the Nicaraguan government is moving backwards by making homosexual relations illegal."[33] Nevertheless, on 8 July 1992, President Chamorro ratified the series of penal reforms. Successive efforts to overturn the law were largely ignored. In their attempts to rescind Article 204, advocates posed incisive challenges and developed critical rhetorical techniques that would animate many elements of the lucha going forward. Indeed, this marked a new era for sexual rights advocacy, explicitly calling attention to human rights, sexual identity, and legal discrimination. New approaches to sexual justice were beginning to take shape, and advocates were developing new arenas for political dissent in civil society activism.

Many Nicaraguans describe the early 1990s as *el boom* of NGOs, a time when the state-based politics of the previous era gave way to new struggles for rights. Long-time activists and Sandinista supporters found themselves freed from obligations to the Sandinista party in the wake of the electoral defeat, enabling them to devise new gender and sexual rights strategies (Fernández Poncela 2001). Activists formed issue-oriented networks such as the Movimiento Autónomo de Mujeres (Autonomous Women's Movement) in a bid to address some of the intractable social problems that the Sandinistas had failed to ameliorate. The network model of political action (Keck and Sikkink 1998; Riles 2000) aimed to address social injustice and negotiate internal conflicts in a more lateral fashion than had been possible under the verticalist, "umbrella" model of power that prevailed during Sandinista rule. Autonomous feminist groups hosted a watershed event in 1991, called the Festival of the 52 Percent, which set forth a series of resolutions, including making violence against women a criminal offense, commemorating International Women's Day, celebrating International Gay and Lesbian Day, and organizing a network of female journalists to establish a radio station dedicated to women's issues (Babb 2001; Randall 1994: 281). Self-identified lesbians at the Festival of the 52 Percent also held a public coming out event, making lesbian rights a more explicit and visible element of feminist and women's rights agendas. The Sandinista party itself faced momentous changes in the mid-1990s when the Sandinista Renovation Movement disengaged from the party proper, taking key spokespersons with it (Hoyt 2004; Walker 2000).[34]

The overlapping politics of gender and sexual rights were invigorated by the new political opportunities of increased civil society advocacy. Spurred by an emphasis on democratization, as well as an influx of U.S. and European development funding, a handful of NGOs formed to address different dimensions of sexual rights and discrimination at the national level. Several of these organizations were founded by activists who had been deeply committed to the Sandinista project as well as feminist principles. Initially conceived by a small group of Nicaraguan women and internacionalistas in the late 1980s, the feminist organization Puntos de Encuentro (Common Ground) was officially established in 1991. Having experienced both the successes and the failures of gender rights organizing during the Sandinista era, Puntos de Encuentro's founders brought a feminist perspective to their work with women and Nicaraguan youth (Howe 2008a). Young people made up more than half of the country's population; the architects of Puntos de Encuentro thus understood youth to be a critical constituency who could provide a foundation for social transformation. Puntos de Encuentro maintained that young people and women shared the conditions of "subordination, discrimination, and patriarchal violence" in Nicaraguan families and in society more generally. Attempting to reach as wide an audience as possible, Puntos de

FIGURE 1.4 *La Boletina* has the widest circulation of any magazine in Nicaragua and has been published for the past two decades by the Nicaraguan feminist NGO Puntos de Encuentro. This issue (Fall 2001) contains an extensive discussion of key issues for women in the elections of 2001 and features a section titled "My Body Is Mine," in which the actress from the popular television show *Betty La Fea* (*Ugly Betty*) moderates a discussion of women's thoughts about their bodies and autonomy. This issue also contains a section on lesbians and *lesbofobia*.

Encuentro also published some of its materials in English and Miskitu for the populations of the Atlantic coast, as well as in Spanish for those residing on the Pacific side of the country. Puntos de Encuentro continues to carry out its work to alleviate discrimination in all forms, and several of its projects are represented in this book.

Fundación Nimehuatzin was established in 1990 to provide information about HIV transmission to vulnerable communities and to provide support for those living with AIDS. Nimehuatzin derives its name from a Nahuatl word that means "rising up for a noble cause." A central part of the organization's mission since the early 1990s has been raising awareness and reducing stigma about HIV/AIDS. After several years of work, Fundación Nimehuatzin was recognized with an award from the United Nations. The NGO Fundación Xochiquetzal, named after the Aztec goddess of female sexuality, fertility, and beauty, was also part of the boom in NGOs in the early 1990s. The organization's perspective on sexual rights insists that gender equity must be established and that the defense of sexual diversity is an issue of human rights. Xochiquetzal founded the magazine *Fuera del Closet* (Out of the Closet), which aims to transform concepts of sexuality, including homosexuality and lesbianism.

Each of these organizations was founded on the principle that civil

FIGURE 1.5 Fundación Xochiquetzal is a prominent Nicaraguan NGO working on issues of sexuality, health, and rights. This poster, showing the goddess Xochiquetzal, promotes the Jornada por una Sexualidad Libre de Prejuicios (Gathering for Sexuality Free from Prejudice) of 1998. The script at the bottom says, "Every one of us has the right to be different and to love differently."

society, rather than state-based intervention, is the most effective route to social transformation. In this sense, the organizations follow a certain neoliberal logic that eschews state management and instead invests social transformation in the private sector. Divesting social justice from state entities also coincides with global trends to create NGOs in the absence of states' interest and ability to ameliorate discriminatory practices (Edelman 2001; Fisher 1997). However, in the Nicaraguan case, these organizations were also developed as a direct response to an increasingly repressive legal regime and socially conservative climate.

Social conservatism and neoliberal economic austerity grew during the Chamorro years and continued to flourish during the presidency of Arnoldo Alemán, leader of the Constitutional Liberal Party (the Liberales). Working closely with the U.S. Agency for International Development, the International Monetary Fund, and the World Bank, Alemán's administration further downsized the public sector, privatized public-sector industries, and instituted provisions that favored foreign investment (Dye and Close 2004; Puig 2004). Following the mandates of neoliberal economic restructuring, the Alemán regime was charged with disassembling the public sector, which led to high levels of unemployment. While he reduced public expenditures and entreated the citizenry to *aguantar* (bear or suffer) more neoliberal reforms, Alemán's personal

FIGURE 1.6 Since the end of the Sandinista revolutionary era, anti-abortion campaigns and Christian fundamentalist messages, many of them originating in the United States, have appeared in greater numbers in Nicaragua. Here a bumper sticker that reads "We Say No to Abortion" is affixed to the gas tank of a motorcycle. Note the brand name on the motorcycle itself, "Genesis."

fortune skyrocketed. Corruption was rampant within his regime from the top down; in 2001, Transparency International dubbed Nicaragua one of the fifteen most corrupt countries in the world.[35]

Beyond financial malfeasance and neoliberal austerity measures, the Alemán regime reflected the results of several decades of influence by socially conservative, right-wing forces and Christian fundamentalism that promoted the political rhetoric of "family values." Alemán's administration, for example, developed new pedagogical materials for Nicaraguan public schools that emphasized what the Nicaraguan Ministry of Education called "Victorian morals." The educational code was revised to state that "sex between people of the same sex and sex with animals . . . are morally repugnant."[36] Alemán's government also maintained a particularly cozy relationship with the Catholic church. The church provided a quotient of moral legitimacy and protection in the face of mounting evidence of the regime's corruption and abuses, as well as a public critique of a rather "unholy" alliance between church and state (Pérez-

Baltodano 2004). Moral engineering of this sort was sustained not only by the doctrine of the Catholic church, but also by transnational Protestant religious movements and international campaigns against reproductive rights. By seamlessly equating bestiality and homosexuality, the Alemán regime seemed to follow the lead of some prominent evangelicals in the United States, who likewise have positioned homosexuality and bestiality as crimes against God and nature. However, the sexual politics unfolding in Nicaragua at the time were not limited to legal codes, textbooks, or socially conservative impulses.

The Daughter of the Revolution and the Child Rapist

The presidential campaign of 2001 made it clear that although the Sandinista Revolution was now history, Nicaraguan politics continued to elicit anxious commentary and recommendations from U.S. policymakers concerned about leftist tendencies in the region. As I followed the elections as both an anthropologist and an international elections observer with the U.S.-based Carter Center, it was clear that political meddling from the North was largely drowned out by accusations closer to home. Indeed, a *denuncia* leveled against the Sandinista presidential candidate, Daniel Ortega, would color the entire electoral ecology of the campaign; it called unprecedented attention to sex, power, and politics in the national imaginary. The race in 2001 between Ortega and the Liberal Party's candidate, Enrique Bolaños, marked Ortega's second attempt to reclaim the presidency since his loss to Chamorro in 1990. The U.S. State Department expressed concern about the U.S. government's worries about an electoral win by the FSLN. In the Senate, Jessie Helms suggested that the United States would need to "rethink" its relationship with Nicaragua should the Sandinistas come to power once again. However, the ink spilled by U.S. government officials was far less interesting to many in the electorate than the media frenzy surrounding the "daughter of the revolution" and "the child rapist." Likely the biggest sexual scandal that Nicaragua had ever seen, the "Zoilamérica question" brought sexuality into political discourse more explicitly than it had been before, both because of the detailed accounts of alleged sex crimes and because the whole country attentively watched as the spectacle unfolded.

Zoilamérica Narváez, Daniel Ortega's adopted stepdaughter, was known affectionately throughout the 1980s as the daughter of the revolution. In 1998, after undergoing years of therapy, Narváez came forth with an accusation that Ortega had sexually abused her starting when she was eleven and throughout his tenure as President of the Republic. Narváez's original allegation made both national and international headlines. Shocking in its own right, the accusation was also fueled by the fact that it coincided with the dalliances between President Bill Clinton and Monica Lewinsky, a sexual conflagration that came to be known as "Monicagate" (Kipnis 1999).[37] Reignited by the political race of 2001, the Zoilamérica controversy was on the minds of many, if not all, Nicaraguan voters. Nicaraguan national newspapers published Narváez's account of the alleged assaults, with all of the lurid details. Partly because of its length (forty-eight pages), Narváez's testimony was published in serialized installments; this editorial decision also made for a very soap-opera-like saga. Some Sandinista loyalists saw Narváez's claim as a neurotic fantasy of a troubled woman. Others believed that Narvaez had been put up to the task by feminist leaders in an effort to discredit Ortega, or that her accusation was part of a larger conspiracy to destroy the Sandinista Party and Ortega himself (Hoyt 2004: 26). More insidiously, some believed that Narváez had been cajoled by the opposing party to come forward with her denuncia for the sole purpose of defeating Ortega at the polls. Many Nicaraguans, including several prominent feminists and women's rights proponents, believed that Narváez had been sexually abused by Ortega; they had little doubt that she was telling the truth (González-Rivera 2011: 170). For his part, Ortega was remarkably and uncharacteristically silent. Instead, he let his (common-law) wife and Zoilamérica's mother, Rosario Murillo, respond to round after round of inquiries. Murillo insisted that Zoilamérica was "troubled" and that the matter was "a family affair."[38] However, for many commentators, the accusation was far from a family affair; it was indicative of the cult of personality that Ortega had mastered, as well as a demonstration of patriarchal values and a refusal to change entrenched ethical failures (Zimmerman 1998).

For many feminists, as well as others who had been sympathetic supporters of the Sandinista project for decades, Zoilamérica's claim was the final straw. On the back of a series of failures and betrayals by Ortega and other members of the FLSN, and given its apparent veracity and Ortega's silence, he had become unforgivable. Feminist and women's rights activists revived the debate about Zoilamérica's accusation during the election cycle by running a series of advertisements in the national newspapers that pilloried Ortega, with statements reading "No Queremos un

Presidente Violador de Niñas—Justicia para Zoilamérica" (We Don't Want a [Girl] Child Rapist for President—Justice for Zoilamérica).[39] The opposing Liberal Party also launched campaigns to highlight Ortega's potentially criminal sexual behavior.[40] For activists involved with sexual and gender rights, Narváez's accusation was divisive. Many activists believed that her story was true, especially following the detailed description that had such wide public circulation. Others were skeptical, believing that Ortega, an ideological hero, was incapable of such behavior and that the accusation was simply a ploy of the opposing party. Whatever views individual activists held about Narváez's allegation, the denuncia itself was an opportunity for the feminist and women's rights community to draw public attention to the problem of rape, incest, and child sexual abuse in Nicaragua. Many activists with whom I spoke believed that Nicaragua suffered from a high incidence of child sexual abuse and that the phenomenon was vastly underreported. Regardless of the electoral outcome that followed, activists found some political traction in Narváez's denuncia and launched campaigns to draw attention to the sexual exploitation of Nicaraguan girls.

Despite a political *pacto* (agreement) that he and former President Alemán had devised—which allowed for a much smaller percentage of the popular vote for victory—Ortega failed to capture the presidency.[41] Enrique Bolaños, the candidate of the socially conservative Liberal Constitutionalist Party, won the election and ruled the country from 2002 to 2007. Bolaños's regime was neoliberal in its fiscal approach but achieved a major political victory against fraud and fiscal malfeasance when the administration prosecuted former president Arnoldo Alemán for corruption, embezzlement, and money laundering. In 2003 Alemán was sentenced to a twenty-year prison term (most of which he has served under house arrest at his palatial ranch outside Managua). The Bolaños administration did little for, or against, the lucha for sexual rights. However, according to Amnesty International, Bolaños allegedly ordered a list of all of the members of his government who were suspected of being part of the "gay–lesbian world" so that he could dismiss them before stepping down as president.[42]

Faith and Payback: Decriminalizing Sex and Banning Therapeutic Abortion

The elections of 2006 returned the Sandinistas to presidential power, though in a much changed form. As President of the Republic once again,

FIGURE 1.7 Daniel Ortega has been the Sandinista presidential candidate multiple times. This photograph was taken by the author a few hours before his victory in 2006 was announced. After a decade and a half out of office, Ortega had retaken his seat in Nicaraguan politics, despite many concerns around electoral law and the accusations of sexual abuse leveled by his adopted step-daughter, Zoilamérica Narváez. In 2011, Ortega was reelected president of Nicaragua.

Daniel Ortega rather unsurprisingly allied himself with the neo-socialist, anti-imperialist values of Hugo Chávez's Bolivarian Revolution.[43] However, Ortega also embraced socially conservative positions favored by powerful religious interests in Nicaragua, the Catholic and evangelical churches. Part of the realignment was Ortega's support of criminalizing abortion in all forms, including when a woman's life was in danger. Article 165 of the Nicaraguan criminal code, the therapeutic abortion provision, had allowed women to obtain abortions if their lives were threatened by carrying a pregnancy to term or if a pregnancy was the result of rape or incest. In 2006, immediately before the elections, the Nicaraguan National Assembly voted to overturn the therapeutic abortion provision, which had been a part of Nicaraguan law for more than a century. The National Assembly's decision to prohibit women's right to therapeutic abortion was a result of mounting pressure from both the Catholic and evangelical churches and the outcome of transnational anti-abortion campaigns that began in Nicaragua in the 1990s. For many observers, Ortega's swift support for the anti-abortion measure, especially given that the country has one of the highest maternal mortality rates in the region,[44] was a shameless political maneuver to secure more socially conservative votes. Before the elections, Ortega was increasingly associating himself with the Catho-

FIGURE 1.8 Feminists and women's rights activists have been actively protesting against banning therapeutic abortion in Nicaragua, a provision that has been part of Nicaraguan law for more than a century and that allows for a therapeutic abortion in the case of danger to a woman's life, incest, or rape, following certification by three physicians. Despite public protests such as this one in Managua (2006), all forms of abortion were banned in Nicaragua just prior to the 2006 presidential elections, making the country one of very few in the world to have such severe restrictions on reproductive health. The text on the banner reads, "Violence against Women also Occurs When We Are Denied the Right to Live. We Demand That Therapeutic Abortion Be Maintained."

lic church, as was his wife, Rosario Murillo. Although they had been co-habitating "in sin" for decades, Ortega and Murillo were formally married in Managua's cathedral before the elections. Ortega proceeded to take seemingly every opportunity to be photographed attending mass or convening with clergy. Murillo was also vociferous about her newly apparent faith; these declarations of piety were a surprise to many Nicaraguans, since Murillo for decades has been known to prefer astrology and the zodiac to Sunday mass and church doctrine. Nonetheless, in an interview on a popular radio station she underscored the FSLN's new political position: "Precisely because we have faith, because we have religion, because we are believers, because we love God above all things. . . . The [Sandinista] Front . . . says, 'No to abortion, yes to life!'"[45]

For many gender and sexual rights advocates, Ortega's support of the anti-abortion legislation was an act of retribution against the country's feminists, who had long lobbied, in both street protests and the halls of government, to prevent precisely such an erosion of reproductive rights. It was, for some, also a form of "payback" for the Zoilamérica campaigns. Indeed, as Karen Kampwirth argues, it appears as though the FSLN was willing to oppose its former allies in the women's movement for the sake of guaranteeing more socially conservative votes. Rather than an ideological shift to the right, banning therapeutic abortion seemed to be a desperate attempt to secure the election after a decade and a half out of power (Kampwirth 2010: 174).[46] Whatever the motive, the law has had its effects. After the abortion prohibition went into effect, several international organizations attempted to persuade the Nicaraguan government to rescind the legislation, to no avail (see Vigil 2006).[47] Within days, maternal deaths were on the rise.

The changes to Nicaraguan law in 2006 had profound effects. In the very same legislative process that criminalized abortion, Article 204 was overturned, and "sodomy" was no longer illegal. Abortion became punishable by up to ten years in prison, and Nicaragua now ranks among six countries in the world that prohibit the procedure for any reason, including saving a pregnant woman's life.[48] If it were not for the tragedy of women's lives lost due to botched illegal abortions,[49] the juridical transformation that occurred in the National Assembly would be *telenovela*-like in its dramatic outcome: Nicaragua went from having one of the most repressive antisodomy laws in the Americas to having one of the most restrictive anti-abortion laws in the world.

The apparent sacrifice of reproductive rights on the altar of sexual rights is a puzzling irony. Set in the context of Nicaraguan politics, however, these political turns appear to be the work of secret deals and political concessions to religious and socially conservative political forces. Since Article 204 was abolished in 2007, I have asked several Nicaraguan sexual rights activists, political commentators, journalists, and academics why the antisodomy law was overturned when it was. None of them have an answer.[50] Clearly, the decision by the Nicaraguan National Assembly to overturn Article 204 and ban therapeutic abortion was linked to the Sandinistas' return to power and, in particular, to Ortega's cozier relationship with the Catholic church. Abortion and lesbian and gay rights also, without question, continue to be two extremely controversial issues for many Nicaraguans, with devout Catholics and evangelicals on one end of the spectrum of public opinion and feminist and sexual rights activists on the other. Many of the people with whom I spoke said that it was certainly possible that some political horse-trading took place in the halls of National Assembly, where "the gays" were given dispensation in exchange for tighter restrictions on women's reproductive freedoms. Daniel Ortega's reelection to the presidency in 2011 suggests that the seemingly contradictory logic that has increased sexual rights while demolishing reproductive choice will probably continue. Even if the jury is still out on precisely how these juridical decisions came about, it is clear that the Nicaraguan state remains committed to a biopolitics that seeks to manage the sexuality of its population, whether in the form of reproductive choice or same-sex erotics.

Sexual rights advocates who fought for years to abolish the antisodomy law can take credit and pride in the fact that the law has been abolished. In their efforts to transform the moral and cultural conditions of Nicaragua, activists have had to engage their own long and complex political history, including various forms of egalitarianism, from Marxism to feminism, as well as an acute understanding of and experience with interventionist politics from el Norte. The antisodomy law may have ended suddenly, and dramatically, but, as I will demonstrate in the chapters that follow, it was only through the painstaking work of advocacy—from the intimate pedagogical work of discussion groups and the epistemological engineering of the lucha to, finally, mediating the politics of sexual rights—that the struggle for Nicaraguan sexual rights was able to take root, thrive, and continue into the present.

CHAPTER TWO

⹀

Intimate Pedagogies

Becoming *Bien Educada*

It was now several years since Victoria had returned to Managua with her new identity. "My consciousness came slowly," she explained, "but now being a lesbian is fundamental to who I am. It is a part of my true identity." As she narrated her experiences living with friends in Mexico City in the mid-1980s when Nicaragua was at war, Victoria recalled these years as a pivotal time in her life: "It was like having my eyes opened and finally being able to see . . . always through talking, through really knowing these other women, these other lesbians." As she and her friends in Mexico shared stories about relationships and the challenges they faced with their families, with their coworkers, and on the street, Victoria said she felt nourished by what she called "a distinct women's culture." It was this culture, she explained, that facilitated her transformative experience and allowed her "to become educated in, and to know, a new consciousness." Victoria wanted to be able to help other women reach similar self-knowledge, and so, together with her partner, Irelia, Victoria organized a lesbian discussion group, Amigas Juntas ([Female] Friends Together). Victoria saw Amigas Juntas as a way to extend her own transformative process and engage in a series of dialogues with other women in which they, too, could achieve a consciousness of their lesbian identity. As she put it, she hoped the women she and her partner worked with would become *bien educada* (well mannered and well educated) and come to "know," in intimate terms, their own sexuality.

Intimate Activism

For Victoria, undergoing a transformation, developing a consciousness, and claiming an identity has been fundamental to her personal struggle; facilitating this transformation in others is also, for her and other activists, essential to the larger political struggle for sexual rights. In discussion groups for *las lesbianas* or *los homosexuales*, activist facilitators hope to create a place where participants gain a deeper understanding of sexual subjectivity and, ultimately, adopt an identity. In this chapter, I focus on three lesbian discussion groups I regularly attended in 2001, one hosted by a Managuan NGO, one facilitated by grassroots activists in Managua, and one held in a rural location also by a grassroots activist.[1] In these settings, I was interested in understanding the pedagogical role of activist facilitators and the didactic decisions that they made in their work with participants. An educational impulse often guided discussion groups as facilitators actively steered conversations, interpreted participants' thoughts and experiences, selected informational material, and chose both topics and projects. The interactions among and between participants, facilitators, and their instructional materials illustrate what I call an "intimate pedagogy." Intimate pedagogies are transacted in small, face-to-face settings and at the same time tread very literally on intimate aspects of people's lives. In these pedagogical spaces, I argue, activists are crafting an "education of desire" (Stoler 1995), an incitement to discourse that aims to produce participants who, as many activist facilitators put it, are *bien educada* in the subjects of sexuality and identity.[2]

In all of the discussion groups I attended, facilitators placed an emphasis on the dialogic nature of their work. They believed that through communication, sharing, and attempting to achieve a consciousness, women in the group would come to co-construct a lesbian identity that both spoke to their experiences and accounted for the social expectations that conditioned their lives. The emphasis on communication and consciousness is reminiscent of earlier consciousness-raising (CR) groups, especially those that were so foundational to the second wave of feminism in the United

Chapter Two

—

62

States. However, the consciousness being articulated in Nicaraguan lesbian discussion groups more closely follows from Nicaragua's historical
legacy. It insists on analyzing sexuality in a forum that is grounded in material relations and a national genealogy, a more "kaleidoscopic" sexuality
that resists essentialist reduction (Roderick Ferguson, quoted in Dinshaw
et al. 2007: 180; Ferguson 2004: 29). Through this mediational process,
facilitators and participants have grappled with local perceptions of gender roles and the values associated with *masculina* and *femenina*, as well as
transnational concepts of sexuality and identity. Rather than cultivating a
singular model of lesbian identity, the discussion groups' facilitators encouraged the participants to question, understand, and, above all, name
their sexuality. In these settings, "lesbiana" came to be a designation that
could (and does) stand for many things.

Xochiquetzal: Hiding Out

During my time in Managua, taxi drivers could take a passenger across the
city for the equivalent of about a dollar. Savvy at negotiating the sprawling
megalopolis that is home to well over one third of the country's population, taxi drivers are often reservoirs of tacit common knowledge: astute
people watchers and ever apprised about what is occurring in their city.[3]
When I requested trips to Fundación Xochiquetzal, drivers often responded with nodding recognition: "Ah, sí. Donde hacen la prueba" (Ah,
yes. Where they do the test).

In addition to doing "the test" (for HIV), Fundación Xochiquetzal, an
NGO that promotes sexual rights and HIV prevention, also hosted monthly
discussion groups for las lesbianas (exclusively for women) and los homosexuals (exclusively for men). The funding proposal for the lesbian discussion group developed by the director and staff of Xochiquetzal and
submitted to a European NGO, made a compelling case for the need to
establish these regular meetings for women. The proposal stated, "The
lesbian discussion group will empower lesbians with knowledge about
gender, sexual identity, self-esteem, sociocultural discrimination, human
rights and internalized *lesbofobia*. . . . Lesbians will develop their self-
esteem which will contribute to their acceptance of their sexual identity,
thereby allowing lesbians to enjoy their sexuality without prejudice. . . .
[As yet,] no information is available, in Nicaragua, other than that information which reinforces 'ideal images' of gender, sexuality, and prejudices
and stereotypes associated with lesbianism."[4] Drawing from a repertoire

of human rights, self-esteem, and identity-formation discourse, the lesbian discussion group is marketed as an antidote to faulty "ideal images" based in prejudice and stereotypes. Empowerment and knowledge are crucial, and interrelated, elements of the group's purpose, poised as a way to generate a more positive and inclusive image of lesbians specifically as "lesbians." While empowerment and the better understanding of one's sexuality are the goals of the group, the proposal also makes clear that there is a preexisting, implicit, and assumed category of person—la lesbiana. Groups such as these, I would argue, are in fact actively creating the category that they claim to represent; activists are constructing *la lesbiana* through the work that they do.

New Girlfriends

Maria Berta, whom I met at the Sexuality Free from Prejudice events of 1999, told me that she was very happy I would be attending the lesbian discussion group she facilitated along with two other women, Elisabet and Sonia, at Fundación Xochiquetzal.[5] Maria Berta was the resident librarian at Xochiquetzal and a part-time writer for the foundation's magazine *Fuera del Closet* (Out of the Closet). We agreed that I would be both a participant in the conversations and "out" as an anthropologist studying sexuality and sexual rights activism in Nicaragua. Maria Berta thought I could bring an international perspective to the group. But mostly, she explained, she wanted me to hear what the conversations were like and meet "the girls."

Meetings do not often begin precisely on time in Nicaragua, and since our meeting was held on Sunday morning, we seemed to be more delayed than usual. As Maria Berta, Elisabet, Sonia, and I waited for the group's participants to arrive, Maria Berta expressed concern about the low turnout thus far. "We sometimes have a little problem here with attendance," she said. "The women come for two or three sessions, and then they quit coming." I wondered out loud why she thought participants might be quitting the group. She and the other facilitators rattled off a litany of concerns: they have to work or attend to their households, babysit for female relatives or care for their own children. "Or," Maria Berta elaborated, "they may not have money for bus fare." "Better yet," she said with her characteristic easy laugh, "they have a new girlfriend who is taking up all their time." The distraction of new love notwithstanding, Maria Berta and her co-facilitators were well aware of the financial concerns and familial obligations that might prevent participants from regularly attending the group. Although the lesbian discussion group hosted by Xochiquetzal was always free of charge, many of the participants were from the *clases populares* (working classes), meaning that at times even basic transportation costs could be prohibitive.[6]

While attending the lesbian discussion group over the course of a year, I met a total of twenty-two participants, all of whom were Nicaraguan and had learned about the group by word of mouth, often from friends in the *ambiente* (lesbian or gay "scene"). As I spent more time with women in the group, I began to see that in addition to the obstacles of baby care, bus fare, and new girlfriends, they faced subtler challenges. Many explained that they had anxiety, and sometimes fear, of a family member or a coworker discovering that they were taking part in a lesbian discussion group. When Eugenia invited me to visit her office for lunch, for instance, she was emphatic about one point in particular: "Do not tell anyone that we know each other from the lesbian discussion group." The group's facilitators were likewise vigilant about disclosing too much information to their families. When Maria Berta and I had dinner together at her house, where she cared for her aging mother, she recommended that we mention homosexuality, lesbianism, and the discussion group only behind closed doors, where her mother would be out of earshot.

For the NGO that hosts these groups, and the activists who facilitate them, taking precautions has been the rule, particularly when the anti-sodomy law was in effect. As Elisabet explained:

> With groups of lesbians, we can't say that they are lesbians, because the government would close the place down. It is the only place that there is that is semi-open. Semi-open. But we can't say directly . . . not openly. For example, we can't do a march in the street for the Sexuality Free from Prejudice events. They would throw us in jail, because of their prejudices and the legal parameters of Article 204. . . . The space is not totally open, but at least it exists. . . . The problem is to be able to get together. For example, we coordinate the meeting by phone. But we don't say who is calling. We have a secret message. The message just says "Elisabet called," but nothing more. Nothing about Xochiquetzal.[7]

Secret phone calls and coded messages about meetings show the primacy of privacy for the group as a whole, as well as among individual participants. The threat of incarceration and the risks of social stigma demanded that sexuality discussion groups obscure their activities to some degree,

Intimate Pedagogies

—

not unlike other national contexts in which potent antisodomy laws operate (Gevisser 2000; Long 1999; Palmberg 1999). Partially "out" and partially clandestine, lesbian discussion groups have been "counterpublic" (Fraser 1989, 1994) spaces in a very literal sense: largely hidden from the gaze of both the public and the state.[8] These groups also reflect the efforts of activists to create counterpublic venues in which discussion and reflection lead to an exploration of the sexual self. By sharing stories, worries, and feelings, participants are encouraged to reflexively engage with their expectations and values around sexuality. With the pedagogical guidance of facilitators, participants are prompted to inquire about their experiences, to obtain knowledge, and to define their sexual identity. The group is also a space of solidarity. As Maria Berta put it, "At least we have the group, and this is important because the girls can see that there are other people who feel like they do. . . . This is the most important thing."

Becoming Oriented to *Opción Sexual*

Taking seats on tiny wooden chairs in Xochiquetzal's library, the group this week was made up of six young women (most of them in their early twenties) and one anthropologist (in the first year of her thirties). At our facilitators' prompting, we introduced ourselves by first name only, preserving some degree of anonymity. Our spatial arrangement, a small semicircle, was part of a larger pedagogical plan to encourage participation, self-reflection, and dialogue among facilitators and participants. Maria Berta, Sonia, and Elisabet asked us to think about our topics for this week, *orientación sexual* (sexual orientation) and *opción sexual* (sexual choice). We were then instructed to write our definitions of these concepts on the small pieces of paper that the facilitators passed around. Most pencils remained motionless as participants traded glances with each other, seemingly a little perplexed. The exercise felt vaguely like a pop quiz for which we had not studied, but soon enough we were crafting our answers. Elisabet then asked us to write our definitions on the white erasable board that had been set up at the front of the room.

The definitions that participants shared with the group described orientación sexual in different ways, but alterity and pedagogy were recurrent themes among them. Hermelinda defined sexual orientation as "when someone helps to orient you toward your sexual path—such as a counselor—so that you can be something different from the normal gender." Haydi wrote, "It is about whether we will go against traditional values or not." And Elena proposed that sexual orientation was "getting oriented and understanding that sexuality can be different from what is around us all the time." Participants did not describe sexual orientation as a biologically predetermined set of desires or drives. Rather, their responses centered on coming to understand one's difference from the "normal gender" and challenging "traditional values." Rather than describing homosexuality as an unchangeable attribute or physical quality, the group's participants imagined orientación sexual not as innate but as achieved. In the participants' responses, sexual orientation was not something that one has; it was something one does. In place of an essential ontology, related to the nature of one's desires, sexual orientation was described as a conscious, engaged, and agentive state of being. This understanding of sexual orientation offered the possibility to challenge social norms such as gender roles and traditional values. In the conceptual schemes offered by participants, sexual orientation had the ability to challenge cultural expectations. But these responses were also conditioned by a guiding principle—that is, a counselor or a facilitator could, literally, get one oriented to a particular "sexual path." Both pedagogy and psychotherapeutic dynamics were at work here.

While orientación sexual was seen as challenging social roles and assumptions, opción sexual was rendered in much more individual terms. The emphasis was on choice. For Luz Marina, opción sexual was "having defined your sexuality" and "identifying what you want to be." For Lelia it was "a sense, a way of being that one knows about their sexual attraction." Irma described it as "our own self-definition." Participants' responses centered on the ability to choose one's "definition" and "what you want to be." Sexual option, in these descriptions, is animated through a process of identification, knowing, and becoming a very conscious sexual subject. The ability to choose and define one's sexuality was fundamental to how participants configured opción sexual.

The facilitators seemed pleased with the participants' responses about options and orientations. However, the discussion of these terms appeared to be a prelude to another concept, identity, to which the facilitators now turned our attention. Elisabet explained that identity was a way in which orientación and opción could be combined. "With the concept of identity," she said, "both 'being' and 'doing' are connected." Maria Berta added to this definition: "With identity, someone refers to who one *is* and who one *wants* to be. . . . It is the self-consciousness and self-image of a person."

As one of the participants deftly echoed, "It is something that we some-times choose to be." In other words, identity was not ascribed from the outside but claimed for, and by, one's self. For facilitators and participants alike, sexual identity was also defined by the liberal registers of individu-ality and choice, where "what you choose to be" is resolved in the matrix of identity. But there were limits to these choices.

In the facilitators' interpretations, refusing an identity had conse-quences. For instance, Elisabet, using the logic of "denial," described that "if a woman who has sexual desire for other women rejects that she is a lesbian, she is acting out of *autonegación* (self-denial)." Desire, in Elisa-bet's reckoning, needed to be codified and named. Failing to recognize one's identity as a lesbiana was bordering on pathology; it was an act of self-delusion. Hoping to put identity in more positive terms, Maria Berta chimed in: "As we understand and begin to know our identities, we see that we are becoming bien educadas."

The participants' voices and the facilitators' interpretations were cen-tral to the dialogic framework of the lesbian discussion group. But in the group hosted by Xochiquetzal, as well as other groups that I attended both in and outside Managua, pedagogical materials were also an important part of the unfolding narrative about lesbian identity. As the facilitators directed us to a photocopied sheet of paper we had received, we found precise definitions of each of the phenomena we had attempted to grasp:

> *Orientación sexual*: inclination of attraction or emotional-sexual con-duct; may be for persons of the opposite sex (heterosexual orienta-tion) or both sexes (bisexual orientation) or people of the same sex (homosexual orientation).
>
> *Opción sexual*: reflects one's choice of someone of a particular sex. Can be someone with whom one affectively or erotically interacts, someone of the same sex, both sexes or the opposite sex . . . though for various social and personal reasons one may choose to be with someone of one sex when in fact their sexual orientation is toward another. (Prison conditions are not the same; this is a case of lim-ited access.)

The small print at the bottom of the document made it clear that the defi-nitions were taken from *El derecho a la propia identidad* (Amnistía Inter-nacional 1999). According to the document's title, it is one's right to have an identity. "The right to identity" and the politics of recognition here are connected to a broader politics and philosophy regarding subjectivity (Taylor 1992). Particular attributes are called forth by bureaucratic bodies as worthy of protection—or, as Elizabeth Povinelli (2004) has put it, there is a certain "cunning" inherent in the language of rights and recognition.[9]

The definitions provided by Amnesty International and the intersection of sexual orientation and sexual option proved complex terminological terrain for the facilitators. Elisabet confirmed that orientación sexual is "how you are" and "how you feel." In the words of the document *El derecho a la propia identidad*, she pointed out, sexual orientation is "an inclination." Sexual option, on the other hand, is the sexual life "you choose to live," as Elisabet put it. Through their discussions of being and doing, or ontologies and praxis, the facilitators worked toward an important point that the workshop was meant to convey: one's ability, and right, to choose a sexual life. To illustrate this pedagogical intervention, Elisabet drew our attention to the following scenario: "Some of us just went into relationships with men because this is what we were supposed to do. . . . We were still searching. Some of us have been married or have been in relationships with men, so that was a sexual choice, or opción. Maybe for the purposes of avoiding society's condemnation, or because we may need some financial help, or for our children, we opt to have a sexual life that is different from our orientación. But our orientation is the same, as lesbians, whether or not we are with another woman." Elisabet's hypothetical situation highlighted the ways in which lesbiana could be understood as a very flexible set of practices and yet also as an enduring identity. In her rendering, one can "be" a lesbian even if one must choose a different sexual life—avoiding condemnation or following social expectations to be in a relationship with a man. Partly due to Nicaragua's social and economic conditions, the facilitators clearly recognized that individuals—perhaps especially women with few economic resources—might not always be able to actively choose to pursue their lesbianness. Although the participants were not exhorted to disclaim, or even discontinue, affective or sexual relationships they had with men, they were encouraged to understand their same-sex desire as evidence of an orientation that was best situated under the mantle of lesbiana.

As they negotiate the nuances of Amnesty International documents and develop a framework of opción, orientación, and *identidad*, the facilitators attempt to reconcile the concepts of choice and identity. Activist facilitators seek to provide a safe communicative space to choose and develop one's sexuality, and in so doing, they closely follow liberal values of free will. However, it is important to note that the facilitators also draw very explicitly on examples that reflect the conditions in Nicaragua—namely, the financial impossibility for (some) women to choose to live their same-sex orientation. Discussions such as these underscore that choice and free will have very real material limits. Activist facilitators see their role as providing the tools, terms, and skills to construct a sense of identity, and they encourage participants to feel confident naming their choices. This exercise is very clearly linked to a larger pedagogical impulse that determines both the content and structure of discussion groups. However, activist facilitators do not insist on a particular set of practices or desires. What constitutes lesbian identity is instead subject to nuanced rhetorical interventions. One's identity as a lesbian can, and should, be acknowledged, even if it is not always possible to live out one's desires for same-sex intimacy. Ultimately, what facilitators work to develop and to inspire is an interest in the sexual self.

Boys Don't Cry

As we gathered around the television set, Sonia pulled a bootleg copy of *Boys Don't Cry (Los muchachos no lloran)* from a colorful homemade cover. Many of the same participants from the previous week had returned, and Elisabet, Sonia, and Maria Berta seemed happy to have gotten hold of a Spanish-subtitled copy of the relatively new film, which had generated a good deal of debate and critical acclaim in the United States. They believed, they said, that the film would be a good way to discuss gender roles and *lesbianismo*. The Oscar-winning film, released in 1999, is based on the life story of Teena Brandon, a transgender female-to-male youth who became Brandon Teena and ultimately was murdered. Throughout the film, Brandon passes as a young man in a small town in Nebraska where he has joined a group of friends whose primary activities seem to be binge drinking and performing a lot of masculine swagger.[10] Brandon becomes involved with a straight woman, Lana, who has some suspicions about Brandon's biological sex but chooses not to confront him. Brandon's male buddies finally discover his biological sex and, apparently to punish him for his perceived gender and sexual transgressions, drag him to a remote location, where he is brutally raped. During police questioning following the rape, Brandon has difficulty accepting that he has been raped and is (as he is throughout the film) loath to identify himself as biologically female. The rape and its aftermath unquestionably uncover Brandon's biological sex, foiling what he had so ably performed up to this point: masculine gender. Soon after, Brandon Teena is murdered by one of his "friends."

Once the blurry subtitles had subsided, there was a momentary pall over the group as participants and facilitators alike gathered their thoughts and, no doubt, managed some of the emotions that a film such as Boys Don't Cry evokes. Before the film's credits finished rolling, several participants expressed their surprise that this kind of violence and lack of acceptance would occur in the United States. With a mixture of disappointment and shock, they turned to me. "But in the United States you are so developed with your sexual freedom," one young woman said. And another participant added, "In the United States, the homosexuals and the lesbians have a much more advanced social situation." I assured them that the film was based on a true story and that such acts of violence and intolerance indeed continue to occur in the United States.

The film provoked a set of questions for the participants, initially, that centered on the differences between the North and Nicaragua. But as the facilitators predicted, the film also generated a lot of conversation about gender roles in Nicaragua. Turning our attention to the plot and characters, Sonia asked the participants what they thought of Brandon Teena. The film itself is attuned to Brandon's suffering, and though this group was a relatively compassionate audience, they did not voice much sympathy for his behavior.[11] Hermelinda, the most outspoken member of the group, declared, "She was a liar. . . . She could not accept who she was: a lesbian." Irma voiced a similar concern, reasoning that "because she is a woman," Brandon should be referred to as "Teena" rather than by his chosen (masculine) name. There was remarkably little discussion about the brutality of Brandon Teena's rape, other than a brief mention of Brandon's inability to cope with the rape "because," as one participant put it, "she still had not accepted the fact that she is a woman." Brandon Teena, by these accounts, was guilty of self-denial: refusing to be the woman, and the lesbian, that he "really" is (or, more accurately, was). Adopting some of the language that had emerged during our lesson on opción, orientación, and identity, Luz Marina asserted that "this woman"—Brandon Teena—was "plagued by autonegación." Brandon Teena's putative failure to accept himself/herself in gendered terms (as "a woman") and in sexual terms (as "a lesbian") provided the grist for more discussion, more mediations on the part of the facilitators, and, ultimately, a deeper engagement with the question of gender roles in women's same-sex relationships.

Brandon Teena's persistent desire to identify as a man — or, at the very least, to insist on a masculine performance of gender — was very familiar to both the facilitators and the participants in our group. In Nicaragua, masculina women, or *cochonas*, are often thought to be "lesser men" or as "wanting to be men." By "playing the man," the figure of Brandon Teena raises concerns about machismo and the qualities of gender roles in women's same-sex relationships. Aura Maria, for instance, used veiled humor to explain that her partner, Eva, with whom she had been in a relationship for several years, was "worse than any man." Aura Maria, as "la femenina," was expected to be responsible for all of their "women's" household tasks, such as shopping, cooking, and cleaning. Eva also insisted that she be served her dinner first, as is the convention with male heads of households. Aura Maria lamented, finally, that while she was explicitly forbidden to go out at night with her female friends, Eva might spend a whole weekend drinking and reveling with her friends. In this context, the film evoked many possible readings. *Boys Don't Cry* was crafted as a commentary about the struggles of transgenderism, homophobia, and transphobia. But in Managua, at the lesbian discussion group, the frame was shifted. Brandon Teena's attempts to be a man (and, perhaps, to draw on masculine privilege) reinforced a familiar stereotype about cochonas and masculina women: they want to be men. Or worse still, they might indulge in an exaggerated form of macho entitlement. Following the lessons of the discussion group, Brandon Teena was guilty of refusing to accept her, or his, true identity as a lesbian. Brandon made for a potent example of failing to come to terms with one's "true" self. The debate about Brandon Teena's identity and performances of masculinity demonstrates that the discussion group's participants apparently are mirroring the lessons and logic of lesbian identity. Brandon Teena, who in an earlier time in Nicaragua certainly would have been considered a cochona, or in the United States likely would be considered transgender, is here redefined as a lesbian. The facilitators, for their part, are engaged in a process of mediating the worries that masculina partners may all too perfectly replicate *machista* behaviors, a concern that is vividly present in the experiences of both the participants and the facilitators.

Femininity, Masculinity, and Gendering Recognition

Following the discussion about *Boys Don't Cry*, our conversation took further turns into the negotiated status of gender roles, masculinity, femininity, and lesbian identity. The facilitators themselves moved into a dialogic mode as they worked through their own, internal debates about the qualities of gender, discrimination, and lesbian subjectivity. Hoping to signal the distinct ways that gendered performances might affect the development of lesbian identity, Maria Berta explained, "Lesbian women who are more feminine must overcome more. They do not fit the stereotype of a cochona. Because they do not wear long-sleeve [men's] shirts and do not have a macho appearance, they are not seen as lesbians, so they are being approached by men all the time, and all of society thinks they are heterosexual. So they have to fight to be recognized as lesbians all the time." Elisabet countered that masculina women face more discrimination because they more overtly transgress feminine gender roles and the social expectations of female comportment and dress. "So," as she put it, "they have to fight even more." Sonia offered her own challenge to the debate—one that took a page from feminist discourses, early lesbian and gay rights movements, and more recent discussions of gender queerness. She argued that "the real problem" is that "there are only two roles from which to choose: 'macho' or 'feminine.'" Instead, she explained, a variety of gendered possibilities should be available, different ways to be a lesbian that are not just masculina or femenina. Whether or not feminine or masculine lesbians in Nicaragua face more hardships may have motivated the discussion, but how gender itself functioned to define lesbian identity was at the heart of the debate. One of the participants, Leda, a young Nicaraguan woman who had spent three years living with her girlfriend in San Francisco—weighed in on the discussion. "I identify as a lesbian," she said, adding rather emphatically, "and I do not want to be with a woman who looks or acts like a man." Leda went on to explain that for her, two femenina women together in a relationship challenged the presumption that feminine and masculine partners somehow naturally belong together. For Leda, an egalitarian model, as opposed to a butch–femme pairing, was a subversive act of gender nonconformity. It was one that implicitly challenged heteronormativity.

Boys Don't Cry, and the ways the film served as a nodal point and mediational device for discussion and debate, illustrates how transnational media is used by activists to ascertain local nuances of gender roles and gendered expectations. In the meetings of the lesbian discussion group hosted by Xochiquetzal, two important dynamics emerged from activists' pedagogical work. First—and in some ways, fundamentally—there was an emphasis on participants' embracing, accepting, and coming to "know" their lesbian identity through a process of self-reflection. However, once the category of lesbian had been relatively securely established, questions about Nicaraguan models of femininity and masculinity followed in quick succession, turning both activists' and participants' attention to the second dynamic animating the conversation: gender. The activist facilitators worked through a series of questions about sexual categories and gender performance that inspired a critical interrogation of sexuality. Through these dialogic engagements, variations of gender performance were played out on, and within, sexual identity. Discussions about the coupling of femenina women and whether or not Brandon Teena was really a woman (and a misguided lesbian who could not accept her identity) challenged gender-based models of sexuality and masculina–femenina same-sex coupling. As facilitators debated whether or not femenina or masculina lesbians face more discrimination, what appeared to be a discussion of gender ultimately became a debate about recognition: whether and how one will be perceived as a lesbian.

Amigas Juntas: How to be a Lesbiana

After spending a lot of time in working-class neighborhoods in Managua, I became accustomed to seeing frail cart horses wandering the streets and grazing on the weeds that grow in vacant lots and in the fissures of broken sidewalks. Nonetheless, as we were all getting ready to sit down for our discussion group at Victoria's house, I was surprised to see a horse stick his head into the cinderblock window of her home before he turned to dine on the grassy bits of her front yard. Victoria, unperturbed, carried on with her opening remarks, looking around to see that we had each brought our supplies: scissors, string, and colored pens.

Amigas Juntas ([Female] Friends Together) is a grassroots lesbian discussion group that, as I described at the beginning of this chapter, Victoria founded with her partner, Irelia. Unlike the lesbian discussion group at Xochiquetzal, Victoria and Irelia had no NGO or other institutional support to run their meetings; they often relied on participants to bring a few coins for coffee and pastries. I met Victoria and Irelia at the Orgullo

Lésbico-Gay (Lesbian and Gay Pride) events in Managua in 1999, where they had mentioned their interest in starting a lesbian group. Over the course of the several months that I attended Amigas Juntas, the number of participants in the group ranged from four to seven women, all of whom came from different neighborhoods in Managua, both middle-class and *barrios populares* (working-class neighborhoods). In their thirties and forties, and many with steady girlfriends or female partners, all of the women in Amigas Juntas were employed. Some worked itinerantly as housekeepers, cooks, or vendors, according to whether or not work was available. Others had more secure professions as secretaries or receptionists. The women in Amigas Juntas explained that they had discovered the group through their involvement with sexual rights activism and women's NGOs or through other lesbians and networks of friends in Managua.

Amigas Juntas, according to the group's mission statement, is founded on the principle that "it is necessary to find one's own lesbian identity in order to find pride and dignity and raise one's self-esteem." The group, as Victoria put it, is a place "for conversation, for reflection . . . and to grow and create an identity." She also insisted, however, that there is latitude in this formulation. "We say that each person, each woman, needs to have her own way of being," she explained. "There are many ways to be a lesbian. We cannot say, 'You must be this and that and follow some rules.' No. Heterosexuals don't have rules about how they must be. . . . It's not about constructing a model. . . . Really, it is about having a consciousness about one's rights . . . that is, that we as lesbians have the right to many things." Insisting that there is no model for lesbian identity, Victoria envisions a framework for Amigas Juntas that is not bound by rules but, rather, that evolves through consciousness-raising. Consciousness and rights are achieved, in Victoria's reckoning, through women's ability to raise their self-esteem and claim their own lesbian identity. Partly because of her own experience and transformation, Victoria is resolute about the value of sexual identity. In her role as an activist and facilitator, she sees herself as committed to fostering the development of this identity among the women in her group. However, it is equally important to her that each woman articulate "her own way of being."

In addition to the value of identity as one's "own way of being," Victoria emphasized the importance of gender. She explained that she tries to integrate questions about gender and how it relates to sexuality as she prepares discussion topics for Amigas Juntas. Victoria showed me several pamphlets about gender equality and women's rights in Latin America that she has collected over the years from conferences, training sessions, and workshops she has attended. She finds the bulk of her pedagogical material at two feminist libraries in Managua, both of which are supported by NGOs. During one of our conversations, I asked Victoria how she chose the activities and discussion topics she used in the group. "I've been working with women for many years," she said, "and I have had a lot of *capacitación* (training), especially on how to run women's shelters. I've also tried to integrate popular participation, as a method, in order to orient our meetings toward the reality, the lives, of lesbian women in Nicaragua." By drawing specific attention to her training, Victoria emphasized her professional preparation for group facilitation. She was also clear that popular participation and a focus on the lives of participants have been critical to her pedagogical approach. She went on to describe that two transnational interlocutors had visited the group: "We also have had two Canadian women come talk to the group about cultural things, . . . and what we try to do is, we sit down, the four of us [Victoria, Irelia, and the two Canadian women], to read and to analyze and to come up with a methodology and design for the workshop and talk about the dynamics and the process. . . . We also have materials to read and analyze and make it appropriate for the women in the group." The "cultural things" the Canadian women had been invited to discuss, according to Victoria, were meant to provide an international perspective on lesbian identity. Her decision to invite input from Northern allies suggests that Victoria values their participation and experiential expertise. She is also adamant, however, that the workshop be appropriate and accessible for the Nicaraguan participants whose transformations she hopes to encourage.

I asked Victoria what she hoped to accomplish with her group. Was it a "training" forum for sexual rights activism? Or was she aiming for a personal politics of transformation? Perhaps it was both or something else altogether. Victoria put it this way: "Amigas Juntas is a way for lesbian women to know themselves . . . to really talk about their sexuality and their feelings and their desires. . . . Because there is so much taboo around lesbian identity, I want these women to be able to have a space to think about and talk about and learn about their feelings, their love. . . . But sometimes it is more complicated, because you have to look at identity, right?" Victoria spoke to the need to create a space where taboos are lifted and women are able to express their feelings and love, translating their emotional worlds and desires into identity. Through the reflexive and dialogical process of the group, the participants are encouraged to find ways, as Victoria says, "to know themselves." To question, to communicate, and to arrive at a particular knowledge about one's self are the bases of the group's work. It is an inquiry into the intimacies of desires, practices, and feelings. Like that of the group hosted by Xochiquetzal, Victoria's description of Amigas Juntas focuses on the ways in which lesbian identity has been understood as taboo and therefore in need of remediation. As the group's leader, she also emphasizes the importance of gender, particularly her professional experience in women's centers and her collection of gender rights materials. However, Victoria also indicates that identity is in itself sometimes more complicated. As she put it, it is something that one "has" to look at. And in Victoria's reckoning, identity appears to be something more than the sum of one's feelings; it is multifaceted and, moreover, something that one can achieve.

Mobilizing Lesbian Identity

Gesturing to several pieces of wire and spools of thread on her coffee table, Victoria explained that we would be making mobiles based on our topic for the morning, "Imagining Our Lesbian Identity." Victoria and Irelia brought out a large box containing photocopied pictures: Joan of Arc on horseback, a statue of Sappho, and the Venus of Willendorf. Also included were a line drawing of the Aztec goddess Xochiquetzal, and several images of nude women embracing. The drawings were the work of the Nicaraguan lesbian artist "Cony," and I recognized the images as photocopies from the magazine *Fuera del Closet*, published by Fundación Xochiquetzal. Symbols appeared on other sheets of paper: the double-headed ax (labrys), two interlocked female symbols, and a rainbow flag (less compelling though still identifiable in its gray-scale photocopied incarnation). Multiple large-font words were also a part of the collection: *orgullo* (pride), *mujeres* (women), *identidad* (identity), *lesbiana* (lesbian), and *amor* (love); all were ready to be cut and pasted onto the mobiles, according to each woman's choosing. Victoria told us about the images, explaining, for instance, how Sappho, the Greek poet from the island of Lesbos, was famous for her amorous poetry directed to other women and that Xochiquetzal, an Aztec goddess of fertility, was recognized for her feminine powers. Victoria encouraged all of us to use the pictures, words, and symbols that most "touched" us and "related to our sense of ourselves."

She wanted us to make a mobile that, as she put it, could be "displayed wherever you want . . . but hopefully, in a place where others can see it."

Attendance was good on that Saturday morning, with six participants in total. We all set to work cutting, coloring, bending wire, snipping thread, and, of course, talking. Conversations moved from topic to topic: the politics of the moment, questions about parents and partners. A woman who had recently ended a relationship with her partner of two years found many nods of knowing agreement among the group as she spelled out the details of her heartbreak. Our mobiles were taking shape, balanced between the physics of wire, paper, and thread and the conversations that animated their construction.

Victoria, with a tray of pastries and cups of coffee, called the group's attention. She wanted each of us to talk about why we had chosen particular images, symbols, or words for our mobiles. We went around individually, with each woman describing her reasoning and Victoria nodding and jotting notes as each of us told our respective interpretations. She began the conversation by remarking that each one of us had made a very important piece of art—one that had the ability to "show our feelings" to ourselves and to others. Victoria's ensuing comments, as well as what she neglected to comment on, said a lot about the pedagogical impulse of the group.

Alejandra had the words "pride," "love," "women," "identity," and "lesbian" dangling from the structure of her mobile, along with the symbol of two interlocked female signs. She explained that she wanted "a very *amplio* (big and comprehensive)" mobile, one in which "you don't have to know the stories of the people but can see yourself in the ideas." Victoria praised Alejandra's mobile for its openness, highlighting particular terms, and explained that "pride" in particular was something that we needed to work toward as lesbian women. "Lesbian and gay pride," Victoria noted, "has been a very important concept all over the world." She then rattled off the names of cities (Mexico City, Buenos Aires, Rio de Janeiro, New York, and Rome) where pride parades had been documented in the Nicaraguan national press. However, Victoria pointed out that none of the women in the group had used the rainbow flag in their mobiles. She seemed surprised, perhaps, but also intent on taking advantage of this teachable moment:

> The rainbow flag is an internationally recognized symbol of pride that we want to uphold. . . . However, this does not mean you cannot fly

el rojo y negro (the red and black [a reference to the FSLN flag]) . . . or *de los liberales* (the Liberal Party's flag) if you like. [Everyone laughs.] With the rainbow flag, we represent all people, of different races and nations, men and women, *los gays* and *las lesbianas*. Especially as the world comes closer together, we need to understand that we are part of a larger community, a larger world of lesbians, and gay men, too.

By referring to the flags of Nicaragua's two most prominent political parties, Victoria staked the rainbow flag of lesbian and gay pride in the terrain of Nicaraguan politics. Given the potency of politics in Nicaragua, Victoria's discursive association ensured that the rainbow flag would be understood as an explicitly political and collective statement, akin to flying the colors of one's political party. Observing that the rainbow flag is intended to represent global diversity and comradeship, Victoria noted that connections with other lesbian- and gay-identified people around the world was important to "us" (using the feminine word *nosotras*). She hoped to extend our identity imaginary by suggesting that women in our group are part of a larger community with collective goals and a shared sense of sexual identity and pride.

We then turned our attention to another mobile, which, according to its creator, Claudia, had the "really important women" represented. Claudia had chosen the images of Joan of Arc, Xochiquetzal, Sappho, and the Venus figure. Included next to them were the words "love" and "women." Victoria agreed that Claudia's creation did feature very significant women from around the world as she pointed to the poet Sappho. Victoria reminded the group that poetry had been an important part of Nicaraguan history and that Nicaraguan feminist poets had global notoriety. "Los Nicas," she explained, "have a lot of pride, rightly, in our poets, male and female." As an icon of lesbian poetry, Sappho, it seemed, dovetailed well with Nicaraguan-ness as well as with lesbianism.[12] Victoria's educational intervention connected the experiences of lesbians in the group to the Nicaraguan political and cultural milieu. At the same time, her pedagogical guidance was premised on linking individual experiences in Nicaragua to larger struggles for global sexual rights. However, Victoria's intervention did not demand a political response; it was not a call to action but a vehicle for women in the group to imagine themselves as part of a global community.

The other women in the workshop had less to say about why, exactly, they had chosen particular images and words for their mobiles. When Victoria went around the circle asking each of them directly, the response was usually, "Because I liked it." Victoria gently admonished those who had demurred from commenting on the significance of their mobiles. She added that she hoped we would really think about what we had created. In her role as facilitator, she wanted to ensure that introspection was a part of our creative project: "We need to think deeply about these things: about who we are, how we want to be, and what it means to us as lesbian women."

Bringing Friends Together

Victoria's affirmation that Amigas Juntas must be made appropriate to the Nicaraguan context illustrates her hope that the group is not simply a funnel for Northern discourses but, rather, a site of identity production that is explicitly marked as "Nicaraguan." Pairing rainbow flags with the flags of Nicaragua's political parties is a way to marry global lesbian and gay politics to the Nicaraguan political context. What constitutes "Nicaraguan," however, is complex. Historical images of women—some from the Americas (Xochiquetzal); others from European history (e.g., Joan of Arc, Sappho) or prehistory (Venus of Willendorf)—and symbols (such as the labrys and rainbow flag) are images that Victoria and her partner have very carefully selected to construct into "identity" art. The art project is a vehicle for reflection about what constitutes one's personal representations of identity, but the images, words, and histories that become narrated are partially predetermined and thus preconstructed. In her role as facilitator, Victoria has a determinative effect on what will be shaped into art, if not identity. Victoria has invested substantial energy in her didactic practice, exhorting participants to do the same: to think deeply about their identities as lesbians. She is also explicit about participants' being explicit. As she said, these mobile self-reflections on sexuality will, she hopes, be made public: a display of values for others to see. Through projects such as these, one is able—and, indeed, encouraged—literally to declare one's sexuality through art in a public way. As the person responsible for prompting, guiding, and educating the group, Victoria faces a complicated task. She hopes to encourage introspection and self-knowledge. She also wants to create a resonance between global and local politics of sexuality. And, finally, she intends for participants to create a sense of resolve around lesbian identity, bringing it "out" to be embraced.

Victoria maintains a pedagogical principle that each woman in the group must find "her own way of being." Choice and self-determination are, according to the ethos of the group, critical elements of each woman's transformation and both are clearly linked to liberal values of modern personhood. The women in the group are encouraged to voice their thoughts, reflections, and reactions; however, Victoria's voice is effectively "louder." She takes the initiative to comment on what counts as lesbian identity, from Sapphic mobiles to the veneration of the rainbow flag. Just as the mobiles are constructed, so are participants encouraged to construct their lesbian identities using symbolic resources, both local and transnational. What remains implicit, and largely unquestioned, is the necessity to adopt the term "lesbian." In the work that Amigas Juntas does the term may be generous in scope, but it is nonetheless a category that is largely taken for granted. Discussion does not center on whether the category lesbian is the best, most appropriate, or most warranted identity available. Ultimately, Victoria's role as an activist and facilitator is to provide a place for participants to engage with the concept of lesbian identity: to translate and transform a particular "feeling" into a more codified "knowing" of the sexual self.

Cochonas del Campo (Country Dykes): Venceremos Juntas (Overcoming Together)

Matagalpa, in Nicaragua's western highlands, is a city known for its coffee, leftist politics, and precipitously hilly streets, so it is unsurprising that some Nicaraguans and many North Americans refer to Matagalpa as the San Francisco of Nicaragua.[13] Venceremos Juntas, a lesbian discussion group, was founded in Matagalpa in 2000 by Catarina. She was inspired to create the group after visiting a male friend in Chinandega who had been involved in HIV-prevention workshops and sexual rights activism.[14] Although Venceremos Juntas had no financial support at the time I attended its meetings, Catarina hoped to continue the group and secure a grant from a Scandinavian NGO with which she had been in contact. Catarina gathered the information she used to facilitate the group from several sources, including material she found at the Internet café in town, online documents published by lesbian and gay rights organizations in Latin America, and Spanish-language websites based in the United States and Spain. Catarina also stayed in touch with friends involved in the Sexuality Free from Prejudice and Lesbian and Gay Pride events in Managua and tried to integrate some of their conversations and thoughts into the work she did with Venceremos Juntas.

As we sat down to talk at a little *comedor* near the city center, Catarina made a point of telling me that Venceremos Juntas was different from the lesbian discussion groups one would find in the country's capital. The women in Venceremos Juntas, as she put it, were "very masculine." After asking them about their reasons for joining the group and a little about their background, it became clear to me that the women in Venceremos Juntas were more solidly working class than the participants in the lesbian discussion groups in Managua. The women who participated in Catarina's group came from the neighboring hamlets and rural zones surrounding Matagalpa. They were all from the clases populares, with the exception of Berta, who worked as a primary-school teacher.[15] Indeed, the women in Venceremos did appear more masculine in their dress and comportment than the women in the lesbian discussion groups in Managua. But perhaps more important, the women in Venceremos Juntas showed more reticence about—or, perhaps, resistance to—the lesbian identity that went rather unquestioned in Managua.

Catarina explained one afternoon what, for her, were the key distinctions: "Here in the country it is different from in Managua, in the big city. The women here are different. . . . They are more masculina in their presentation. They are more *hombruna* (manly) in their demeanor. But they are also different in how they think about these modern things. Identity, a more egalitarian path, is hard for them to understand." Why, I asked, did she think these women were "more masculine," and why did they find it hard to understand identity and so-called "modern things"? Catarina replied without hesitation: "There are deep roots here, strong beliefs about how women and men are supposed to act. Maybe this is because of tradition, but also because there is no model for lesbians, only the cochona, only the *machista* model. In this, how can a lesbian see that there are other ways to be? Other possibilities—not just machista or femenina?" Catarina's group, by her reckoning, was burdened with tradition and the shadow of machismo. The "deep roots" of tradition seemed to be particularly embedded and intractable when it came to refiguring new possibilities for gender and sexuality. For Catarina, the contingencies of gender, class, and, importantly, rural and urban distinctions signaled profound differences between the discussion work that was possible in the city versus the country. Her aspiration to establish what she called "egalitarian identity" was an uneasy pedagogy, fraught with tension between desire, practice, and the politics of naming. As in the other lesbian discussion groups, the women in Venceremos Juntas were happy to talk, share, and reflect but not always in the ways that their facilitator wanted them to. The *cochonas del campo* (country dykes), it seemed, were not as assimilable to the hegemonic registers of urban, modern, and supposedly egalitarian sexual identity.

Female Machismo and an Education in Desire

It was quite a trek to Catarina's house on narrow roads and paths, soggy from a thunderstorm the night before. As our group gathered in the small front room of Catarina's cinderblock house, I was surprised to see how many women were present. Usually inundated roads and thick mud prevent people from venturing very far, and they make only the most necessary excursions. As we settled into white plastic chairs arranged around the room, all of the nine women present were talkative and enthusiastic for the discussion to begin.

Today, Catarina began with, "We are going to talk about gender and sex." To set the stage, she informed the group that gender was a concept that described a social "way of being—either masculine or feminine." In contrast, sex was biological, determining whether one was male or female. Everyone in the group nodded. Carmen, one of the participants, posed a question to clarify these distinctions further. "Gender, then, is masculine and feminine? So, for example, I have a masculine gender and a female body?" Catarina responded with "sí . . ." (yes), drawing the word out in an almost audible ellipsis. It appeared as though our facilitator wanted to address Carmen's interpretation, but instead, with a thoughtful expression, she left the comment aside. She opted instead to poll us on what, exactly, femininity and masculinity are. With ease, participants rattled off the qualities of femininity and masculinity. Femininity was defined as "pretty, soft skin, quiet, passive, curves shaped like a guitar, needs a lot of attention, gossip, jealous, crying all the time, submissive in sex, honest, with a lot of patience, fragile and attracted to strength." Masculinity was defined as "an inclination to drink too much, fight over women, possessive, always in control, strong, *mujeriego* (womanizer), and machista." Benita, a woman in her early thirties, wanted to make a point about the definitions of femininity and masculinity that the group had devised. "But, you know," she said, "you don't have to be a man to be a macho. . . . God knows that cochonas—or, that is, lesbians—can be *muy* machista, too. Sometimes I can be more macho than any man. The worst!" With lively nods of agreement and a round of laughter, the group made it clear that they appreciated Benita's comment, one that oscillated somewhere between self-deprecation and self-satisfaction.

Catarina, however, wanted to make a different point. "Lesbians can become trapped in these roles of masculine and feminine," she explained. And she queried further, "Why follow the same way of being, feminine or macho, that we see traditionally here in Nicaragua? We need to be more equal in our relationships with our partners. We see around us, around the world, that things are changing and that we can also, all of us, work to change with them. . . . There is no need to subscribe to the old ways of being." The women in the group considered Catarina's point about change, equality, and shifting values regarding sexuality. In a pedagogical mode, she contrasted tradition and the "old ways" with changes occurring around the world and, presumably, in Nicaragua. According to Catarina's pedagogical intervention, one way that participants could adopt a more global and putatively modern sexuality was to refuse the gendered distinctions of femininity and masculinity. As in the group hosted by Xochiquetzal, Catarina's comment provoked questions about the legitimacy of a dual masculine–feminine gender system.

Following Benita's comment about machismo, Alba, a boisterous woman in her forties confided that it was hard for her "*not* to be a man in bed." She explained to us, "I don't want my girlfriend to touch me sexually, not *ever*." Catarina seemed very taken aback by Alba's comment. Her dismay, however, did not seem predicated on Alba's narrating an overly intimate experience—indeed, reflection and sharing were part of the group's larger pedagogical plan. Rather, taking the role of teacher and counselor, Catarina wanted to offer Alba some advice. "You need to allow yourself to enjoy sex," she suggested. Alba appeared interested in the proposition but was equally resolute about the nature of her desire. She wanted only to be the *activa*, never the *pasiva* partner. "I am always the machista in bed," she said with a satisfied grin. The other women in the group nodded in agreement. Alba's smile suggested that she did in fact enjoy sex, though not necessarily in the sort of "egalitarian" way that Catarina advocated. Following Catarina's lead, Lelia, another participant, added her experience to the conversation. "I used to be like you [Alba], and it is hard to change," she said. "But you can. Now I can enjoy my own sexuality more. But it costs. It doesn't come easily. . . . But still, in the end, I feel better now that I am able to give and to receive sexual pleasure." Catarina nodded emphatically in agreement with Lelia's intervention. Eliciting psychotherapeutics, Catarina explained that our initial sexual experiences are fundamental to how we perceive our sexuality. She asked Alba whether her first sexual experience had been traumatic. Alba shrugged her shoulders and replied that her first sexual experience was good; still she did not want to be touched "down there" by her girlfriend.

Both gender roles and sexual desire emerged as important touchstones for Catarina, as well as for the participants in Venceremos Juntas. Catarina's and Lelia's intervention, encouraging Alba to embrace pleasure by refusing the gender role of the solely activa sexual partner, was an attempt to equalize Alba's sexual relationships and, by extension, that of other participants. The interaction between Catarina, Lelia, and Alba illustrates the pedagogical directive of the group: to discover one's sexuality. However, putatively machista gender or sexual positionings, in this scenario, are anathema to a more subtle impulse within the discussion group. Whether explicitly stated or not, there is a very clear pedagogical preference for an egalitarian form of sexuality and sexual behavior. The education of desire that Catarina proposes is a very particular understanding of equality in terms consonant with liberal values — namely, that pleasure is supposedly best experienced under conditions of equality between partners. Gender roles of femenina and masculina, in Catarina's configuration, are highly suspect not only because they represent what is seen to be outmoded tradition and hierarchical domination, but also because they obscure the pursuit of "true" (and non-traumatic) paths to mutual satisfaction and pleasure. Lesbianism, in this model, is explicitly equal and, indeed, pleasure-centered; it is an education of, and about, desire that attempts to render a lesbian sexuality that is not bound by the conventions of femininity and masculinity. This mode of instruction, however, did not go unquestioned.

Rolling Up One's Sleeves and Being *Muy Muy Campo*

After our meeting that afternoon, Blanca, who had been attending the meetings of Venceremos Juntas for about a year, explained to me, "Here we are *campesinas* (peasants, farmers, country folk)." She chuckled a little and added, shaking her head slowly and grinning, "Really, *really* 'country,' you know?" The *campo*, or countryside, evokes a certain humble nobility, pastoral romance, and sense of tradition for many Nicaraguans. Country folk in Nicaragua, as in many other places, also are often stereotyped as being less sophisticated and less educated than their urban counter-parts. I asked Blanca what it was that she thought was so "country" about the lesbian discussion group she was attending. She had a ready example. "See," she said, "we had this conversation in the group, maybe a couple of months ago, where we were talking about what it means to be a lesbian, how we know we are one or not, how we talk about it, feel it, live it. And we were talking about our love for other women, about attraction, about how women like to be treated. And it was so clear to some of us, this is what being a lesbian is about: it's about how you feel, and also feeling proud about those feelings, having a name for it, lesbian." Blanca, still smiling, leaned forward to emphasize her point. "But you wouldn't believe it, my friend, how many women in that group didn't want to say they were a lesbiana. No. They said, 'Well, so I like women, and what of it?' . . . *but like a man* likes women, sexually, possessive, macho. . . . This is what they were thinking was the best! Now if you ask me, these women—*mangas largas* (long sleeves) all of them, of course—just don't get it. It's a case of *autonegación* (self-denial) about their lesbian identity." Blanca's com-ment, as well as Catarina's original diagnosis, that participants are "very, very country" echoes many of the stereotypes about the "backwardness" of campesinos and campesinas. In the context of the lesbian discussion group, the significance of the campo is not simply quaint and antiquated. It is a mode of sexuality that is explicitly un-modern and retrograde. Based on their masculine presentation, these women appear to have failed, from some participants' point of view, to achieve the elusive goal of egalitar-ian behavior and identity. They are, rather, trapped in a cycle of supposed autonegación where both sexual identity and sexual performance are de-termined by gender roles. These narratives of the campo and masculina women are, of course, tied to the ways in which lesbian identity is being imagined—and at times challenged. For Blanca, the "long-sleeve" disposi-tion is really simply a matter of self-denial and not "getting it." The evoca-tion of the campo and manly lesbians is taken as evidence that the women in Venceremos Juntas are somehow less willing, or unable, to accept the putative truth of their sexuality. But it is also in these figures and their stories that lesbian identity is most thoroughly critiqued and challenged as a category befitting very different sexual subjectivities, practices, and, importantly, social location.

The women in Venceremos Juntas faced criticism for being overly in-vested in the "old ways" of sexuality. From the point of view of the activist who facilitated the group, the participants either failed to fully understand or, at the very least, were reticent to embrace a supposedly "more educated way of being": a lesbian. As in the lesbian discussion groups in Managua, in Venceremos Juntas, refusing to adopt a lesbian identity was seen as a sure and troubling sign of self-denial. However, the participants in Venceremos Juntas asked pointed questions that undermined the desirability of adopting a lesbian identity at all. Although they did not quite provoke their facilitator, they did offer several challenges to the supposedly gender-neutral egalitarian model. With their bold claims to performing a masculine role in both their gendered and their sexual behavior—in public and in bed—the women in Venceremos Juntas were rather unapologetic about who they are, how they appear, and what they do. One might say they were less willing to be bien educada in the subject of sexuality. The conversations in Venceremos Juntas, the activist interventions and the pedagogical moments, complicate what it means to be sexually well mannered and, in turn, what it means to be a sexual subject.

Intimate Instruction and Being Bien Educada

Whether they are located in the capital city or in rural locations, and whether they are convened by grassroots activists or by advocates working within NGOs, Nicaraguan lesbian discussion groups are invested in cultivating participants who are bien educada: women who are well-educated and well-mannered in how they speak about and understand sexuality. In lesbian discussion groups, women who historically have been designated cochonas can now subscribe to a new moniker: lesbiana. But who may count—or, better yet, who may *want* to be counted—as a lesbian is a question that remains unresolved in discussion groups. In the intimate pedagogical space of discussion groups, sexual rights advocates must actively manage the tensions between older, more familiar Nicaraguan "folk" terms such as "cochona" and newer, globally circulated terms such as "lesbiana." Activists' mediation of this process involves defining and, importantly, redefining the meanings, both positive and negative, that particular terms embody. The work of discussion groups and the mediations of the activists who convene them represent a complex fusion of political strategies and pedagogical methods. They are a forum for consciousness raising, echoing both feminist and Marxist calls to consciousness. They are dialogic in their method, calling for both instruction and the exchange of ideas and experiences. Simultaneously, they emphasize choice and they are structured by liberal individual values of self-help and self-esteem. Through this process, activist facilitators craft a sense of sexual identity that is meant to codify a range of affective and performative moments, transforming "feeling" into "knowing."

The pedagogical work of discussion groups demands acquiring a specific set of ethics, discourses, and interpretations of sexuality that more often than not are glossed as "modern," "educated," and sophisticated. Pierre Bourdieu (1984) theorized a similar phenomenon within certain socioeconomic classes in which "distinction" was rendered through lifestyle choices rather than through economic capital. Becoming bien educada in Nicaraguan sexuality discussion groups involves cultivating a similar "mannered" (Elias 2000 [1994]) distinction, one linked to middle-class and upper-middle-class values regarding proper comportment. The behavioral gestures described by Bourdieu and Elias serve to mark class hierarchies; Nicaraguan lesbian discussion groups' focus on the acquisition of an "egalitarian," "modern," and "educated" sexuality follows a parallel logic of comportment and hierarchical distinctions. It also appears to reflect an entrenched, if unconscious, bias toward putatively developed forms of gay and lesbian sexual citizenship that have become hegemonic in many places (see, e.g., Cantú 2009; Gopinath 2005; Manalansan and Cruz-Malavé 2002; Reddy 2005). Whether this is a sign of cultural imperialism (Massad 2002) or an accommodation to a global context in which both ideas and identities rapidly circulate (Boellstorff 2005; Sinnott 2004), what is clear is that activists facilitating discussion groups are calibrating their pedagogy to reflect certain kinds of sexual subjectivity. As they operationalize certain kinds of discursive tools and seek to manage the sexual imaginary, facilitators recreate the process that Michel Foucault (1979) found with the emergence of homosexuality as a category and marker of personhood. The proliferation of sexual discourse and modes of categorization and control that were of such interest to Foucault are, in discussion groups, refocused through articulations of transnational human rights discourses (Howe 2009). Although Bourdieu's analysis of distinction and Foucault's analysis of the history of sexuality address more general structural phenomena of modern society, what is most striking in Nicaraguan lesbian discussion groups is how activists serve as agents of articulation in these phenomena. Activist facilitators hope to engender an exchange between themselves and participants, to create a space where experiences, opinions, and thoughts can be shared. But facilitators also have cast themselves in the role of teachers with a pedagogical mission. While participants' thoughts are welcomed and encouraged, activist facilitators are ever ready with carefully planned pedagogical responses. They are quick to present the "right" answers, many of which favor egalitarian models of homoerotic desire. They are also ready with global symbols such as rainbow flags and rights-based logics such as those found in Amnesty International documents. As they interpret participants' experiences, activist facilitators are effectively convening lessons in sexual subjectivity that, with their ideological emphasis on rational understanding, are also intimate lessons in liberalism. *Knowledge Production based on Neo-Liberal (Western/Northern) pedagogical ideas/frameworks?*

For facilitators, knowledge is acquired through a process of sharing, obtaining consciousness, and becoming empowered. Both consciousness and empowerment, as pedagogical frameworks, have cultural and political genealogies in both Latin and North America. Consciousness, as a politically honed self-awareness, has been a cornerstone of many Marxist projects encouraging revolutionary citizens to recognize their political agency and to claim their true position in history. The concept of consciousness was foundational to both Paulo Freire's "pedagogy of the oppressed" (Freire 1973) and the values of Liberation Theology that inspired many to action during the Nicaraguan revolution.[16] In a similar way, promoting a sense of empowerment was a fundamental aspect of the U.S. Civil Rights Movement. Feminist consciousness-raising (CR) groups in the United States also relied heavily on the concept of empowerment. During the second wave of feminism in the United States and elsewhere, CR groups encouraged women to meet, talk, and realize that "the personal is political" (Firestone 1970; Morgan 1977). Feminist CR groups never enjoyed the same level of popularity in Latin America that they did in the United States because structural conditions, poverty, and the political legacy of *caudillo* leadership in much of Latin America led Latin American feminists to become more immediately and directly involved with revolutionary movements and opposition politics (Craske 1999; Saporta Sternbach et al. 1992). Feminist CR groups did not appear in Nicaragua, for example, until the late 1980s, when small groups of intellectual women met to discuss the feminist limitations of the FSLN, as well as "women's disempowerment" (Field 1999: 159). However, shades of feminist CR appear in contemporary lesbian discussion groups when facilitators advocate the use of personal narrative and focus on participants' developing self-esteem. Self-esteem, according to the logic of discussion groups, is accomplished through an individual and psychotherapeutic development of the sexual self. The language of self-esteem, self-awareness, and sexual choice favored by activist facilitators—and, eventually, often discussion group participants themselves—mirrors many of the values associated with liberal individualism and an "autological" subject (Povinelli 2007).[17] The autologics at work in discussion groups draw from multiple political histories, including survivals of Sandinismo and a situated form of identity politics.

Transforming cochonas and lesbianas into rights-bearing subjects has been central to activists' attempts to challenge the antisodomy law. However, the law itself did not identify particular categories of sexual identity or subjectivity as criminal. Instead, it very plainly designated any same-sex sexual *practice* (or the promotion of it), by any name, to be illegal. Promoting lesbian identity therefore cannot be understood as simply a lever with which to overturn policy. Rather, it is an exercise in the semiotics of sexual identity. The term "lesbiana" has only very recently found wide popular usage in Nicaragua. Therefore, the emphasis that activists place on identity adoption—as a "sure sign" that participants have become bien educada—slips rather easily between international discourses and the specificities of Nicaraguan experience. Because the term "lesbian" is now familiar in many places in the world, it is important that activist facilitators attempt to keep the category capacious and polyvalent. It must be capable of representing many different things, including, for example, the experiences of lesbians who have lived in the queer epicenters of the North with their girlfriends as well as the experiences of women who love other women, feel that they are part of the campo, and at times refuse to assimilate their sexual practices to a hegemonic logic of *lesbianidad*.

Identity politics have faced a great deal of criticism, from both scholars and pundits, for their dependence on essentialism—prioritizing one aspect of personhood rather than allowing for a more complex and heterogeneous understanding of the self. However, in the case of Nicaraguan lesbian discussion groups, the impetus to adopt an identity is better understood as a political and processual exercise. Discussion groups and the pedagogical interventions that inform them are a way to comprehend social relationships rather than insist on an inner state of mind or essential personhood (Alcoff et al. 2005). Lesbian identity is a framework and a mechanism that activists use to encourage participants to make sense of their experiences; it is a way for participants and activist facilitators alike to engage with sexuality as both an analytic and an affective category.

Discussion groups are a forum for personal transformation and lessons about identity, but they are also a space where activists foster an explicit conversation about sexuality. These groups, above all, are an education in desire. They are a pedagogical space to assess affective states and the experience of sexual being. Activist facilitators hope to create participant-citizens who will acquire and maintain sexual self-esteem and who will come to consider themselves worthy of rights. However, activist facilitators do not necessarily expect participants to become involved in the lucha for sexual rights. The discursive exercises in sexuality, identity, and empowerment that take place in discussion groups may ultimately result in participants' taking to the streets. Yet the activist facilitators I have observed and spoken with have been more concerned that participants engage with the intimacies of self-acceptance and explorations of the sexual self. It is tempting to see discussion groups as transmission points where relatively private conversations become the impetus for public dissent. In the case of some participants, this may be true. But it would be overly simplistic to follow a linear trajectory from intimate pedagogies to political protest. The "overturning" that takes place in discussion groups is centered on the self rather than on the state. Ultimately, activists' mediations, in these spaces, are intimate pedagogical interventions that do not insist on explicitly challenging legal regimes or rousing overt protest against sexual injustice. Public demonstrations of sexual and gender rights that take place on the street and in the media—the focus of subsequent chapters—both reflect and inform the intimate pedagogies of discussion groups. In the next chapter, activists negotiate questions of *declaración* and debate how best to articulate sexual rights in the public domain. The desire to transform consciousness remains, but the scale of intervention and the intended impact are much greater as activists attempt to move the lucha out of the closet and into the public sphere.

[handwritten margin note: Argues intent of Activist lead discussion groups do not solely surround that of a political agenda.]

CHAPTER THREE

=

Pride and Prejudice

Engineering Epistemologies

When you are dressed to the nines and ready for a night on the town, Nicaraguans are apt to say, "Andas bien armada" (You're going out well armed). Those attending the grand finale fiesta for the Jornada por una Sexualidad Libre de Prejuicios (Gathering for Sexuality Free from Prejudice) were definitely that: bien armadas. Sponsored by several NGOs and smaller advocacy groups in Nicaragua in late June every year, the fiesta concludes a weeklong series of events to promote a better understanding of sexual diversity and rights. As the party got under way at a local restaurant, plates of *bocas* (snacks) made from deep-fried cheese and salty slices of green plantain were passed around, and Flor de Caña, Nicaragua's popular national rum, began to flow.[1] As guests arrived, they were greeted by friends with kisses on the cheek, and conversations erupted across the room as updates were exchanged and people shared all their latest news. Everyone seemed to know someone, and some knew just about everyone. By the time we were ready to begin, the audience numbered close to one hundred, and as the disco ball overhead was geared up and the stage lights beamed, cheers and whistles filled the darkening room. Squinting in the spotlight, with microphone in hand, the host shouted out a boisterous greeting: "Welcome! Welcome to you all! We are all so glad to be here because this is our party, for us, for the solidarity of lesbians and homosexuals in Nicaragua!"

The host of the Sexuality Free from Prejudice (SFFP) party rallied much heartfelt enthusiasm for the ideal of solidarity. The fiesta was a space and a time to celebrate "us." However, creating solidarity and establishing a unified agenda for sexual rights in Nicaragua has not been a goal that is easily accomplished.[2] It is an aspiration that requires a great deal of mediation. As sexual rights activists endeavor to shape their distinct approaches to local and trans-local political paradigms, they find themselves in conversation, and sometimes in conflict, with the agendas of other advocates, even when they all share a commitment to establishing greater public tolerance and appreciation for sexual difference. The discussion groups described in the previous chapter focused on intimate pedagogies and constructions of subjectivity among relatively small groups of individuals. The political interventions I describe in this chapter are grander in scale and scope, including fiestas, press conferences, lectures, and public events. These political performances are also intended for a much larger audience: the greater Nicaraguan nation. Activists are, necessarily, acutely aware of the distinctions between relatively private disclosures of sexual identity and public claims for sexual rights. As they maneuver the politics of sexual rights from the intersubjective spaces of discussion groups into the bright light of public scrutiny, activists must strategize how to go public. However, before their political interventions can be scaled to reach a broader audience, activists must work through their priorities for the *lucha*, and account for dramatic differences in how to approach the political history and imagined future of sexual rights advocacy. In this chapter, I consider how, in their quest to create a coherent message and foster social change, sexual rights advocates have grappled with the politics of both presentation and representation. Or, to put it in the parlance of lesbian and gay disclosure, I examine how the struggle for sexual rights "comes out."

In public venues and behind the scenes, three debates have been central to the struggle for sexual rights in Nicaragua: the differences between Lesbian and Gay Pride and Sexuality Free from Prejudice; the politics of *declaración*; and the gendered dimensions of power within the lucha. In the first part of this chapter, I contrast the distinct political frameworks of Orgullo Lésbico-Gay (Lesbian and Gay Pride) and SFFP and explain how these political positions are established, contested, and negotiated. In these deliberations, activists must engage in negotiations, often backstage, to render and refine their public presentations of sexual rights. As I describe in the second part of this chapter, transvestic performances have had a long-standing place in Nicaraguan folkloric traditions and the country's history. Transvestics, however, have a unique significance within the lucha. "Drag" performances have been a source of entertainment at many sexual rights events and celebrations, but the rather spectacular shows also uncover gendered power dynamics in unexpected ways. In the final section of this chapter, I turn to the politics of declaración (lit., a "declaration" that serves as an index of one's "outness"). As in some other sexual rights struggles in other parts of the world, the mandate to be out of the closet has met with an uneven reception within Nicaragua. What counts as being "declared," to what degree, and in which specific settings all determine the qualities attributed to the closet and the legitimacy of sexual rights activists themselves. As they debate, modify, and ultimately perform their political interventions, sexual rights advocates must collectively define how sexual rights will come to be known and understood by the Nicaraguan public. It is precisely because these politics are intended to reshape public understandings of sexuality that activists' interventions demand a carefully crafted representational strategy. Rather than simply seeking to change policy (such as overturning the antisodomy law), activists have aimed for a remapping of the cultural logics of the country. It is through these political performances and discourses, I argue, that activists are engineering the epistemology of the lucha, carefully constructing how the struggle will come to be known and understood.[3]

In the late afternoon, the streets of Managua are often crowded with bicycles, taxis, and recycled American school buses that have been refashioned into the capital's commercial transportation system. On a fading afternoon in late June 2001, a local HIV/AIDS prevention organization decided to take advantage of the streets' evening bustle by rallying a coterie of twenty young men to commandeer the sidewalks. Carrying banners proclaiming "Everyone Has a Right to Their Sexuality" and chanting "Human Rights Are Our Rights," the troupe made its way down a crowded boulevard toward the Nicaraguan National Assembly and the Office of the President. Armed with yellow balloons that read "No al artículo 204" (No

FIGURE 3.1 Holding bumper stickers that say "No to Article 204," Nicaragua's anti-sodomy law, these two protestors are part of a larger group organized by a local NGO as part of the Sexuality Free from Prejudice campaign, Managua, 2001.

FIGURE 3.2 Protestors marched through the streets of central Managua as part of the Sexuality Free from Prejudice campaign in 2001, passing important government offices and momentarily blocking traffic. Here they have draped a banner from a pedestrian bridge. The sign rejects Article 204 and says, "Homosexual and Lesbian Rights are Human Rights."

FIGURE 3.3 This well-known statue located on a busy thoroughfare in Managua was erected by the Sandinistas and is officially known as "El Guerrillero sin Nombre" (The Unknown Soldier) in remembrance of soldiers who died during the Contra war. Commonly referred to as "Rambo," the statute was an important symbolic location for anti–Article 204 protestors to affix their message.

to Article 204), the protesters managed momentarily to fill the skies with their demands. The group then found its way to an iconic figure in Managua: the hypermasculine statue of a revolutionary soldier that towers above one of the city's main thoroughfares. Erected by the Sandinistas, the statue honors Nicaragua's fallen soldiers in the Contra war. Although his official designation is "El Guerrillero sin Nombre" (The Unknown Soldier), he is commonly referred to as "Rambo." The public sculpture was meant to stand in opposition to the kind of U.S.-centered imperialisms that the original "Rambo" represents, but the statue embodies much more than one designation alone can capture. In an effort to ensure a more durable message for their cause than was possible with balloons and banners, the protestors decided to plaster the base of the figure with "No al artículo 204" stickers. Rambo's raised AK-47 cast an imposing shadow over the endeavor, but the young men were much more interested in commenting to me about how clearly "well-endowed" this particular Rambo was. Beyond the commentary on the statue's groin, however, the young men saw purpose in placing stickers at this particular site. Affixing their message against Article 204 here was, as they put it, *un mensaje simbó-lico* (a symbolic message). It was a way to make their opposition to the antisodomy law very visible and to provide a more subtle rebuttal of ma-chismo and the masculine prerogative that the protesters believed, im-plicitly, bolstered the antisodomy law.

The protestors' symbolic message, in the simplest terms, was a sign of dissent against the antisodomy law. But the march, and the messages, hold other significance, as well. It is no coincidence, for instance, that the NGO and the young men orchestrated their *manifestación* (demonstration or rally) in late June. This attuned their protest temporally with LGBT pride celebrations around the globe that themselves are often timed to coincide with the Stonewall Rebellion of 1969, which inaugurated the gay and les-bian liberation movement in the United States (see, e.g., D'Emilio 1983; D'Emilio and Freedman 1997; Epstein 1999a, 1999b; Marcus 1992; Plum-mer 1992; Stein 1997; Weeks 1989). Using the rainbow flag and reiterating the position that "everyone has a right to their sexuality," the protest was saturated with globally recognized markers of lesbian and gay movement politics and discourses of human rights. And while these components, in sum, appear to be sure signs of Nicaraguan gay and lesbian pride, this would tell only part of the story. The protestors' balloons and banners on that afternoon were part of Nicaragua's annual Sexuality Free from Preju-dice (SFFP) events, which stand in some distinction to the politics of Les-bian and Gay Pride, both in their origins and in their ideological purpose.

[handwritten margin note: mirroring western innovations?]

The lucha for sexual rights has not been a singular project and activ-ists involved in the struggle often envision very different ways of how to navigate and structure the lucha going forward. Some sexual rights pro-ponents insist that Lesbian and Gay Pride is the ideal approach to sexual rights advocacy. Pride, for them, has the possibility of radically transform-ing how Nicaraguans understand same-sex sexuality. Other sexual rights advocates, however, believe that SFFP is the more effective framework. It is, for them, a better method to establish equality for sexual minorities as well as a way to embark on a larger, national discussion about sexuality for both gay and straight Nicaraguans. Both approaches share the goal of promoting respect and social justice for sexually marginalized people, and both are predicated on ideals of rights and freedoms. However, these strategies of social transformation are quite distinct and at times are epis-temologically divergent. The premises and principles on which they are based draw from different ways of envisioning both their constituencies for sexual rights and the political values and discourses that will be presented, and performed, in the Nicaraguan public sphere.

For Sexuality Free from Prejudice

The Gathering for Sexuality Free from Prejudice was launched in the early 1990s by sexual rights activists, feminist allies, and Nicaraguan NGOs in an effort to challenge the newly virulent antisodomy law. Since that time, however, it has become much more. The SFFP events have become the largest, most well-known, and best-funded representation of sexual rights in the country. The focal point for SFFP is the capital city, but events have also been held in other parts of the country. The city of Matagalpa, a longtime Sandinista hub in Nicaragua's coffee-growing region, holds SFFP events. Chinandega, a city near the Honduran border with a high incidence of HIV/AIDS, and San Juan del Sur (a favorite beach enclave of the Somozas, Sandinistas, and, now, expatriates) have all hosted SFFP events. The gathering has grown dramatically, in both scope and scale, since its debut. Initially it ran a day or two of events, but by 1999, the gathering's activities stretched for nearly a week and featured call-in radio shows, television appearances by activists, press conferences, research presentations, magazine canvassing, and the screening of films such as *Fresa y chocolate* and *Ma vie en rose*. Each of these public presentations demanded a careful crafting of both content and form.

During the SFFP events of 2001, the film *Antes que anochezca*, based on the life of the gay Cuban writer Reinaldo Arenas, was screened for an audience of fifty or so people at the Coro de Ángeles (Chorus of Angels), an old Sandinista haunt in Managua. Following the film, a Cuban intellectual discussed the persecution of Cuban homosexuals and the relative tolerance found in Sandinista Nicaragua. In addition to screening educational and entertaining films, local NGOs hosted research presentations such as reports on HIV transmission in Nicaraguan cities and findings on depression and suicide among gay male youth. The magazine *Fuera del Closet* (Out of the Closet),[4] published by the HIV-prevention and sexual rights organization Fundación Xochiquetzal, was distributed around the city. Making an appearance on an early morning TV talk show, "a homosexual" and "a lesbian" discussed their experiences of discrimination in the job market and the social stigma surrounding homosexuality in Nicaragua. Radio shows such as "Derechos Humanos de Homosexuales y Lesbianas: La Pareja Perfecta también Puede Encontrarse entre Personas del Mismo

Sexo" (Human Rights for Homosexuals and Lesbians: Your Perfect Match May Be Someone of the Same Sex) and "El Amor Verdadero no Tiene Prejuicios" (True Love Knows No Prejudice) were broadcast on youth radio programs. To create maximum attendance and public visibility, the SFFP events have been advertised in the national newspapers, on leaflets and posters, and through the broadcast media.

The educational presentations and gatherings for SFFP are financed by a handful of feminist, sexual rights, and HIV/AIDS-prevention NGOs. The organizations that sponsor SFFP, such as Fundación Xochiquetzal and Puntos de Encuentro (Common Ground), are largely responsible for choosing the content, timing, and scale of the events. While NGOs are the primary architects of SFFP events, additional planning, suggestions for activities, and the volunteer labor needed to make it all possible are often provided by less institutionally embedded advocates, such as avowed feminists, university students, long-time homosexual rights activists, and parishioners from the Iglesia de la Comunidad Metropolitana Comunitaria (Metropolitan Community Church), often called the "gay church."[5] *church originated u.s.*

To frame the political priorities of SFFP and encourage participation in the events held in the summer of 2001, Puntos de Encuentro circulated an announcement by e-mail and had copies printed and distributed. The text of their circular described how "the Jornada por una Sexualidad Libre de Prejucios has become a space where sexuality is demystified in order to speak about sexuality as a natural entity, with the end result of learning, understanding, and creating, overall, respect for the human species, all of whom are diverse and equal. The Jornada has always promoted the need to have a sexual scientific education. This helps us to recognize that there is sexual diversity and that its existence is an undeniable right." The mission of the Jornada, as the announcement indicates, is to highlight sexual diversity and equality as broad social concerns. Notably, the announcement does not refer to gay and lesbian rights specifically; nor does it mention homosexuality, male or female. While this can be read partly as a concession to the antisodomy law (so that the government cannot claim that the gathering is promoting or propagandizing same-sex intercourse), it also speaks to a larger set of claims. Establishing sexuality that is "free from prejudice" is, in this narrative, not a concern unique to sexual minorities. Rather, it is equated with a fundamental "respect for the human species." Positioning sexual rights as intrinsic to humanity, and placing sexuality within the greater scope of human rights, activists

fuera del **closet**

Revista trimestral No. 25, marzo 2001

Ocho de marzo, día internacional de la mujer

FIGURE 3.4 *Fuera del Closet* (Out of the Closet) has been published by the Nicaraguan NGO Fundación Xochiquetzal since the early 1990s. It is distributed in several locations around the country, particularly during sexual rights events. The authors are primarily Nicaraguan, although the magazine does reproduce stories from abroad. For this issue, published in March 2001, the artist "Cony" has illustrated a woman freeing herself from a cage and leaning toward another woman who is located in a lotus flower. Cony's art is used extensively in *Fuera del Closet*; some of her drawings were also used during a consciousness-raising exercise for a local lesbian discussion group.

propose that sexual diversity is not simply a "minority" concern but one that implicates all of society. As they draw specific attention to the process of "learning," "understanding," and "demystifying" sexuality, advocates create an epistemological framework that intends to change the way that Nicaraguans think about sexuality, diversity, and desire. Advancing the possibility for a "sexual scientific education," one that is based on the proposition that sexuality is a "natural entity," the proponents of SFFP also gesture to notions of progress, modernity, and the putative objectivity of science. These naturalizing discourses situate sexuality as a quality that is universally inherent and biological. At the same time, sexuality must be left amenable to social intervention, education, and the promise of demystification. The political logic of SFFP, on the one hand, is a subtle approach, treading carefully before the law; but it is also meant to promote broad transformation and a general social tolerance rather than emphasize minority politics. The constituency that SFFP seeks to convince and to educate is the larger Nicaraguan population, not only *lesbianas*, *gays*, *homosexuales*, or others who would consider themselves part of a sexual minority. It is the greater collective of the nation that, for the advocates of SFFP, is the proper subject of sexual rights. Put another way, the goal of SFFP is to promulgate the notion that all Nicaraguans have a sexuality and, in turn, a right to it.

Advocates of SFFP have been very attentive to how sexuality and rights are combined and interrelated to one another as epistemological devices. They have also been vigilant about how sexual rights are presented to the Nicaraguan public. Lilia, a lead organizer for the SFFP events, for example, carefully sketched how the proceedings were to be presented in an upcoming press conference. She wanted to ensure that each member of the organizing committee was well-versed in how to speak with journalists, who would, in turn, be communicating with the Nicaraguan public through newspaper, radio, and television coverage. "When you talk to the press, when you approach them, you don't tell them the event is for homosexuals and lesbians," Lilia explained. "Approach it *suavemente* (gently or mildly). Don't scare them right away. Ease into it. This is *sexuality free from prejudice* [drawing out the phrase]. Please, don't start by telling them about the *cochones* and *cochonas*!" Emphasizing the phrase "sexuality free from prejudice" and gesturing with a wink and a nod (and appropriating the derogatory terms "cochón" and "cochona" in the way only a true insider can), Lilia discouraged her comrades from highlighting "the fags and

FIGURE 3.5 This sticker, created for Sexuality Free from Prejudice events, was affixed to a file cabinet in a sexual rights activist's home. The script at the bottom says, "That's how I like it!" Given that the young woman pictured appears to be nude and is holding the bare leg of another woman, the sticker has a double meaning, evoking both lesbian sexuality and Sexuality Free from Prejudice.

the dykes" in their conversations with reporters. She wanted to be sure that "sexuality free from prejudice" was articulated in a very particular way. Her recommendation fell on appreciative ears among the committee members, and everyone nodded in agreement. Lilia's intentionally delicate discourse for the press was not meant to deny that SFFP advocates are committed to promoting sexual rights and invested in remediating prejudice against homosexuales, lesbianas, cochones, and cochonas. However, she did want to underscore that the framework for sexual rights needed to be presented to the public in carefully calibrated ways—that is, suavemente. Lilia is a very publicly declared lesbian. But her goal of fostering greater public tolerance for sexual rights called for a more seductive subtlety around the issue of "the fags and the dykes."

At the SFFP press conference a few days later, I was curious to see whether Lilia's message would be received in the way she intended. The press conference was very well attended by most of Nicaragua's prominent media sources, and journalists were gathered in a large room at a local NGO. After we had heard an overview of the SFFP events from Lilia and another lead organizer, I asked two male journalists (one from a national daily and the other from a local television station) for their thoughts about the upcoming activities. "The way I understand it is that one shouldn't have anything against other people, like homosexuals or lesbians," one of the journalists said, "because this is the kind of sex that is most criticized. So we need to value people not for their sexuality but for who they are." His colleague also weighed in: "I would say the same thing: that we can't be prejudiced against people just because they maintain relations with people of the same sex. . . . And we need to recognize that there are people who have relations with people of the same sex. This is something that we need to understand." Although they were supposed to leave the meeting with the understanding that SFFP was "not all about the cochones and cochonas," the journalists seemed convinced, nonetheless, that the events were oriented toward the concerns of sexual minorities. One journalist used polite and non-derogatory terms ("lesbianas" and "homosexuales," as opposed to "cochones" and "cochonas"), and the other named the practice (maintaining relations with people of the same sex) rather than the personage. Lilia's *suave* approach thus proved more difficult in practice than in theory. The journalists' default assumption was that SFFP was, essentially, for lesbianas and homosexuales (or cochones and cochonas), the marked categories within the rubric of sexual diversity. In the estimation of the reporters, homosexuality seemed to stand in for all sexuality; this is precisely what the organizers had hoped to avoid. The activists who convene Sexuality Free from Prejudice events aspire to create a broad-based campaign that will promote sexual tolerance and cultivate the understanding that sexuality is something that is embodied in, and of interest to, all Nicaraguans. Defining this national constituency may meet with uneven results. However, as they endeavor to broaden the purview of sexual rights beyond minority politics, SFFP advocates reveal their affinity with the communitarian impulses of Sandinismo. Theirs is a political imaginary that privileges a national ethical and epistemological transformation rather than focusing on a particular marginalized population. In addition to echoing Sandinismo, expanding the range of sexual rights to include the Nicaraguan nation follows a democratizing and human rights-based narrative that reflects the country's broader political climate.

Revolutionary Sexology

As I arrived at a large lecture hall at the Universidad Centroamericana, the well-respected Jesuit University in Managua, I could see that the event would be standing-room only. More than three hundred students were filing into rows of chairs, and the mood was high. Two renowned Nicaraguan sexologists took their places on the dais at the front of the room. As part of SFFP's educational mission, the sexologists' presentations would explain the influences of both "nature" and "nurture" in the development of homosexuality, and overview the topic of childrearing by lesbians and gay men. Before the speakers embarked on their talks, I asked several students what they thought of the day's subjects. One young woman said: "I believe that it is very important, and I think that young people need to eliminate these myths and dogmas that force us to close ourselves off. It is an idea that limits us, and so we need to have more choices in order to develop ourselves." Hoping to better understand what she meant by these limitations and enclosures I asked what she meant, exactly, with the term "dogma." She responded, "Dogma is like a recipe: there is no way out; it is boxed in. You can't get away from it. It's, like, the same as prejudice. That's what dogma is. We have to get out of it. And to develop ourselves and to see sexuality as something that is very natural. It is part of human development." Her friend standing next to her explained that, for him, "It seems like an opportunity to choose whichever sex [a man or a woman] that each person likes without prejudice, without any social impediment." Another student added, "I agree, because nowadays, nobody can repress the choices of others. This is something of the past."

The students agreed with many of the values animating the SFFP events: overcoming prejudice and viewing sexuality in terms of human development and science. More important, perhaps, they averred that choice (or whatever "each person likes") was an important value. It was, from their vantage point, a more contemporary worldview that relegated anti-homosexual bias and dogma to the past. Liberal values of choice and tolerance are interwoven in the students' narratives, and they phrase their thoughts in terms of temporal movement and progress: to be free from prejudice is to be more personally "developed." Their narratives, not unlike the principles of SFFP, follow a modernist logic and, in particular, underscore the belief that it is the responsibility of individuals to advance their own levels of tolerance and open-mindedness.

Promoting progress and overcoming antiquated dogmas was also a central element in the lecturers' presentations. During the question-and-answer period following the talks, one of the speakers, a clinical psychologist who specialized in sexuality, called attention to a student's question about the effect of the revolutionary period on sexuality and marriage:

Someone just asked a question that is very important, because probably many of you were either very young or just born in the 1980s. She asked if the 1980s marked changes in people's lives, and if we think about the word "revolution," it is a *revuelta* (an uprising or a mixing up) of everything. This was a social revolution, where the social structure and political structure was radically changed, but obviously there were a number of changes. There were a lot of people who got divorced. And [there were] a lot of people who couldn't stand these changes. But those who were really committed kept their relationships, and those who weren't lost them. But it wasn't the revolution that did this: people getting divorced or people becoming lesbians.[6]

What the revolution did was open a space. The people who had been living hidden lives because of the censorship with this new space [were] now able to be less isolated; they got together in groups and they got organized. The women got organized, everyone got organized, right down to the young people, they got organized. And so the homosexuals got organized, too. And it wasn't with the intent to just have a bunch of homosexuals, but it was because they had more opportunities to be open about themselves. The rights that one has and the ability to exercise those rights are two distinct things.

The revolutionary history of the nation, in the sexologist's recounting, constituted an era of radical change for both social and political structures in Nicaragua, from the emergence of homosexual rights to changing relationships. Linking the country's socialist past with contemporary articulations of rights, the speaker emphasized both the opportunities for political organizing and the shape of those projects. In essence, the revolutionary period is characterized as a social space in which many found themselves provided with, or confronted with, the "opportunity to be open about themselves." For both the students and the speakers, the ideals of "choice," freedom from "impediment," and "the ability to exercise [one's] rights" are explicitly related to the revolutionary era as well as the contemporary moment. Prejudice and censoring sexuality, for the sexologists and the students, become a kind of premodern, or less developed, survival from Nicaragua's past.[7] Discrimination, in other words, is antithetical to the aspirations of a more liberated present marked by a discourse of rights.

As students were filing out of the hall, I was curious about what they had learned from the presentations and the question-and-answer session.

One young woman responded with a somewhat surprising answer. "Well," she said, "I learned that we need to have a campaign to protect the homosexuals, because in one way or another, in some form, we have to protect them, because they are like kids. They can't take care of themselves, or that is, they need help." Although she seemed well intentioned in her response, her condescending, protective intervention was not what the panelists or the organizers were hoping to achieve. As with the journalists at the press conference, this particular student had understood that homosexuales and lesbianas were the intended recipients of sexual rights. She did not mention a more expansive contingent of sexual-rights-bearing subjects, as SFFP proposes. Her comment was interesting in other ways, too. In one sense, her response, though condescending and infantilizing, was not wholly anti-homosexual; she seemed to have digested a broader message that, minimally, calls for tolerance. Her rendering of tolerance, however, demonstrates the ease with which rights may slip into a different register: one of patronizing support and a rhetoric of protecting the weak (Fassin 2011).

As the largest and best-supported forum for sexual rights in Nicaragua, the Gathering for Sexuality Free from Prejudice has been an important site for activists to perform very public and visible claims for sexual rights. Because of both its scale and its educational orientation, SFFP has managed to generate and sustain an enduring epistemology for sexual rights advocacy. The values that appear in the narratives of the SFFP campaigns—choice, individual decision making, tolerance, development, progress, and the value of scientific knowledge—are explicitly crafted by activists who present sexual rights in a particular way, drawing heavily on liberalism and pluralist multiculturalism. This epistemic space aligns liberal discourses of subjectivity with the nation's Marxian, nationalist history and these collective forms of political expression. By advocating for SFFP, activists emphasize that the Nicaraguan nation as a whole is the constituency of their rights-based work. While it may not be singular or monological, the nation is invoked as a site for activist remediation and intervention. Like the Sandinista era's national communitarian ethos, SFFP envisions sexual rights for all, not just for lesbianas and homosexuales specifically. It is a set of discourses and practices that marks the nation as subjects of, and for, sexual rights.

For other sexual rights activists, however, the logics that animate SFFP are too opaque, and ultimately too *suave*. Primarily, SFFP has failed to present a sufficiently bold critique of the antisodomy law. This failure, from the point of view of Lesbian and Gay Pride activists, rests on the fact that, in its attempt at breadth, SFFP obscures that it is Nicaraguan lesbianas and homosexuales who are the primary victims of sexual intolerance and marginalization.

Pride and Praxis

It was around midnight at a *disco gay* in one of Managua's working-class neighborhoods that I first met proponents of Nicaraguan Orgullo Lésbico-Gay. As is often the case, there were few women at the disco that evening, but one young woman came to our table with an invitation for the Lesbian and Gay Pride festivities. When my friend and I arrived at the event, held at Galería Praxis, later that week, we were greeted by Humberto, who was working as the "door diva." Bedecked in gold lamé and wearing a glitter-covered fedora and shoes to match, Humberto shuttled us to a table in the courtyard. As we waited for the night's activities to unfold, Bernice, one of the event's primary organizers, came to the table to welcome us. The stage was set: a microphone for the *travesti* lip-sync performances and a table at the back for poetry readings and a *charla* (talk, discussion) that the coordinators had planned. The banana trees that bordered the courtyard were festooned with multicolored Christmas lights, an ironic yuletide in June in the tropics.

The Lesbian and Gay Pride event, as with the SFFP events, is intentionally scheduled in late June to coincide with LGBT pride events all over the world. In 1999, the Nicaraguan pride party featured a travesti lip-sync competition in which biologically male, "cross"-dressed contestants performed their feminine poise and received awards based on audience appreciation; similar performances have also been a staple of SFFP events. Poetry readings, however, were unique to the pride event. As participants read their own works to much applause and appreciation, the pride event was steeped in the long tradition of Nicaraguan poetry, from Rubén Darío to the present.[8] This added a particularly "Nica" slant to the event. Like the SFFP events, the Lesbian and Gay Pride event is coordinated by a handful of groups. But unlike the organizers of the SFFP events, the planners of the Lesbian and Gay Pride events have little institutional support: they are not NGO staff members but individuals and small activist groups. Some of the groups that have worked to promote pride events are composed solely of Nicaraguans. Others, such as Grupo Arcoiris (Rainbow Group), are a transnational mix of foreign nationals and allies. Humberto explained that both women and men were involved in organizing the pride events. In one of our many talks over the next two years, Humberto noted that placing "Lésbico" first in "Lésbico-Gay" was intentional, an attempt to overcome the relative invisibility of lesbians in Nicaragua.[9] Rather than the week-long series of events hosted by SFFP, Lesbian-Gay Pride was largely limited to one fiesta. The pride event also attracted far fewer attendees than the final SFFP party. As Bernice lamented in an interview a couple of weeks after the pride event took place, "The talks and discussion that we planned for the pride event did not happen. . . . It is easy to get people to come and party but hard to get them to do political work." This, I said, is likely true just about everywhere—and perhaps, I offered, there is no shame in "party" politics.

As one of the primary organizers of the pride events, Bernice was a firm believer in the political principles of pride, and she and I spoke many times about the meaning of Orgullo Lésbico-Gay in Nicaragua. Bernice was adamant that Lesbian and Gay Pride was a "more visible" way to both publicly challenge Article 204 and make clear that Nicaraguan lesbians and gay men were being denied their human rights.[10] "Lesbian and Gay Pride," she explained, "really provokes the government much more dramatically than Sexuality Free from Prejudice." By naming a constituency under the mantles "lesbian" and "gay," pride presented an overt challenge to a legal regime that criminalized same-sex relationships. Because they called attention to lesbians and gays specifically, the pride events certainly fell under the category of "promoting" or "propagandizing" same-sex intercourse that the law explicitly forbade. Thus, Lesbian and Gay Pride, for Bernice, put Article 204 to the test. But more than that, framing sexual rights in terms of Lesbian and Gay Pride was important, she explained, "so the Nicaraguan people know that we are not going to stand for this homophobia." Bernice was quick to acknowledge that pride was a project that needed to speak to the national level. However, rather than pursuing the SFFP ethos of investing the larger body politic with sexual rights, Bernice believed that political attention needed to focus on the discrimination faced by lesbianas and gays as lesbianas and gays. The task of the Nicaraguan nation was not to recognize their own investments in sexual rights but, rather, to overcome and confront their *homofobia*.

The activists involved with the politics of pride often used categories—*lesbiana, gay, orgullo*—that correspond to a global episteme of gay and lesbian rights discourses, in both the global North and the global South.

However, proponents of Nicaraguan pride did not consider these terms to be derivative discourses; instead, they narrated their convictions in more complex vocabularies. Activists with whom I spoke described their sense of pride in terms that went beyond sexuality. They often gestured to a national pride that echoed the anti-imperialist sentiments for which Sandino was so famous. Holding their events at the Galería Praxis, Lesbian and Gay Pride activists created a symbolic association with the Marxist values of praxis. Activists involved with Lesbian and Gay Pride also shared a keen awareness of the inequalities between the global North and the global South. They were always watchful for potential political imperialism. Ivo, for example, had received funding from a U.S.-based NGO to develop a pride-oriented pocket calendar (*agenda*). In describing how he chose the images and quotes for the calendar, he was very clear that he had developed the project without ideological input from the funding agency. His support, he explained, "had no strings attached." Many of the pride activists with whom I spoke, including Bernice and Humberto, did not consider the term "pride" appropriated, derived, or borrowed from LGBT pride politics in the global North. As Bernice pointedly put it, "Everyone has pride. This is not just something that the gringos have."

Potency and Palatability

Activists committed to SFFP conceptualize their project in broad social terms; it is an attempt, writ large, to establish a concept of sexual rights that is free from prejudice. The Jornada por una Sexualidad Libre de Prejuicios was born in reaction to the antisodomy law, and since that time, the SFFP campaign has been committed to alleviating the quotidian discrimination faced by those marked as sexually "other"—cochonas, cochones, homosexuales, and lesbianas. But perhaps more important, SFFP embodies an epistemological perspective that locates sexuality within the national body and (bio)politic, not simply in the bodies of sexually marginalized populations. With this communitarian ethos, the discourses and practices of SFFP mirror the revolutionary principles of an earlier era that sought broad social transformation. Indeed, many of the activists responsible for crafting the public politics of SFFP were part of the revolutionary struggle and the social transformations that took place during the Sandinista decade, including a politics of sexuality that was broadly based and not limited to those who identified as lesbian or gay (Randall 1993; Thayer 1997).

The logic underlying SFFP is similar to at least two other formulations of sexual rights. It reflects many of the tenets of lesbian and gay liberationist approaches that have sought to transform social conditions rather than define and defend a sexual "minority."[11] Sexuality Free from Prejudice also shares kinship with queer political approaches that have envisioned an inclusive, post-identity imperative.[12] Because SFFP aims to provide an approach that includes both sexually marginalized people and their straight allies, SFFP activists have developed a polymorphous subject for sexual rights. However, unlike many other queer political projects that emphasize a comprehensive or an "umbrella" approach, SFFP does not stress radical difference from a heteronormative status quo. Sexuality Free from Prejudice is quite the opposite of the grassroots queer political paradigms that gave birth to queer theory; it is a subtle, perhaps even careful approach to sexual rights. It is an approach that "normalizes" more than it queers (Warner 1999).

By employing the terms "lesbiana" and "gay," Nicaraguan pride activists have made semantic and symbolic links to a now globally recognized form of identity politics. By demarcating a constituency under the signs of lesbian and gay identity, Lesbian and Gay Pride reflects what has been called a "minoritizing" approach—one that defines a minority (and marginalized) population as its subject for rights-based claims. Although Lesbian and Gay Pride gestures to these sorts of global impulses, it is also an epistemological position firmly rooted in opposition to the (local) antisodomy law and cognizant of potential political imperialisms. Lesbian and Gay Pride, then, suggests a double quality of pride. First, it is a quality to be venerated, shared, and deployed among, for, and on behalf of lesbian- and gay-identified people, in Nicaragua and around the world. Second, it is a sentiment and political ideology that resonates with and has the ability to capture some of the spirit of national patrimony. Lesbian and Gay Pride may use familiar frameworks of identity and pride, but, according to the activists involved, this line of thinking is not a mere replica of Northern identity politics; it is not solely the provenance of the "gringos."

Both "pride" and "prejudice" are hybrid ways to articulate trans-local political values, placing them in conversation with local political logics. The differences between these strategies reveal how activists engage political values and how they create epistemological frameworks for the sexual rights struggle. Each approach is distinct in both structure and scale, but where they diverge most fundamentally is in how activists imagine the subject of their interventions. Both Lesbian and Gay Pride and Sexuality Free from Prejudice aspire to create a collective sensibility, an "us" around which to rally political sentiment. For Lesbian and Gay Pride, this "us" is lesbians and gay men. For SFFP, the "us" is envisioned as the Nicaraguan nation in all its diversity and in its entirety. "Pride" and "prejudice" both posed challenges to the legal regime of Article 204; each articulated a critique of the legislation and, to different degrees, advocated for the sexual rights of same-sex-attracted people. For proponents of SFFP, Lesbian and Gay Pride may have overtly confronted the law, but its formula of minority rights failed to appeal to the larger population—an important audience for those who have hoped to change the country's moral climate. Activists committed to the politics of pride, for their part, often found the SFFP approach too conciliatory because it failed to draw attention to the specific ways in which gays and lesbians have faced legal and social marginalization. While pride may be more potent and SFFP more palatable, their distinct epistemic values demonstrate how activists manage, mediate, and carefully engineer the category of sexual rights.

The Gendered Pageantry of "Drag"

The grand finales for both the SFFP party and the Lesbian and Gay Pride celebration each have one, particularly climactic, event: the *concurso travesti* (transvestite or cross-dressing contest). In their bids to be crowned *la reina* (the queen) of the night, the biological men who competed in the *concurso* in June 2001 had to excel in three separate competitions: bathing suit, evening gown, and *la exotica*. Each performance demanded rapid costume changes and carefully practiced feminine poise on the catwalk. Backstage—an area constructed by draping long pieces of cloth from the ceiling—the contestants struggled for space at steamy mirrors in makeshift dressing rooms. It was clear that the contestants had invested a good deal of time in their regalia, and every detail had been carefully planned. The evening gowns were often sewn by the contestants themselves, and some had been crafted from relatively expensive fabric such as velvet, satin, and taffeta. One contestant, Veronica, had re-fitted one of her sister's dresses, and after saving money from her work as a street vendor, she added sequins and lace to add an extra quotient of glamour to her gown. Most of the contestants in the *concurso* told me that they were from the *clases populares*, but, they explained, it was important to them that their look be "perfect"; hence, they were willing to scrimp and save to add the appearance of upper-class elegance to their performances.[13] In the second round of the competition, the bathing suit contest, contestants donned bikinis as well as the more familiar one-piece bathing suit favored by many Nicaraguan women. Both demanded a careful arrangement of male genitalia. The final category of the concurso, the exotica, involved several feats of costume engineering: contestants balanced towering headdresses while performing a seamless gait in platform heels. With music and applause to accompany them, contestants glided down the promenade as enthusiastic onlookers whistled and cheered their costumed finery as well as contestants' ability to appear wholly feminine.[14] Arlén, one of the contestants, said that her primary objective—and the one that would win her the title—was to be a true or real woman.[15]

The concursos travestis that have taken place at the SFFP and Pride parties have a particular political purpose including glossing travestis as gay or homosexual subjects. However, transvestic performances themselves have a rather long history in Nicaragua. They have been a popular form of entertainment in the ambiente (scene) and discos gay. And as in the concurso, they have occupied an important role in public displays of sexual rights, making them a good example of "drag as protest" (Rupp and Taylor 2003: 213) or an effective way of "redrawing the boundaries between aesthetics and activism" (Fox and Starn 1997: 10). Before they appeared in sexual rights activism, transvestic performances were enacted annually in the Torovenado, a long-standing cultural event honoring San Geronimo, the patron saint of Nicaragua's folkloric capital, Masaya. The San Geronimo celebrations in Masaya attract several thousand Nicaraguans each year. The parade that is the hallmark of the festivities is commonly called the "parade of the cochones." Torovenado participants, many of them male, don flamboyant women's garb, wigs, and garish makeup to march through the streets, making exaggerated and often ribald gestures along the way (Borland 2006). Featuring representations of Spanish conquistadors and political figures (such as Ronald Reagan and Margaret Thatcher in the 1980s), the Torovenado has been a parodic political space. But it has also been a carnivalesque opportunity in which, at least temporarily, the norms of gender, race, class, and social hierarchy have been inverted in ways that both challenge and recapitulate the dominant normative order (Bakhtin 1984; Turner 1969). While the inversions of the Torovenado have been a source of ongoing cultural commentary since the Sandinista era, the Torovenado has also become a lively and (re-

FIGURE 3.6 A contestant who is *bien armada* and awaiting her turn backstage in the evening gown portion of the *travesti* competition during the Sexuality Free from Prejudice party in Managua, 2001.

FIGURE 3.7 Another contestant with platform heels ready on the shelf and press-on fingernails and lipstick already in place. Backstage is a less than glamorous space, but *travestis* invest time, effort, and, when they can, money in creating the appearance of well-coiffed femininity.

FIGURE 3.8 A contestant competing in the *exotica* portion of the *travesti concurso* in Managua 2001. Padding and false appendages (e.g., breasts and buttocks) were not used in the *concursos*, but displaying one's feminized body was certainly part of the show.

invented) tradition in which the public enunciation of Nicaraguan homosexuality can be expressed (Blandón 2003; Borland 2006; Dávila Bolaños 1973).[16] Cochones are central protagonists—indeed, the "stars"—of the Torovenado. Their ability to occupy gender transgression exceeds those of their straight competitors. Therefore, according to Erick Blandón, the Torovenado is a "moment of escape from oppressive heterosexual masculinity and a dialogic engagement between different sexual subjects where homoeroticism becomes the center of attention for both homosexuals and heterosexuals."[17] While transvestics are not the quotidian norm in Nicaragua, it is clear that the country has had a public and symbolic space for these kinds of gendered performances. The settings in which transvestic pageantry are now being performed—for SFFP or on behalf of Lesbian and Gay Pride—illustrate one way in which these performances of femininity have become refashioned and rearticulated in support of sexual rights.

Backstage at the SFFP concurso as travesti performers made their final preparations, I was charged with fetching last-minute necessities such as safety pins and duct tape. My lipstick also ended up playing a prominent role in the final show, as several of the performers borrowed it for touch-ups. The competitors' boyfriends also lingered backstage, talking with one another and admiring the dramatic transformations that were taking place behind scanty pieces of cloth. Travesti's boyfriends were also engaging in performances of their own. The hypermasculinity of these *hombres hombres* (real men) provided an important foil for the contestants' carefully displayed femininity.[18] The coupling of hombres hombres with travestis reinforced a well-honed assumption in Nicaragua—namely, that *machos* couple with *femeninas* even if the couple consists of two biological men (or women). Indeed, rather than challenging gender norms, if exaggerated for the stage, the transvestic performers in glamorous women's regalia and the macho affectations of their boyfriends mirrored commonly held assumptions about femininity and masculinity in Nicaragua. The audience members with whom I spoke during the concurso did not, in fact, find any dissonance with the proposition that biological men were performing "true womanhood," and no one suggested that the performances were a critique of idealized gender forms. There was, rather, very little gender trouble here.

The *travesti* performances staged for sexual rights campaigns are not easily categorized. They are neither a critique of gendered forms nor a reification of them. They are "drag" performances and, at the same time, they are not. The rendering of femininity in the travesti concurso is certainly similar to the body manipulations and dramatic countenances seen in drag performances in the United States and elsewhere: a little too much makeup to approximate a "real" woman. However, these performances are not campy, comedic, or cabaret-like.[19] The transvestic events in Managua are more like pageant than camp. They share a closer affinity with Miss America than they do with the famously witty performances of drag queens. The bathing suit and evening gown competitions, for example, are signature beauty pageant categories in which attention is focused on the perfected display of femininity rather than the requisite comedy of drag or the parody of camp. However, the travesti concurso is not simply a gender-bending beauty contest. Unlike the usual format of beauty pageants, the travesti show involves few or no speech acts. Contestants are asked to give their names and, perhaps, the name of their neighborhoods, but they are not asked a series of questions, as is the norm in beauty pageants. There is no talent competition, and there are no "What I would do if I were queen of the world" speeches. Nor is there the flip or scathing commentary that is common in many North American drag performances. The travesti concurso has been, rather, an event that is purely visual except for the pop anthem invariably playing in the background. It is a scopophilic feast that places a spotlight on "true" femininity.

Always spectacular, the travesti performances I attended were received by audiences with much enthusiasm. Onlookers were generous with their cheers and whistles. Indeed, the only complaints I ever encountered about travesti competitions came from North American and European allies of the struggle, some of whom would lament, "Why do they always have to do these drag shows?" Some of them opined that drag was, at its core, an act of misogyny. The exaggerated performance of femininity in travesti contests made some foreign interlocutors suspicious: were travesti performances another iteration of (gay) men's hegemony or a prurient patriarchy? While I had not heard Nicaraguans question the validity, inclusiveness, or entertainment value of transvestic performances, by the early 2000s this was beginning to change.

Who Wears the Pants?

In anticipation of the upcoming week of SFFP events, feminist and sexual rights NGOs, along with a handful of activist groups, convened a planning committee to discuss the program they would be hosting. Based on my previous organizing experience and my now well-known identity as a "student of sexuality," I was also invited to participate and offer suggestions. Once the meeting was under way and the logistical questions had been resolved, the NGO director heading the committee suggested that it was time to change the focal point of the event: the entertainment. She said that the travesti contests of previous years had been the source of "too much drama" and "competition" between participants. What she, and others, saw as cattiness on the part of contestants led her to propose that the travesti competitions be discontinued. "From now on, we will do *danza*," she said. Danza features a troupe of young men in matching spandex outfits dancing in unison behind an exquisitely attired travesti lip-syncing the latest pop music hit. Replacing the travesti concurso with danza did not eradicate transvestics — or, one might argue, "competition" — from the event. However, there was remarkably little discussion about the decision to switch to danza, suggesting that it was a fait accompli.

The politics of transvestics gesture to several dynamics regarding gender and how representational power is being staged in Nicaraguan sexual rights campaigns. The travesti concursos, as political and performative events, occupy a hybrid place between the paradigmatic beauty pageant and the dramatic gender parody of drag. Although there are few comprehensive ethnographic studies of "drag,"[20] scholars of gender and sexuality have been involved in an extensive debate about the significance of drag and transvestic performance and what this may indicate about gender in political, social, and cultural terms (Altman 2001; Butler 1990, 1993; Garber 1997; Halberstam 1998; Morris 1995). Judith Butler (1990) rather famously applauded drag as a signifying practice and parodic form of illocutionary performance. She attributed it with the potential to destabilize forms of gender that have become naturalized through infinite repetition and performative reiteration. The travesti concurso can be understood, on the one hand, as an event that recapitulates a dualistic model of gender as it relies on ideal types of femininity and masculinity. Yet it is biological men who appropriate feminine attire and become — rather unproblematically, from the point of view of the audience — "true women." In this sense, the travesti concursos have mirrored Butler's hopeful prognosis — that is, that transvestics have the potential to challenge much of our thinking about gender identity, most pointedly "the distinction between appearance and reality" (Butler 1988: 527). From a very different vantage point, Dennis Altman has questioned the continuous presence and durability of drag in lesbian and gay communities. "I remain unsure just why 'drag,' and its female equivalents, remains a strong part of the contemporary homosexual world," he writes, "even where there is increasing space for open homosexuality and a range of acceptable ways of 'being' male or female" (Altman 2001: 91). Drag, in his interpretation, has historically operated as an escape mechanism from restrictive gender and sexual norms. Following this logic, as new ways of being homosexual or inhabiting gender roles are legitimated, drag should naturally disappear. The fact that it has not in Nicaraguan sexual rights campaigns, and in gay and lesbian communities elsewhere, suggests that drag may be less a protest against gender and sexual conformity than an ongoing reinterpretation of gender and sexual aesthetics.

Transvestics are complex stagings that are both mimetic and disruptive of gender and sexual norms. For those who have analyzed the significance of drag, one persistent question has been whether or not gender is reified, or imbued with essential and seemingly immutable characteristics, through these performances. This question is a provocative one. However, it is also a query that is incomplete unless other factors are brought to bear on the question. In her discussion of drag and camp performances, for example, Esther Newton underscores the political economic dimensions of drag. She writes that "the most important historical situation in which drag and camp have been implicated has been the greater power of gay men than lesbians within every socioeconomic class and ethnic group" (Newton 2000: 66). In contrast, the travesti concursos at Nicaraguan sexual rights events have been largely financed, produced, and engineered by self-identified lesbian and feminist women. This suggests a different kind of gender subversion in which lesbians challenge the stereotype of their structural powerlessness. With their organizational acumen, lesbian and feminist women are demonstrating power inversions rather than gender subversions. Or, to occupy a more campy register, biological men in women's clothing may be the stars, but lesbian women are the ones wearing the pants. The winners of the travesti concurso in 2000, for example, were determined by audience approval. Yet, due to the imperfect metric of applause, close calls were decided by the staff of the NGO that hosted the event. Irelia, a staff member, explained to me that the NGO provided the cash prizes, and when the crowning took place, it was the NGO's director, a long-time lesbian activist, who did the honors. Gender conventions that often designate women and lesbians as structurally powerless are challenged here not by the gender-bending of drag but through financial and managerial control over the representation of sexual rights events.

As the aesthetics and content of performances are reformatted and repackaged—from drag to danza—decisions about what is performed and by whom uncovers the infrastructures of power within the lucha. By engineering the key symbolic moments of sexual rights events, women—lesbian women, in particular—exercise their representational powers in very public ways. As they manage the aesthetics of drag performance, they are also establishing a distinct epistemological position that is supposedly "less competitive," situated within an institutional framework. Through these epistemological acts to re-gender the performances associated with sexual rights, activists demonstrate how the politics of representation are carefully crafted to develop what they hope is a perfected public presentation of the struggle.

The Politics of Declaración

I first met Federico in the summer of 1999, but his reputation long pre-ceded him. In the 1980s, Federico founded the group Colectivo Shomos.[21] As one of the early architects of the lucha for sexual rights, he had an especially long view of the transformative processes that had taken place in Nicaragua. Sitting in front of his sister's pink house in 2001, Federico offered me the same sweet coffee he drinks whenever we meet; he has always been generous with his coffee but cannot afford to be too gen-erous now, because he has been unemployed for several years. His in-ability to get work, he explained, was a result of Nicaragua's poor econ-omy and employment discrimination against homosexuals.[22] Federico had been evicted from his brother's house because his brother "didn't want co-chones meeting there." He now lived in an adjacent working-class neigh-borhood with his sister, who was "*tranquila* (cool, mellow)" with the Colec-tivo Shomos occasionally meeting at her home. "Here," he said, "we don't have any trouble with the neighbors." Federico then took me on a tour of the group's makeshift office, which was also where Federico slept. He proudly showed me a wall decorated with magazine pages and postcards depicting muscular men in briefs and short shorts. I told him that his col-lection of images, more elaborate than it had been in the past, rivaled any of the postcard and calendar shops in the Castro District in San Francisco. He seemed pleased.

According to its mission statement, Colectivo Shomos's purpose is to establish *respeto* (respect) for lesbians and homosexual men.[23] Long before there were SFFP campaigns or Lesbian and Gay Pride events in Managua, Colectivo Shomos was hosting parties for, as Federico put it, "us homo-sexuals." During the Sandinista era, Colectivo Shomos took part in the Collective of Popular Educators Concerned with HIV/AIDS (CEP-SIDA) to enhance awareness about sexual health and prevent the spread of HIV/AIDS. The members of Colectivo Shomos spent their nights in the meeting places of homosexual men, such as the abandoned cathedral in downtown Managua. They spent their days in the gathering places of sex workers, such as the Mercado Oriental, distributing condoms and educational ma-terials about HIV/AIDS. "We did *capacitación* (training) in the parks and in the street about AIDS and about lifting self-esteem for these people in the street," Federico said.[24] Beginning in the early 1990s, the "minimal con-ditions" for outreach no longer existed, according to Federico. Colectivo

Another of form of Intimate Activism

Shomos was not affiliated with or financially supported by an NGO, and when the small amount of funding that the group had received through a handful of European grants dissipated, Colectivo Shomos could no longer buy condoms or HIV/AIDS educational materials. With the enhanced antisodomy penalties, members of Colectivo Shomos were increasingly afraid that they would be identified as "known homosexuals." For his part, Federico had continued to participate in events and offer recommendations to campaigns such as the Gathering for Sexuality Free from Prejudice. However, Colectivo Shomos, he said, had become "more social" and sporadic than militantly political. "Nevertheless," Federico explained, "we have decided that as men, as homosexuals, we are going to live and die as men with a sexual preference."

Reflecting on his early years of activism, Federico explained that lesbians and homosexual men had originally worked together on HIV/AIDS education and prevention. But now things had changed, he said. "Now lesbians do a little about AIDS, but they don't have much interest because AIDS doesn't affect them directly . . . supposedly. But we don't have any fights with them, the lesbians."[25] I asked Federico why he thought NGOs and grassroots groups headed by women—some of them declared lesbianas and many of them self-proclaimed feminists—have been relatively well funded, primarily by foreign allies and agencies. Federico began with history. He explained that during the Sandinista decade, some women achieved notoriety as political leaders and *militantes*. During the NGO boom, some of those women were able to draw on their revolutionary-era experience and networks with international allies to finance their projects and establish their own organizations (Randall 1994). Federico pointed out that in the early 1990s, Nicaragua saw an increase in feminist organizations, including new NGOs dedicated to women's health and reproductive health. "However," he said, "those feminists are, you know, Cymene, all just a bunch of lesbians who won't come out of the closet."

Federico's contention that "those feminists" are all lesbians echoes opinions one might hear on the street in Managua, although it would likely be phrased as, "Those feminists are all cochonas." Federico's comment also recalls rumors of lesbianism that have orbited around powerful female leaders in Nicaragua since the 1980s (Collinson 1990; Ferguson 1991; Randall 1994).[26] Federico, however, seemed to have a touch of antipathy (perhaps "funding envy") toward the feminists/lesbians. In a place with scant resources available for political organizing, his reaction was not unexpected.[27] Federico conceded that he did not know exactly why Colectivo Shomos had not secured funding or institutional support. Grassroots lesbian discussion groups and feminist NGOs, he said diplomatically, "have been luckier."

As the afternoon turned to evening and Federico's sister replaced our coffee with *gallo pinto* (fried red beans and rice) and glasses of ice for the small plastic bag of rum we bought at the corner *pulpería*, our conversation about "outness" continued. A particular challenge for Federico seemed to center on feminist and lesbian identities. He was suspicious about how one obscured the other and about how feminists might in fact be muddying the cause of sexual rights. In blunt terms he explained, "These lesbians hide behind being a feminist, behind being a woman. The problem is that they won't come out of the closet. Not publicly. That's the problem. That's why we can't get anywhere with *derechos homosexuales* (homosexual rights) here."[28] While Federico is certainly not the only Nicaraguan sexual rights activist who has advocated that public and political declarations of sexual identity are vital for the struggle, he was a particularly fervent proponent. I raised the issue that claiming a lesbian or gay identity and publicly declaring oneself as "out" could involve serious consequences, since having a same-sex relationship in Nicaragua at the time was illegal. Federico was adamant, however, that the antisodomy law did not constitute a significant threat: "The antisodomy law? It's not the law that they are afraid of. Look what we did to overthrow Somoza, the dictatorship, and you think we should be afraid of some little law?" By evoking the overthrow of the dictatorial regime, Federico linked the symbolic capital of the revolution to declarations of identity in the struggle for sexual rights. He explicitly connected the sexual politics of the present to the heroics of past struggles, indexing where they overlapped, if not where they were equivalent. His reference to the country's popular insurrection rather seamlessly replaced the socioeconomic and nationalist motives of Sandinismo with a new paradigm of identity that is explicitly declared.

Federico's out-of-the-closet logic illustrates a political orientation in which declaración and outness are fundamental epistemic criteria. But from a more pragmatic point of view, Federico's disregard for the antisodomy law also underscores some of the structural differences between NGOs and small groups such as Colectivo Shomos. *Personería jurídica* (the legal right to operate as an NGO in Nicaragua) is a status granted or rescinded by the state—the same state that instituted the antisodomy law.

For advocates who work as staff or directors of NGOs, the law seems to have warranted a modicum of caution. As I showed in the previous chapter, NGOs often went to some lengths to obscure the identity of their meetings for lesbian and homosexual discussion groups. Colectivo Shomos's lack of institutional affiliation means that the men's group is more sporadic and financially at risk. But it also allows the group a degree of freedom regarding the politics of *declaración*. Federico, it seems, can afford to be cavalier about "some little law." Somewhat ironically, a lack of institutional power may facilitate personal freedom for activists such as Federico who want to publicly represent their sexual identity. For those with a greater public, institutional visibility (such as NGO leaders) and activists such as Federico, the possibilities for declaración are very distinct. This suggests that the "epistemology of the closet" is not predicated solely on individual choice or conviction. Rather, it is contingent on one's structural location within the struggle for sexual rights.

Cracking the Closet?

Federico's position about declaración is—for him, as well as for others—not simply a personal question. It is a political one. It is a proposition about how the lucha will be presented publicly. As an epistemological basis for "homosexual rights," as Federico put it, the politics of declaración underscores both the individual and the collective visibility of declared lesbians and homosexual men. Political projects that lobby for an "out" sexual identity have found traction in many places and in some cases have successfully lobbied for legal change (Blasius and Phelan 1997; Rosenbloom and Bunch 1999). Among lesbian and gay political movements in the United States and Europe, for instance, coming out has been an "inaugural event and pivotal, enduring fixture" (Lancaster and di Leonardo 1997: 3), if not *the* inaugural and pivotal fixture. However, coming out, or a politics built on declaración, has not found equal utility or appeal in all sexual rights campaigns everywhere. In her analysis of lesbian identity and politics in Mexico, Norma Mogrovejo (2000: 73) describes how *el salir del closet* (coming out of the closet) has been a phenomenon primarily modeled on "the industrialized first world." While Mogrovejo does not dispute the utility of closet exiting for some social movements or its potential to empower certain individuals, neither does she consider it to be "universally valid." The impetus to come out of the closet can erase other forms of recognition, such as tacit acknowledgment of one's sexuality by family and friends (Carrillo 2001; Decena 2011). In other cases, marking projects as explicitly "gay" or "lesbian" can have the unintended effect of excluding those who might not identify with these terms (Wright 2000).[29] The directive to be "out" might also be interpreted as the result of cultural imperialism, an outcome that erases other forms of sexual practice and replaces them with Western, hegemonic understandings of identity and sexual citizenship (Massad 2002).

For sexual rights advocates such as Federico, claiming an out or *declarado* identity may be the ideal, but what precisely counts as "out" can be difficult to define. Federico declared his identity as a homosexual in the 1980s and is well known in the sexual rights community as declarado. From his perspective, activists for sexual rights—especially leaders—ought to declare themselves as lesbians or homosexual men in a very overt, clear, and public fashion. Refusing to do so, for him, is a betrayal of the cause. Yet many sexual rights leaders have been quite visible in their dedication to sexual rights, even if they have not publicly declared themselves lesbianas, homosexuales, or gay men. Several NGO directors, for instance, have appeared on national television in support of SFFP or provided commentary to the national press on issues regarding HIV/AIDS and sexual rights. While they may not begin their media presentations with the declaration "I am a lesbian," their personal visibility on issues of sexual health and rights is far from clandestine. Discussing these topics in the Nicaraguan media certainly provokes speculation about one's sexual identity. In the public imagination, those involved with sexual rights or working toward HIV/AIDS prevention are often, rightly or wrongly, assumed to be lesbians or homosexual men; they are covertly recognized. Involvement in the struggle for sexual rights is, in some sense, a de facto declaración in itself. As sexual identity gets mapped onto sexual rights advocates—and onto leaders, in particular—nominal declarations of identity may be less significant than they at first appear. Yet for Federico and others, a validity and validation comes with coming out.

Nicaraguan activists' debates about declaración ultimately are epistemological exercises about the politics of visibility. As some activists lobby for individuals to become declarado, the question of declaración, in and of itself, raises an important, and collective, issue: How should the struggle for sexual rights, as a whole, come out to the Nicaraguan public? Individuals may declare themselves, implicitly or explicitly, but ultimately it is the lucha itself that must be recognized and justified as a valid political project. For individuals, coming out is a process, as family, friends, colleagues, and others may become aware of a person's sexuality over time. The ways in which the sexual rights struggle itself becomes declarado is likewise "not simply a single act" (D'Emilio and Freedman 1997: 323). Rather, it is an iterative and uneven process that occurs over time in *fases múltiples* (multiple phases) (Mogrovejo 2000: 73). Although there is no singular moment in which a political struggle comes out, activists' mediations around the very question of declaración help to illustrate the fraught politics of going public. The contingencies of declaración prompt activists to engineer their public presentations strategically and to debate deeply how the lucha will come to be seen and known.

Epistemically Engineering "Us"

This chapter began with the host of the SFFP party's effusive words making an apparently simple statement: that the celebration was "for us." But it is worth asking who, exactly, "us" is. Does "us" refer to all sexually marginalized people in Nicaragua—or, for that matter, around the world? Or does "us" represent only those who subscribe to certain tenets of transformation, whether embodied in Sexuality Free from Prejudice, Lesbian and Gay Pride, or commitment to declaring one's sexual identity? For activists defining the contours of a constituency, the "us" of sexual rights is a complex set of representational questions and political priorities.[30] The distinctions between "pride" and "prejudice," the contingencies of declaración and the negotiated status of gender all shape the ways in which Nicaraguans will come to know and understand the lucha for sexual rights. As part of their interventions, sexual rights advocates must balance the exigencies of funding streams, NGO affiliation, declaración, gender differences, and revolutionary histories. As scholars of social justice have found, social movements often face challenges, fissures, and contradictions whenever, and wherever, political actors attempt to create a comprehensive and coherent set of messages for social change (Agamben 1993; Badiou 2012; Hale and Calhoun 2008; Jackson and Warren 2005). The distinct approaches that activists take, as collectives or as individuals, illustrate, again, many advocates' assertion that their politics are not "a movement" but a polymorphous set of practices to establish sexual equality. This plurality of epistemological frameworks and equivocations is not, then, evidence of an impasse or of incoherence (Brown 2005). In fact, as Deborah Gould (2009: 332) has put it, "Social movements are typically filled with contentiousness; conflict and debate are a primary means by which movements analyze the political terrain and figure out what to do." Defining a constituency, performing for a particular audience, and attempting to "go public" draws attention to the multiple ways that activists conceptualize the lucha for sexual rights. The mediational work in these processes demonstrates not only how activists attempt to institute social change, their sites and acts of intervention, but also, and just as importantly, the epistemological work and knowledge production that is foundational to these politics.

In the classic formulation of vanguardism, intellectuals, artists, and other cultural experts take a preeminent role in constructing particular "visions" for their respective movements. For anthropologists (and others), interest in how systems of meaning and action are produced—and, in particular, in how particular forms of knowledge get validated while others are left to the wayside—has been long-standing (see, e.g., Allen 2002; Boyer and Lomnitz 2005; Herzfeld 1997; Povinelli 2004). Kay Warren (1998) found, for example, that Mayan intellectuals played an instrumental, if sometimes fraught, role in creating the agenda of the Pan-Mayanist Movement in Guatemala. Mayan activists were explicit about the need to craft an intellectual armature that emphasized language preservation and placed ideological attention on indigenousness. Their goal was politically efficaciousness, even if this meant reviving essentialist tropes.[31] As intellectuals and other experts, like activists, are tasked (or task themselves) with producing ideological infrastructures, they face the challenge of demarcating identities, whether national, ethnic, regional, or sexual. Indubitably, as activists, who are operating as experts in the sexual rights struggle, seek to promote their own "version of social reality" (Verdery 1991: 18), contentions and conflicts, perhaps unsurprisingly, often arise.

Nicaraguan sexual rights activists are engaged in a reflexive process in which there is acute awareness about which specific political tropes are being operationalized, from pride and prejudice to declaración and danza. There is little question that structural factors condition sexual rights activists' conversations, as well. As Rafael de la Dehesa (2010) has documented in his comparison of LGBT politics in Mexico and Brazil, each movement has had to establish alliances with political parties to advance its agenda. Each country has also had to contend, as has Nicaragua, with a neoliberal economic context and transformed state and civil society relations. These shifting alliances and allegiances show themselves most clearly in Nicaragua around the issue of declaración and the differences between small activist groups and large, state-sanctioned NGOs. Each of these permutations of sexual rights activism is situated within a broader transition to democratic forms and an expansion of rights discourses.

The deliberations about how to "best" present the politics of sexual rights in the public domain reflect many of the principles of Nicaragua's contemporary democratic era. These approaches rely on the power of civil and human rights to transform not only law but also culture (Comaroff and Comaroff 1997; Paley 2001). In turn, these political processes highlight the importance of understanding activists' strategies, not just the policy outcomes (de la Dehesa 2010: xiii); sexual rights activists are both managers of political logics and strategists of struggle. Focusing attention on choice (to be declared) and freedom (from prejudice), activists very consciously draw on key tropes of liberalism. They privilege choice, instill their faith in freedom, and invoke democratic ideals. Tacking back and forth between explicit declarations and inferred identities, activists craft a set of diverse principles. Through this process, they structure an epistemological framework for sexual rights in multiple registers, including those of universal liberation and minority rights, as well as the communitarian ethos of Nicaragua's revolutionary era. Like the lesbian discussion groups profiled in chapter 2, in which lesbian identity was constructed in broad terms, the public identity of the struggle here is broadly inclusive, though not necessarily unitary or agreed on. Often, it is open to interpretation. Questions of private selves and public manifestations however, are linked by at least one epistemic thread: the goal of tolerance for sexual difference.

Bringing the lucha out of the closet, engaging with a broader public and the mandate to represent sexual rights in very precise ways, raises the stakes; activists are, and must be, committed to "getting it right." Indeed, it is the overtly public forum of these politics that makes the epistemological exercises that precede them so fraught. Going public with the lucha involves deep mediational work to configure how the lucha will be declared and become known in the eyes of the public. However, in both backstage deliberations about declaración and gendered performances of power, and in the reified spaces of public performances such as Lesbian and Gay Pride and Sexuality Free from Prejudice, a certain limit is apparent—that is, activists present the lucha and its goals to very particular audiences. Beyond the passer-by on the street when banners are displayed, these performative politics usually reach those who are already affiliated with, or have an affinity for, the struggle: those who attend SFFP or pride events. By presenting sexual rights to university students and journalists in press conferences, activists are able to gain access to another strata of the country's population. As the nation's up-and-coming intelligentsia and professional class, students are an important constituency for activists to reach. Journalists, for their part, have the ability to disseminate information widely and, one hopes, positively. However, given the structural limits of scale in these face-to-face presentations, activists have understood the need to expand their mediational reach. Taking the lessons they have learned through the politics of public engagement, activists have chosen to expand their epistemic potential by broadcasting their messages of sexual tolerance and sexual rights. Using mass media platforms, and remaking them into dialogic systems to promote their social justice goals, activists have attempted to create an "erotiscape" that speaks not only to the greater Nicaraguan nation, but to a larger transnational audience, as well.

≡

CHAPTER FOUR

Mediating Sexual Subjectivities

The Revolution Will Be Televised

Latin American *telenovelas* (soap operas) have become rather famous for their epically emotional sagas of passion, heartbreak, and betrayal. *Sexto Sentido* (Sixth Sense), a telenovela produced by the NGO Puntos de Encuentro (Common Ground) which debuted in early 2001 on Nicaragua's most popular commercial TV station, never wanted for melodrama. But *Sexto Sentido* was not simply another well-loved telenovela; it was instead a social justice soap opera. Supported by funds from the U.S. Agency for International Development (USAID) and other international development agencies,[1] *Sexto Sentido* broached many controversial issues over the course of eighty episodes, including sexual identity; abortion; intra-family violence; sexism; racism; classism; homophobia; discrimination against disabled people; prejudice against *costeños*;[2] and bias against *campesinos* (farmers, country folk). The telenovela treated nearly every "-ism" imaginable in Nicaragua, but it managed to do so without sacrificing its entertainment value. In fact, at times it seemed as if everyone in Nicaragua was enthralled with *Sexto Sentido*. One Sunday afternoon, for example, while the family I lived with gathered around the household TV for an anticipated episode, I volunteered to get cold Cokes at the corner store. As I headed toward the nearest *pulpería* (convenience store) in a working-class neighborhood in Managua, I could hear the opening scenes of *Sexto Sentido* unfold as the show's dialogue emanated from the open windows of the cinderblock houses I passed along the way. After six months of Sunday afternoon screenings, prime time for family viewing, *Sexto Sentido* was rated the most popular TV program among Nicaraguan youth, its target audience. According to polling data, 80 percent of thirteen- to seventeen-year-olds tuned in to watch the show. The program also had some of the highest television ratings in the overall national market, claiming 70 percent of the *entire* Nicaraguan viewing audience (more than double the percentage of Super Bowl Sunday viewership in the United States). For the activists who produced the program, *Sexto Sentido* would serve an educational purpose by bringing sensitive issues to a wide Nicaraguan audience. At the same time, the show was meant as a device to stimulate conversations in Nicaraguan households, particularly between youth and their families. As an explicitly dialogic forum for advocacy, the TV program was intended to transform how Nicaraguans thought about, and talked about, the controversial issues being "aired" in the show's plotline.

Popular media in Nicaragua—in the form of newspapers, magazines, radio, and television—have long played an influential role in national politics, and activists have understood the political potential of various forms of media (Buchsbaum 2003; Jones 2002).[3] The Internet and digital communications have transformed both the Nicaraguan public sphere and activists' use of it in recent years, particularly as more Nicaraguans have acquired Internet access. However, long before "new" media proliferated, older forms of media were an important catalyst for articulating political messages at the level of the state and that of civil society.[4] Popular education pamphlets—featuring illustrations and accessible wording to reach illiterate populations—were a staple of the revolutionary era. These printed materials were widely circulated as a way to promote social welfare programs and raise political consciousness. Radio also figured prominently in Nicaragua's revolutionary project, partly because it was an easily accessible and inexpensive medium for disseminating the messages of the Sandinista movement to large sectors of the population at minimal expense to both producers and consumers. During the Somoza era, U.S. and other foreign media interests came to dominate the Nicaraguan television market, but local political talk shows did gain popularity during the Sandinista era.[5] In addition to television programming such as *Sexto Sentido*, several radio programs about sexuality are broadcast by individual activists and NGOS. Many feature listener call-in shows in which the audience can talk with the hosts, live, about topics such as dating, monogamy, sexually transmitted infections, pregnancy, and same-sex sexuality. Following the legacy of popular education pamphlets, the feminist magazine *La Boletina* features graphics and photographs, as well as accessible articles, covering topics such as human rights, women's employment, and intrafamily violence. *La Boletina* is also, notably, the most widely distributed magazine in Nicaragua.

Sexual rights activists have made extensive use of television, print, and radio in their efforts to transform how Nicaraguans understand sexuality and sexual rights. Activists' media interventions target a very broad audience, and compared with sexuality discussion groups and the epistemological engineering of the lucha described in chapters 2 and 3, it is a qualitatively different kind of activism. In this chapter I analyze how sexual rights activists have strategically combined politics and popular culture in order to speak with a broad, national, and diverse public. The advocacy messages that they have endeavored to create are intended to both entertain and serve as the impetus for social change. The television program *Sexto Sentido*, for example, illustrates how plot, character development, and sexual subjectivity are carefully integrated and evoked with both a national and an international political public in mind. The sexual rights activists who produced the show created TV characters that embody particular forms of sexual subjectivity and the performative affect of these characters is intended to have a social justice effect.

The radio program *Sin Máscaras* (Without Masks) and the first Nicaraguan lesbian magazine, *Humanas* ([Female] Humans), were also developed by sexual rights activists in an effort to circulate positive messages about sexuality and the lucha. Drawing from a global mediascape of news stories and human rights discourses, the activist who produced *Sin Máscaras* and the group that published *Humanas* used material that addressed the particularities of life and sexuality in Nicaragua; they were also committed to an engaged conversation with their audiences. Whether their messages are circulated in print, on the airwaves, or on Nicaraguan television screens, activists have sought to promote a greater *visibilidad* (visibility) for issues surrounding sexuality, including those of sexual rights. Through this process, advocates are mediating sexuality in a dual sense. They are using communications media to convey particular images and ideals about sexual subjectivity and at the same time are seeking to establish a dialogic and responsive relationship with viewers, listeners, and readers.[6] In their attempt to create more fully dialogic modes of communication through media activism, I argue, Nicaraguan sexual rights advocates prefigured contemporary modes of digital activism (such as facebook and twitter), and simultaneously, reflected the dialogic ethic that has been the foundation of *educación popular* since its inception.

Screening Social Justice

The studio where *Sexto Sentido* was produced was located across the street from one of Managua's most famous cemeteries. At first glance, it was a strange setting for a TV studio. However, it was also a very logical place to have television stars spend time — necessarily a little clandestine.[7] Hidden behind a fifteen-foot-high corrugated metal fence (a typical and inexpensive form of security in Managua), a large cinderblock building housed the sets, props, and equipment for the show. Although the building was supposed to be sound-proof against the drone of aging taxis and ambient street noise, in the time I spent watching the show's taping, the cameras were often halted while dogs barked or muffler-less motorcycles passed. Two cameramen with MiniDV cameras were charged with capturing the show's drama. But before the action could begin, the huge silver fans that made the temperature inside the studio almost bearable had to be switched off; their whirr was too loud for the microphones to overcome. Iliana, the show's director, sat at a long table with her eyes fixed on two monitors, where she was able to scrutinize the performances as they unfolded on the screens. Rising from her semi-lit position behind the table, Iliana occasionally consulted with the actors and often encouraged them to make their performances "more real." Once she was satisfied with a scene, the metal fans were reignited, and brows were swabbed with the small washcloths that Managuans carry to contend with the city's tropical swelter. To reiterate a well-worn truism heard in the world of television and film, everything seemed much smaller on the set, in real life. But at the same time, everything also appeared more dense and vivid. Television is a medium with the power to both magnify and diffuse.

When it debuted, *Sexto Sentido* was the first dramatic television series *ever* to have been produced in Nicaragua. The funding proposals that were submitted to USAID for the show described how the program would focus on the friendships among a group of young people living in Managua. The proposal likened it to the U.S. television comedy *Friends*, though needless to say, the show was far less costly to produce than its North American counterpart. One of the producers of *Sexto Sentido* estimated that the budget for one episode of *Friends* would fund more than four hundred episodes of *Sexto Sentido*. The program was also distinct from the majority of Nicaraguan television fare that is imported from the United States, Mexico, Colombia, and Brazil (see, e.g., Benavides 2008; La Pastina 2004; López 1995; Martín-Barbero 1995; Sinclair 1999). It was different partly because it did not focus on the lives of the elite.[8] Instead, it featured local actors and was shot entirely on location in familiar locales around Managua. The show was peppered with Nicaraguan *dichos* (colloquial expressions); as many people explained to me, one of the reasons they loved the show was "because it is *puro Nicaragüense*"—that is, "really and truly Nicaraguan." The activists who created the show were well aware of how important it was to produce a sense of locality, and they intentionally incorporated "Nica"-ness into the plotlines and dialogue. Reflecting well-known places, expressions, and values, the producers believed they could encourage viewers to more readily engage with the show's controversial content. It was a strategy that used familiarity to promote difference. The telenovela followed the logic of so-called edu-tainment programming, in which pedagogical lessons are integrated into the narrative.[9] While *Sexto Sentido* incorporated readily apparent messages about equality and tolerance, it did not do so at the expense of entertainment or humor. Entertainment value, and the consequent ability to attract and retain viewers, was an explicit element of the activists' goals for the show. As one of *Sexto Sentido*'s producers put it, "By entertaining, we are best able to get our message across." The telenovela provided a platform to both portray particular forms of sexual identity and generate more dialogue about sexuality in general. It was a vehicle for social change that was both subtle and spectacular as it used the familiar form of the telenovela to engender new ways to imagine social relationships through the use of images (Debord 1995 [1967]: 12).

Sexto Sentido was part of a larger, multiyear campaign called "We Are Different, We Are Equal," which was developed by Puntos de Encuentro to promote greater equality and diminish discrimination of all kinds. Following Puntos de Encuentro's mandate "to change culture, not just be-havior," *Sexto Sentido*'s director explained to me one afternoon that the TV show aimed "to impact public opinion and promote values and rela-tions of justice and equality." To transform social values, she continued, the TV characters themselves had to undergo "a process of self-discovery." The self-discoveries that the director described were those of "identities, the changing roles of men and women, romantic and sexual relation-ships, and self-esteem." By linking self-discovery with social transforma-tion, the activists who created *Sexto Sentido* followed in the footsteps of Freirian *concientización* practices that were part of Nicaragua's revolution-ary period. But in the TV series, personal and political transformations are married to discourses of identity, self-fulfillment, and subjectivity. The show is predicated on the characters' conversations and their transforma-tions, and viewers are entreated to do the same: to engage in dialogue and begin to imagine themselves, and Nicaraguan society, in transformative terms.

The sexual rights activists who produced *Sexto Sentido* emphasized the power of dialogue within the program; as characters modified their sub-jectivity, the audience, presumably, would also take the opportunity to express their thoughts about sexuality. However, the producers took the methodological tool of dialogue a step further still as they sought direct feedback and invited audiences to engage in direct conversation with them. During the credits shown at the end of each episode, for example, viewers were invited to e-mail, call, or write with suggestions for the pro-gram. The NGO also held a contest in which teenagers were asked to write letters about the impact the show's lesbian and gay characters had on their lives.[10] By encouraging a reciprocal relationship between their audience and themselves, and by providing the means to communicate with view-ers, the producers of the show hoped to generate a more democratic and egalitarian approach to media production. By promoting conversations among viewers as they watched the show and by establishing venues for audiences to actively influence the show's content, the activist producers of *Sexto Sentido* demonstrated a commitment to both a strategy of elicita-tion and a dialogic mode of engagement.

Angelic Gay Men and *Declaraciones* in the *Campo*

Historically, television programming in Nicaragua has subsisted on the syndicated television shows and mass-distributed blockbuster movies that appear throughout global mediascapes. Caricatures of effeminate gay men or outrageous queens are familiar enough fare on Nicaraguan TV, whereas lesbian characters are rarely, if ever, depicted.[11] *Sexto Sentido*, however, did attempt to offer something different: its aim was to produce novel sexual subjects and to promote a dialogue that interrogated commonly held assumptions about the lives of gay Nicaraguans. As *Sexto Sentido's* director very plainly described it, "The issue of homosexuality has always been discussed openly [in the show] because one of our principal characters is gay." The program's producers also developed a prominent secondary character who would ultimately declare herself a *lesbiana*. The trials faced by the lesbian and gay characters on the show, as well as the triumphs they attained, were intended to overturn some of the stereotypes that surround *cochonas* and *cochones*. At the same time, the characters' travails and transformations were meant to amplify and deepen Nicaraguans' quotidian discussions about sexuality and equality.

Sexto Sentido's gay protagonist was named, interestingly enough, Angel. Although the producers assured me that the name was purely coincidental, Angel was indeed quite angelic. Or, as one of the telenovela's scriptwriters put it, "He is so damn likeable, it's impossible to hate him for anything." From the point of view of the activist producers of the show, "[Angel] is the kind of gay character we have to create: one that is beyond reproach." Angel is not particularly covert about his identity or his sexual preference among his friends, but neither is he fully declared to everyone in his social circle. For instance, one of Angel's close pals, Eddy, is unaware of Angel's homosexuality. Eddy is the show's "bad boy," and he often makes biased and prejudicial comments. Although Angel has not intentionally hidden his sexuality from Eddy, Angel's sexual ambiguity provides a narrative space for other protagonists to make derogatory comments about homosexuality. These challenging moments, in turn, offer opportunities to incite dialogue among the viewing audience. For instance, in one episode Eddy chides Angel about one of their female friends. "Hey, aren't you in to Sofía?" Eddy asks. Angel obliquely answers, "Nah . . . she's not my type." "Well, then," Eddy unwittingly teases, "Vos sos un cochóncito" (You're a little fag). Eddy continues to be unaware — or perhaps unwilling to recognize — that his good friend is gay. The plot steadily builds toward a dramatic confrontation in which Eddy finally realizes his friend's sexuality and, in turn, is made to face his own bias. As Angel bluntly puts it, "The problem with you, Eddy, is that you have too many prejudices." Gabriel,

FIGURE 4.1 The actor who played Angel on *Sexto Sentido* posing with a promotional banner for the television show.

another central character, is aware that Angel is gay, but even knowing this, he reveals his prejudice against cochones at various points during the show. When Gabriel sees Angel washing clothes at the backyard *pila* (a cement sink used to wash clothes by hand), he says, "If it weren't for the fact that you wash your [own] clothes, no one would suspect that you're a fag." Angel asks what Gabriel is talking about, and Gabriel responds, "Well, you seem like a man." Angel retorts, irritated, "I am a man. Can't you see that?" Gabriel is not convinced, however, and confidently declares, "Fags aren't men. Real men like women."[12] Angel, glaring at Gabriel, offers a firm corrective in a very self-assured voice: "Just because I like men doesn't mean I'm not a man." Gabriel's comment and Angel's rebuttal illustrate a very familiar set of beliefs among the viewing audience—namely, that cochones are not truly men; the discrimination they endure is not only based on the sex they practice but also for the masculine gender they fail to perform. Angel's gender presentation is masculine (though not *machista*). He never uses the effeminate gestures that are associated with cochones. Because he is not the cochón with whom everyone in the viewing audience is familiar, Angel is not readily identifiable as a "queer."

Indeed, his masculinity performs an important ambiguity. The only way anyone can know Angel is gay, in fact, is when he declares it. It is his masculine affect that allows viewers, presumably, to identify him as a "normal guy" and therefore identify with him. For the producers, it is important that these sorts of conflicts and ambivalences take place on the screen so viewers will continue the conversation in their living rooms. The hope is that those watching the show will side with the very reasonable, angelic character, despite his sexual difference. Angel's gendered behavior and his particular performance of sexual identity are further complicated when Angel has a new love interest.

Prior to declaring himself to Eddy, Angel tells his friend that he has a date with someone new: Cristian. The gender-neutral and ambiguous name "Cristian," of course, has Eddy assuming that his friend has a date with a woman. Just as Angel is about to tell Eddy that Cristian is not a woman but a man, he finds that Eddy has fallen fast asleep on the couch. Despite his good intentions, Angel has missed his chance to declare himself to Eddy. Once the relationship between Angel and Cristian has become more public and out, viewers are shown that neither partner is more macho than the other. Neither behaves like a cochón or a *loca* (queer or queen) or acts in a way that would evoke the *mano quebrada* ("broken-handed," effeminate) gestures associated with the cochón. In their gendered mannerisms, neither Angel nor Cristian fits the stereotype of the cochón. Angel's and Cristian's relationship also appears to be the epitome of egalitarianism, mirroring a Northern liberal model of homosexuality. While their relationship, in the Nicaraguan context, is a relatively novel representation of male homosexuality, the characters also embody a form of masculinity that subscribes to Nicaraguan expectations of gender normativity. The characters of Angel and Cristian were intentionally crafted in these ways to challenge the homoerotic relationships based in gender roles that typically have been associated with cochones. The relationship with Cristian also gave Angel a higher degree of legitimacy: cochones, many Nicaraguans believe, cannot have "real" affective and lasting relationships with other men. According to pervasive stereotypes, cochones are in search of sexual encounters, never commitment. Added to this is the prevalent fact that many, though not all, *hombres hombres* are themselves only interested in an *aventura* (affair or fling) rather than an ongoing relationship with another man. The egalitarian and gender-normative relationship between Cristian and Angel challenged many of the qualities associated with cochones as effeminate, submissive, and stigma bearing, but their pairing also confronted larger misconceptions about the nature of love and commitment between gay men.

In addition to properly performing masculinity and an egalitarian model of the sexual self, Angel is an affable guy and an exemplary friend, student, and son. His moral credentials are crafted to counterbalance any negative interpretations the viewing audience might have about him as a cochón. For instance, in the show Angel has accomplished goals that many Nicaraguans would admire, including earning a scholarship to study in Mexico. However, before leaving for his studies farther north, Angel decides that he wants to declare himself to his parents, both of whom are *campesinos*. On an afternoon visit to their very humble home, with chickens foraging on the porch and his mother and father seated in a pair of artisanal wooden chairs that are synonymous with the campo, Angel explains, "I want you to know so that you understand me. I like men. I am a homosexual." Angel's parents react negatively at first to their son's overt statement about his sexuality. His father glares at him and walks away while his mother breaks down in tears, asking how they failed as parents. Ultimately, however, they accept their son's declaration, most poignantly through his father's comment, "*Sos mi hijo* (You are my son). . . . May God bless you." Indeed, Angel has been an exceptionally good son, even if his parents are concerned about his newly explicit sexual self.

Bringing his declaración to his parents in the campo is a bold act on Angel's part because it explicitly challenges the traditional social values associated with the campo. His declaration also points to several other important dynamics at work in the sexual subjectivity being enacted through Angel's character. The fact that Angel's parents were not aware of—or, at least, had not acknowledged—his sexual orientation suggests that Angel had been performing a presumed heterosexuality and masculinity very well. Angel was passing as straight, and moreover, he was about to leave Nicaragua, where he would be far from his parents' gaze. Angel was not being confronted or challenged with questions about his sexuality. In other words, he didn't "need" to tell his parents about his sexuality, even if he (justifiably) wanted to. However, in Nicaragua, as in many other contexts, Latin American and otherwise, "Don't ask, don't tell" is often taken as the socially acceptable way to negotiate sexual difference. Angel's direct declaration to his parents, for many *Sexto Sentido* viewers, would be a somewhat unusual act. Rather than speaking openly and overtly about a family member's sexuality, many Nicaraguan families would instead "tacitly" acknowledge or covertly recognize homosexuality rather than naming it out loud and publically (Carrillo 2001; Decena 2011). By including a declaración by Angel to his parents in the show, the activist producers presented a challenge to tacit or covert forms of recognition. They opted instead for a performance of a very explicit and identified "out-ness." Angel's *autodeclaración*, moreover, is a complex eliciting device because it marries the tradition associated with filial piety and the campo with a relatively novel sexual identity. Clearly, Angel's explicit act of declaración is closely tied to one of the show's key goals: "to openly discuss homosexuality." How this gets aired—the specific gestures, terms, and performances that frame the issue of sexuality—is, of course, a complicated proposition.

Angel's character overall performs a very particular kind of queer being: the *homosexual* rather than the cochón. It is not that homosexual subjects such as Angel do not exist in Nicaragua, but his experience, though fictional, is a significant departure from the character (or caricature) of the more locally familiar cochón, maricón, or loca. Given that the activists who produced *Sexto Sentido* did not know whether or not the show would be funded for a second season, choosing to have Angel declare his homosexuality suggests that this was a high-priority political performance. Angel's pronouncement follows the logic of the closet, an "epistemology" (Sedgwick 1990) that has proved fundamental to both public and private discourses about homosexuality in the West. Angel, his relationship, and his revelatory process represent a very particular configuration of a homosexual subject that may have been more familiar to the development professionals at USAID than to most Nicaraguans. The show's producers were invested in highlighting the liberatory potential of a specific sexual subject: the self-identified, "out," and gender-neutral gay man. However, by placing Angel at center stage, the show elides—or, perhaps, erases—the cochón. As they broadcast a particular kind of sexual subject, advocates are deliberately mediating sexuality and eliciting a particular set of conversations around these sexual subjects.

[handwritten margin note: does not necessarily add up w/ local Nica means of homosexuality]

Focus Groups and the Girl Next Door

Wearing spaghetti-strap tank tops, tight jeans, and flower-shaped barrettes in her hair, Vicki, *Sexto Sentido*'s lesbian protagonist, epitomizes Nicaraguan ideals of feminine youth. As I sat down for a conversation with Jacinta, the actress who played Vicki, I was curious about what she thought when she was told during her audition that the character she would be playing was a lesbian. "I liked it," she said, laughing.

It made me really happy . . . to break with all the *normal*. This is something that I had never done, and I was interested in doing it as a personal goal—to break with my own prejudices and do something public like this and to go out in the street and say, 'Look, this is the work. Watch it. Analyze it. Take in the message, and if you can't do that, at least take away something.' This is what made me really excited about doing it. If I had been some other way, then maybe I wouldn't have been so interested in it.

Without prompting, Jacinta turned to the social impact she felt her character would have:

And commentaries, yes, we're going to hear those from people here on the street. [When they see these characters] on TV, these lesbian or gay roles are difficult. The people take it like this [she exhaled loudly and threw her hands up, mocking a reaction of being scandalized]: 'This girl is a dyke or I don't know what!' But it also so happens, on the flip side, that this is positive, because people are learning, with these little details and examples, how to handle this.

Jacinta's reaction to discovering her new character, like the ideological aspirations of the show's producers, follows a pedagogical curve where new identity forms are seen to challenge older conventions around sexuality and gender. In good activist form, the actress is up for the challenge of facing her own prejudice. She is excited to perform the role of a TV character that teaches people "how to handle" the subject of lesbianism. Although her performances take place on the screen, it is notable that Jacinta sees her work as taking place, if only metaphorically, on the "street" of Nicaraguan public consciousness.

Norelí, the actress who played Vicki's best friend, Alejandra (or "Ale"), explained that a potential romance between Vicki and Ale had already provoked some reactions from the viewing audience even prior to anything explicit being screened:

I remember in the first episode when Vicki appeared, someone wrote an e-mail and said that it wasn't believable that Ale would have a relationship with a lesbian girl. It wasn't possible that Alejandra would have an affair or fling with a lesbian girl . . . I remember one person said that it was nice [that the show featured a lesbian character]. Also, we were asked why, . . . if there was already Angel, who is homosexual, . . . we had to have a lesbian. What was our interest, specifically, to reinforce this issue about sexual options?

Even though Vicki had not yet been declared a lesbian, the viewing audience was clearly tuned in to her queer potential. But, as Norelí went on to explain, Vicki's femininity generated questions among those who watched and commented on the show: "People said that the lesbian character was *linda* (nice, pretty) and *guapísima* (very attractive). And people asked me about this. . . . There are a lot of people watching who don't want Vicki to be a lesbian because she looks like a *chavala* (feminine young woman), very pretty and all of that." Vicki's status as *guapísima* and a "feminine young woman" made her a laudable subject in a place that, like so many, values youth and beauty in women. Like Angel, Vicki performed a gendered norm that established a narrative space to broach the topic of sexual difference. However, Vicki's femininity also prompted some resistance. She was, in essence "too pretty" to be a dyke for some of the audience members with whom Norelí spoke. Vicki's character from the outset was both appealing and suspect. Her relationship with her best friend Ale would eventually uncover more gender complexities being screened in the sexual subject of the *lesbiana*.

Despite the simmering story line between Vicki and Ale, and the potential to read their relationship "queerly" (Gopinath 2005), Alejandra is quite surprised, even shocked, in the episode in which Vicki makes her identity clear. Following a series of missed communications, Vicki finally has to pose a direct question to her friend: "Ale, you know that I'm a lesbian, right? I mean, we talked about the topic, . . . and I thought you knew." Alejandra's jaw seems to drop and she is clearly deeply troubled by the news. She decides to turn to her other friends for advice. Ale wants to find a solution that allows her to continue her friendship with Vicki and assuage her worries about Vicki's sexuality.

However, before Vicki's *declaraciones* were publicly screened to the television audience, Vicki's disclosure was subjected to a trial run. In search of audience feedback and in order to facilitate a more dialogic engagement with viewers, *Sexto Sentido*'s producers organized a series of focus groups for the show's upcoming episodes. For the episode featur-

FIGURE 4.2 The actress who played Vicki, *Sexto Sentido*'s lesbian character, backstage looking over her script.

ing Vicki's controversial declaration of her lesbianism, the focus group consisted of female viewers age fifteen to twenty-four. The organizers believed that in a single-sex setting, young people would be more likely to respond openly and honestly. The group was intended to gather information and provide a better understanding of girls' reactions to Vicki's disclosure. Depending on the girls' responses, the producers explained, amendments could be made, such as an epilogue at the end of the show. While focus groups are often the stuff of corporate marketing strategies, convening the focus group for Vicki's disclosure also mirrored the ideological underpinnings of the TV show's politics: it was another installment in the producers' ongoing quest to engage their audience dialogically, seeking a more reciprocal relationship between creators and consumers.

After viewing scenes of Vicki's declaration and Alejandra's ensuing reaction, the focus group participants were asked to comment on the characters and their behavior. One young woman said, "Well, I see Vicki as normal and that she should be treated like a normal person, like one of us." Another added, "We should accept her like a normal person." The facilitator questioned further: "So, Vicki is not normal because she is a lesbian?" One girl answered, "Yes, she's a normal person. The only thing is that she likes women." But another disagreed: "In this sense, because she likes women, she's not normal, but the rest of her, yes, is normal." Clearly, the young women were still processing the idea of Vicki's normalcy; they were, as a group, undecided as to whether Vicki was really, or only partly, normal in terms of her sexuality. Vicki undoubtedly appeared normal to the focus group because of her feminine mannerisms and appearance. For the activist producers of the show, Vicki's gender conformity and embodied femininity were intentional strategies to subvert her sexual difference.

The next set of questions probed more deeply and encouraged the focus group's participants to apply the TV lesson to their own lives. After screening the scene in which Alejandra is disturbed by Vicki's confession, the facilitator asked the group: "What do you think about the way Alejandra acted toward Vicki? What would you have done?" The question brought a pause. After some thinking, one young woman responded, "Ale should help Vicki to not be a lesbian anymore." Another participant countered, "Ale should accept Vicki." It was also suggested that "Ale should tell Vicki to go out with guys so she can get rid of this lesbian thing."

The participants were then asked whether anything similar had happened to them or anyone they knew. A long silence followed, but finally, one young woman responded: "Last year at school, there was this girl, Corelia. She always dressed like a guy, and I think she was a lesbian. They said that she was with this other girl, Luisa, and one time, Corelia, la cochona, invited the other one over to her house, and she invited her in her room . . . and [Corelia] told [Luisa] that she was in love with her. Then Luisa took off and told Corelia she never wanted to see her again. So Corelia left school right after that and disappeared, and no one ever saw her again."

Beyond the mysterious disappearance of Corelia, the girls in the focus group were able to translate the events on the small screen into their real-world encounters. Corelia is described alternately as both a "lesbiana" and a "cochona" in the girl's retelling of the events. However, there is a substantive difference between the real-life gay girl, Corelia, and Vicki, the televised lesbian. Corelia "dresses like a guy," while Vicki always wears girlish clothes and makeup. Vicki's superficial markers, her carefully deployed feminine appearance, effectively create a dyke who looks like the girl next door. Vicki, like Angel, embodies a homosexual character that is unlike the neighborhood cochona so familiar to the Nicaraguan audience.

Rather—and again, like Angel—Vicki represents a novel form of being: a lesbiana. Indeed, more than a few times during the discussion, the focus group's participants referred to Vicki as "la coch—" only to correct themselves, "I mean, la lesbiana." Their slippage between the terms "cochona" and "lesbiana" is one indicator of the tensions between the concepts and the characters. The girls may have been performing these corrections for the facilitator and the *gringa* anthropologist. The corrective here, however, is important because it suggests changes in discourse and, perhaps, meaning. The girls in the focus group seem to have accepted that lesbianas represent a didactically privileged and perhaps more "modern" and television-worthy form of female homosexuality than the cochona. Their reactions, at the same time, demonstrated acts of translation. These young female viewers very quickly equated Vicki's sexual subjectivity as a lesbian to that of the "gay girl who dresses like a guy" of their past experience. They did not accept that women "liking women" was normal. But Vicki's ascription to Nicaraguan values of well-groomed girlishness conformed to the girls' expectations about femininity. Her gender performance was normal even if her sexuality was not.

As the episodes of *Sexto Sentido* unfolded, Vicki's character became more multifaceted. Viewers discovered, for example, that in addition to being a lesbian, Vicki was a recovering alcoholic and a survivor of sexual abuse. These two elements of her character, coupled with her lesbianism, are sensitive subjects. According to popularly held beliefs in Nicaragua, homosexuality can be "caused" by childhood sexual abuse. It is also not uncommon to hear pathologizing narratives about homosexuality—that like alcoholism, homosexuality is a sickness or disease. While it may not be one's fault, it is a debility that is, nevertheless, morally suspect. The scriptwriters and activist producers of *Sexto Sentido* determined that Vicki ought to embody some of these stereotypes in order to create a space in the plot in which they could be eschewed. Because Vicki's character spoke openly about commonly held assumptions about women's same-sex sexuality, she worked to resolve, reverse, and re-frame the stereotypes that the show treats. Her character proved useful for eliciting discussions about abuse, both sexual and substance-based. Vicki's character also provided narrative space to consider the question of sexuality and culpability.

Angel is a character who is the epitome of beneficence; he is "all good." By contrast, the activists who produced *Sexto Sentido* took some risks with Vicki. She is more complex and, indeed, less angelic.[13] The audience is

FIGURE 4.3 On the set of *Sexto Sentido*, the characters Eddy and Vicki await the director's signal to begin filming a scene. Two posters on the wall in the background feature Nicaraguan cultural events. Also note that the well-known poster produced by ACT-UP (New York) hangs next to them.

privy to Vicki's struggle with alcoholism, and while she finds a solution in Alcoholics Anonymous, the difficulties she faces in the course of overcoming her disease serve as a potent message in a place where alcoholism is a challenge within many families. Vicki eventually must face the psychological wounds of her childhood sexual abuse, raising the specter of another well-known social ill. Vicki is a victim in each of these plot devices and comes to represent a figure whose identity is configured as wounded (Brown 1995). However, it is also through these tropes of injury that Vicki is made more believable and "real." Having faced dramatic challenges that will soundly resonate with the viewing audience, Vicki is not simply the girl next door in terms of her gender comportment but more authentically the girl next door because she has struggled with the nefarious side of Nicaraguan girlhood. While neither alcoholism nor sexual abuse is unique to Nicaragua, the ways in which they are emplotted in the storyline allows Nicaraguan viewers to interpret Vicki as a sympathetic, if sexually different, subject.

As they did for the carefully crafted relationship between Angel and Cristian, the producers did a great deal of pondering about Vicki's love life. Should she have a girlfriend on the show? If so, how should that girlfriend look, and how should she behave? "We don't know if Vicki should have a feminine girlfriend to break with the stereotypes or whether she should have a more masculine girlfriend," Martina, a scriptwriter for *Sexto Sentido*, explained to me. If Vicki had a female partner who was visibly *masculina*, a common stereotype would be reinforced—that is, that *femeninas* (such as Vicki) always couple with cochonas (masculine dykes). This configuration would bolster the notion (and misapprehension) that masculinity and femininity require their romantic foils. Alternatively, if Vicki had a female partner who was equally feminine in appearance, the relationship would take on a different cast, suggesting that feminine-appearing women can, and do, have romantic lives together. This particular pairing would also have been the most challenging to the viewing audience because it would have been a departure from gender-role-based coupling between same-sex partners. While the question of Vicki's girlfriend would have to wait for a future episode, the sexual scripts (Gagnon 2004; Kimmel 2007) being developed by the show's producers and scriptwriters were very carefully crafted to either challenge or uphold stereotypes and expectations about women's same-sex relationships and gendered behavior. As with Angel's very visible, apparently egalitarian relationship and gendered behavior, Vicki's performance of gender and the representation of her relationship were intended to trouble expectations about how cochonas ought to act and with whom. The scripting of sexual rights in Vicki's character was a way to mediate the category of "lesbian" by explicitly tampering with social expectations that imagine only masculina and femenina couplings.

The Limits of *Normalidad*

For many Nicaraguan sexual rights advocates, including those who produced *Sexto Sentido*, visibility and an open conversation about homosexuality are fundamental to the struggle for sexual rights. But precisely how this visibility appears and how this conversation unfolds is of equal importance. How normal, or "beyond reproach," must Nicaraguan homosexual or lesbian TV characters be for respect to replace a history of *burla* (mockery), invisibility, and the criminalization of homosexuality? Partly in response to the antisodomy law that was in place at the time,

FIGURE 4.4 The title screen for the television show *Sexto Sentido*, which is painted on a cinderblock wall outside the program's production studio.

and partly because of their goal to create more tolerance for sexual diversity, the advocates who produced *Sexto Sentido* opted for a particular kind of homosexual subjectivity. Through the vehicle of a social justice soap opera, homosexual subjects are carefully coiffed in a dramatic process of normalizing homosexuality. Gay men and lesbians are crafted to meet ideal types of monogamy, gender conformity, and social success, even if obtaining these successes may be out of reach for many Nicaraguans, both gay and straight. The strategy behind *Sexto Sentido* relied heavily on "normalizing" (Warner 1999) rather than "queering" sexual subjectivity. The telenovela cultivated characters that would perform gender, as well as gay and lesbian relationships, that were relatively new to the Nicaraguan public sphere. However, the sexual subjects who regularly transgress gender ideals and who are the most visible and often the most vulnerable to discrimination—namely, cochonas and cochones—do not appear in the show's political plotline. By virtue of their absence, cochonas and cochones are seamlessly absorbed into the transnationally familiar categories of lesbian, gay, and homosexual. *Sexto Sentido*'s gay characters codify a certain kind of sexual subjectivity and performance of gendered normalidad.

The characters in Sexto Sentido fit well with late liberal U.S. and European concepts of egalitarian gay and lesbian identity. However, they also reflect many values that Nicaraguan viewers would find familiar, acceptable, and sometimes laudable. Vicki and Angel were scripted with Nicaraguan sexual and romantic ideals in mind, including gender normativity and a commitment to monogamy. This is a strategy of invoking the international validity of gay and lesbian subjectivity, to be sure, but with a firm ethical core of puro Nicaragüense. The carefully calculated representations of homosexuality in the figures of Angel and Vicki, for the activists who have created the show, were the most politically efficacious way to circulate ideals of tolerance and create opportunities to promote sexual rights. The cost of these decisions, however, is the continued erasure of the cochona and the cochón. Sexual rights activists are able to create sexual subjectivity as spectacle through the medium of social justice television, but these representations are subject to certain ideological limits. Selecting particular performances and situating an open dialogue in the ways that they have, activist producers have mediated sexual subjectivity—one that oscillates between locally familiar tropes and the transnationally translatable figures of lesbian and gay identity. However, a broader range of sexual subjectivity does emerge as activists engage the political and communicative medium of radio.

Questioning Callers and the Sexual Rights Sonoscape

Luis has spent many nights as a volunteer on the campus of the Jesuit University in Managua hosting his radio show, Sin Máscaras (Without Masks). One evening, sitting in the cramped booth and waiting for the broadcast hour to arrive, Luis explained that he has had a long involvement in the struggle for what he called "the rights of homosexuals and lesbians." He had spent a good part of the previous decade involved in the lucha, working with different groups and organizations and conducting HIV/AIDS education. The free airtime he received for his weekly news, music, and call-in radio show was granted by a relatively powerful administrator at the university whom Luis described as "gay" (but who was not declaredly so). Luis compiled his programming from gay and lesbian news stories from around the world lifted from the Internet. His shows highlighted gay marriages in the Netherlands, Romania's antisodomy law, Gay and Lesbian Pride marches in Ecuador, and controversies about gay men and lesbians adopting children in the United States. Between reports, Luis would play mainstream Latin pop music—the latest from Christina Aguilera, Luis Miguel and Shakira. Luis described his work as a way "to make visible many important issues about homosexuality, lesbianism and bisexuality" in Nicaragua. And yet the "visibility" that Luis generated occurred not on a screen, or even in an ocular mode, but through disembodied voices.

Luis and I had many opportunities to talk, sometimes over the ubiquitous *cafecito* and sometimes hunched together in the tiny studio where *Sin Máscaras* was produced. During the time we spent talking about the sexual rights struggle, it was clear that Luis was well aware that radio is a political medium that travels well: it is inexpensive to both produce and receive. Long a staple of the Latin American public sphere, radio has served as a platform for various kinds of advocacy in Nicaraguan political history (Buchsbaum 2003). Pundits, dictators, revolutionaries, and itinerate entertainers have all aired their positions on radio. It would also be safe to say that every household in Nicaragua has a radio, including households in remote, non-electrified, and rural areas. Radio, Luis explained, has the ability to reach sectors of the population who might not interact with activists or declared lesbians or homosexual men in any other way. Luis's show, as he saw it, was a way to broadcast the cause of sexual rights in the broadest terms possible and to connect with a vast audience, even if it was largely anonymous.

Luis's radio show is a political forum, but it serves another, more dialogic purpose. "It is a place for people to talk about their worries and concerns and ask questions," he explained. The questions, it seemed, were many. Men and women phoned in to Luis's show from all over the region to ask questions and air their concerns. During one evening we spent in the control booth, callers wondered, for example, whether it is a sin to be homosexual, whether they should tell their wives they were having sex with men, and whether kissing women and liking it meant that one was a cochona. Some calls, Luis hypothesized, were being made from public pay phones or private cell phones so that family members, boyfriends, girlfriends, husbands, or wives would be none the wiser. Other calls, he surmised, might be made from the family phone, but "only after the family is asleep and the caller himself or herself is carefully hidden under a desk, table, or other sound-blocking device." Based on his experience over time,

Luis was sure that much of the communication he received was clandestine, and the voices he aired needed to be kept confidential. Callers to his radio show, he assured me, were keenly aware of potential condemnation from their families. They might also fear losing their jobs or facing ostracism if they were found out. Yet they wanted to know more. It went without saying, but Luis told me anyway to emphasize his point, that the callers were "scared, but they are curious."

Radio programs such as *Sin Máscaras* work to establish a dialogic space that may be particularly productive, partly because it is anonymous. Luis's show and others like it allow callers and listeners to explore questions about sexuality relatively safely, at the other end of a telephone receiver or a radio speaker. Although they are not visible themselves, these curious callers do make audible, and heard, complex questions surrounding sexual difference and desire. In addition to the *Sin Máscaras* show that Luis has produced, several NGOs host weekly radio programs about sexuality. Fundación Xochiquetzal has produced a weekly radio program addressing topics such as monogamy, homosexuality, orgasm, dating, virginity, and pregnancy. Puntos de Encuentro has aired the *Programa Joven sin Nombre* (Nameless Youth Program). Broadcast live every weeknight, the show has featured segments such as "Es Mi Vida, No Quiero Cambiar: Responder Mitos sobre Homosexuales y Lesbianas" (It's My Life and I Don't Want to Change: Discussing Myths about Homosexuals and Lesbians) and "Derechos Humanos de Homosexuales y Lesbianas" (Human Rights of Homosexuals and Lesbians). Teenagers were encouraged to call in with questions and were prompted to discuss issues that might be taboo in other settings. The evenings I spent in the studio during the live broadcast of *Programa Joven sin Nombre* were entertaining. The two or three youths who answered the calls live on the air needed to be quick-witted and funny and at the same time sympathetic to travails that came across the phone lines. Prepared with a list of services and various agencies, the radio hosts sometimes encouraged the callers to seek help (in the case of an abusive boyfriend, for instance). But more often, the studio was filled with boisterous energy, and a blush or two, as the hosts attempted to navigate the sometimes graphic questions callers asked.

Radio shows such as *Sin Máscaras* and *Programa Joven sin Nombre* serve to air speculations about sexuality, and in so doing they provide a space for dialogue. Pop music anthems, merengue, and *Rock en Español* (Spanish rock music) share the sonoscape with radio talk shows, filling the airwaves with conversations about sexuality while callers remain protected by anonymity. Callers to radio shows may feel more empowered because they are effectively disembodied and thus unidentified. They effectively create a public sphere, albeit an anonymous one, for stories and queries about sexuality to emerge. The sexual visibility that *Sin Máscaras* and *Programa Joven sin Nombre* established was, ironically, transmitted through the very invisible medium of radio. However, these radio programs also allowed for an intimate engagement between listeners and broadcasters, allowing local concerns and questions to emerge over the collective airwaves. Rather than reacting to carefully produced personas on a telenovela, listeners shared their personal experiences directly and in their own words. In turn, they received an immediate response from an actual person, live. The sexual discourse that unfolded on the air was not only tolerated but solicited by the activists who created the radio programming. Radio, despite its apparently unidirectional broadcast technology, proved to be an exceptionally dialogic space for activists and their audiences.

Humanas: Grupo por la Visibilidad Lésbica

When we first met in 1999, Monica presented me with a copy of *Humanas*, the magazine that she and her grassroots organization, Grupo por la Visibilidad Lésbica (Lesbian Visibility Group), had just published. *Humanas* was specifically dedicated to increasing "the visibility of lesbians and their human rights" in Nicaragua. It was also Nicaragua's first and only lesbian magazine. The magazine had a print run of only one thousand copies. Nevertheless, Monica said that she wanted to mail a copy of the magazine to every member of the Nicaraguan National Assembly to directly criticize the legislature's passive support of the antisodomy law. "If I get the money to do it," Monica said, "I will." Like Luis's desire to highlight homosexuality on the airwaves and the youth radio program's emphasis on dialogue and disclosure, Monica spoke about her wish to make lesbianism and lesbian rights a very visible issue.

The cover of *Humanas* is a full-color reproduction of Gustav Klimt's painting *The Virgin* (1913). Below Klimt's sensual depiction of women entwined is a drawing of an Aztec deity whose caption designates her the "goddess of duality." By combining the aesthetics of early-twentieth-century European art with a pre-Columbian image of women's power, the activists who produced *Humanas* drew from both local and global renderings of women's sexuality. The Aztec goddess is, however, somewhat

Humanas
Revista Trimestral Enero - Marzo 1999 - No. 1
Por la Visibilidad Lésbica
y sus Derechos de Humanas
¿Quiénes somos?
Lesbianas diversas
Diálogo entre cuatro lesbianas y su experiencia de ser madres.
La legislación nicaragüense y la ley más arcaica del fin del milenio.
Los Gay Games en Amsterdam.
La marcha mundial del orgullo: ROMA 2000.
Poesía lésbica.
Primer certamen de *Poesía y Narrativa*.

FIGURE 4.5 *Humanas* magazine, published by Grupo por la Visibilidad Lésbica (Lesbian Visibility Group) in March 1999, the first lesbian magazine in Nicaragua. The publication was meant to do precisely what the organization's name suggested: promote lesbian visibility.

crushed by the European art image that occupies most of the cover's space. The first pages of the magazine call Nicaragua the "shame of Latin America" because of its antisodomy law, closely followed with details about how Article 204 violates Nicaragua's constitution. Following the political tenor of the magazine's initial pages, an unnamed lesbian from Costa Rica provides a testimonial, which she signs with the pseudonym "Me llamo Humana" (My Name is [Female] Human); her anonymity again calls attention to Nicaragua's repressive penal climate. The Nicaraguan women who contributed to the magazine also used pseudonyms to avoid potential prosecution under the antisodomy law or to prevent inadvertent declarations of their sexuality to a larger audience of families or employers. In later pages, the magazine features profiles of Amnesty International and the International Gay and Lesbian Human Rights Commission, fulfilling one of its mandates to highlight the importance of sexual rights. *Humanas* also includes several poems by Nicaraguan lesbian women, all of which have bylines such as "Venancia" (likely a reference to the famed Sandinista *guerrillera*), "Carmen," "Janette," or simply "Anonymous." Drawing on Nicaragua's history of poetical patrimony and the pride surrounding it, *Humanas* issued a call for contestants to submit entries for the "first national lesbian poetry contest," sponsored by the magazine. The magazine contained a "dialogue between four diverse lesbians" and a "*lesboróscopo* (lesbian horoscope)," with all of the usual zodiac signs. The centerfold featured a tasteful, though definitely not puritanical, black-and-white image of two nude women kissing.

As we spoke further about the magazine's purpose, it became clear that Monica did not equate lesbian *visibilidad* with exiting the closet. Instead, she explained that it was important for lesbian women to "remove the mask, to come out from behind a mask of invisibility." Indeed, the magazine's frontispiece, bordered by the editor's message, is an image of a Nicaraguan mask leaning alone against a white wall. The mask suggests a revelatory process, involving removing the mask, setting it aside, and ultimately coming forth with one's sexuality. In its isolation, against a stark wall, the mask also makes this appear a rather solitary endeavor. Monica's masking metaphor, like *Sin Máscaras*, the title of Luis's radio show, is a departure from the trope of the closet that has so structured Western interpretations of homosexuality and heterosexuality. There is no threshold of a closet door to step beyond; instead, there is a fictive face, and a self, that needs to be placed to the side to reveal one's "true" self. Removing the

Grupo por la Visibilidad
NICARAGUA

FIGURE 4.6 The centerfold from *Humanas* depicts two nude women kissing who are possibly Nicaraguan, based on their appearance. However, the image was reproduced from a North American photographer, Judy Francesconi, and the models were not Nicaraguan, thus the image itself and its placement in *Humanas* illustrate how global media is used in localized claims for sexual rights. It is indicative of an "erotiscape" where sexuality serves to link distinct places across time and space.

mask, like stepping out of a metaphorical closet, involves discursive practices of revelation and identifying one's sexual self publicly. It is an act of declaración, although the metaphor for doing so evokes Nicaraguan patrimonial associations. The mask—indeed, the particular mask of a fictive conquistador that the magazine features—is one that is deeply linked to the country's long tradition of masking in folkloric festivals (Field 1999).[14] Because it is considered such an important part of Nicaragua's folk history and resistance to imperial incursions, the mask evokes a strong sense of *lo nicaragüense*, or Nicaraguan-ness. In addition to serving as a route toward personal declaración, the mask is an affective metaphor with patriotic resonance.

Monica was deeply convinced that Nicaraguan lesbians ought to be recognized for their distinct identity and that they needed to become "unmasked" and publicly visible as lesbians. Her position, however, was not without critique from other activists, who accused her of trying to "move too fast" on the issue of visibility. Her stance, like Federico's demands for declaración in chapter 3, entails a philosophy of revelation. However, not all activists are comfortable with the difficulties that they might face if they were to inhabit a public mode of being "sin mascara." Many activists committed to a Sexuality Free from Prejudice (SFFP) approach, for instance, found Monica's invocation too risky, premature, or simply ill-conceived. Whether because of "personal" preference for discretion or "political" positions regarding ideology, some advocates found Monica more of a provocateur than an ally. While Grupo por la Visibilidad Lésbica intended to establish a greater modicum of visibility for lesbians in Nicaragua, what the organization was actually able to accomplish in the end was somewhat limited. A member of *Humanas* had secured funding for the magazine from a Dutch nonprofit organization she contacted during the Gay Games in Amsterdam in July 1998. Unfortunately, because no further funding was available, there was no second edition of the magazine, and ultimately *Humanas* had less impact than the Grupo por la Visibilidad Lésbica and its Dutch patrons originally intended. In 2001, with the Grupo por la Visibilidad Lésbica rarely meeting and without any economic support for the project, Monica turned her attention to other things and enrolled in law school. The fact that an issue of *Humanas* exists at all, and that it was both published and distributed in Nicaragua, demonstrates that Monica and her group were able partially to fulfill their goals for lesbian visibility. That visibility, however, was based on anonymity, pseudonyms, and disembodied subjects, much like the listeners and callers to sexuality radio shows who remained both nameless and bodiless.

Rather than marking particular bodies with precise identities, activist projects like Luis's radio show and Monica's magazine redefine sexual subjectivity by taking identifiable people (who can be marked, mocked, and incarcerated) largely out of the equation. Sexual subjectivity is made visible in these media spaces—or, as Monica or Luis might put it, it is "unmasked." But this visibility is accomplished through anonymity. These politics of anonymity create a sexual subject that may be literally disembodied but is not without a voice, telephonically or textually. In comparison to the face-to-face politics of SFFP or Lesbian and Gay Pride, the media-based interventions of radio and print allowed for nearly complete anonymity and a modicum of spectacular visibility at the same time. While sexual politics in many places around the world have advocated the power of coming out of the closet, Monica and Luis's strategy is notably different. They have largely separated people from identities. At the same time, they have established a place of dialogue and discussion about homosexuality in very public forums. These strategies, predicated on anonymity and dependent on opacity, may not directly challenge heterosexism or critique repressive legislation in the ways that the more explicit ideologies of pride and sexuality free from prejudice do. However, publishing magazines that feature poetic lesbians and airing radio shows with questioning callers produces a form of mediated sexual subjectivity that is simultaneously both visible and clandestine. Voices on nighttime airwaves, poets with pseudonyms, and tales from the World Wide Web work to create an audible and textual tapestry of sexual subjects who are in one sense everywhere, but who are no one in particular. They are ubiquitous but anonymous.

Channeling Transnational Identities and Politics

As I sat down with the director of USAID's Managua office one afternoon, I was only slightly surprised when he "outed" himself as a huge fan of the TV show *Sexto Sentido*. He went on to explain that USAID considered *Sexto Sentido* an ideal model for development, an exemplary way to bring about social change. From his perspective, the show promoted autonomy and a sense of personhood grounded in human rights—values that are well suited to USAID's development agenda.[15] The fact that the show was broadcast on Nicaragua's most popular television station and therefore accessible to large sectors of the population made it that much better. *Sexto Sentido's* method of social transformation does have a fiscal appeal: it is social engineering on a shoestring budget. From this perspective, media activism can be seen as development on the cheap. When compared with large infrastructure projects that are the traditional hallmark of development projects in the global South, the television show provides potentially broad interventions at a fraction of the cost. It allows digital cameras to replace drop-in clinics and low-salary local actors to stand in for costly technicians. As charmingly local expressions that are inexpensively produced and transnationally distributable, these media productions can be seen as the culmination of neoliberal development desires. They are, in a sense, an off-shoring of social justice. However, I would argue that media activism such as *Sexto Sentido* appeals to development agencies like USAID not simply because of its fiscal efficacy but also because it fulfills a modernizing and democratizing impulse. The local stagings and *dichos* of *Sexto Sentido*, the voices aired on *Sin Máscaras*, the unmasking and poetry included in *Humanas* all evoke a sense of *puro Nicaragüense*. Nicaraguan audiences are able to see themselves represented here, but these locally focused productions also appeal to Northern liberal aspirations for a less imperially laden approach to development. They represent a possibility of development that involves co-participation by the global North and the global South. These interventions produce a sense of locality that effectively serves to market globally circulated identities, as well as liberal values regarding choice, subjectivity, and sexuality.

The ability to produce a sense of locality and familiarity while also attending to globally legible forms of subjectivity was part of *Sexto Sentido's* phenomenal success, at home and abroad. The telenovela received several international awards, and *Sexto Sentido* was the subject of a documentary (Miller 2002) that was screened at lesbian and gay film festivals around the world. The fact that the show circulated well beyond the borders of Nicaragua is likely to have increased its impact. Since its debut, *Sexto Sentido* has been syndicated in ten Latin American television markets, and it became available through DirecTV in the United States in 2007. Nearly three hundred video clips of the show were uploaded to YouTube, making a good portion of its episodes globally available on the Internet for a period of time.[16] The saga of *Sexto Sentido* demonstrates an important articulation of sexuality, media, and rights. For while Nicaraguan advocates do use global discourses of identity and sexual subjectivity, the advocacy materials they have produced are also readily disseminated in this same global sphere. This is not a one-way importation of values, from the global North to the global South, but a circular exchange between public cultures and political spaces in both the South and the North.

Sexual rights activists have made extensive use of media forms to advance their advocacy goals. However, it is worth asking who is supposed to be convinced by these interventions. Are these performances for the Nicaraguan nation, intended to turn the tide of public opinion? Are they for the Nicaraguan National Assembly, to influence the legislative halls of power? Or are activists performing these politics for an international audience, such as the benefactors at USAID, who fund the development projects on which the country has come to depend? The answer, of course, is all of the above. Several of the activists I spoke to said that media activism proliferated to counter the antisodomy law. However, many activists also emphasized the need to redirect the national dialogue, to move sexual rights away from a conversation about criminality and toward a discussion of tolerance. Like activists' work to establish a broad notion of sexual subjectivity in lesbian discussion groups and the negotiations surrounding the identity of the lucha, media-based activism has been premised on refining and redefining the conceptual space of sexuality within the Nicaraguan context. While sexual rights activists' focus may be local or national in scope, understanding global dynamics and articulating select discourses is also critical to their work.

By combining politics and pop culture with entertainment and education, Nicaraguan sexual rights advocates have endeavored to transform the Nicaraguan public sphere. Activist interventions such as *Sexto Sentido*, *Humanas*, and *Sin Máscaras* use mass media as a promotional platform in an attempt to make gay and lesbian identity part of the Nicaraguan national imaginary. As they articulate particular messages about sexuality and seek a responsive relationship with their audience, activists mediate their advocacy goals in a dual sense. They both promote certain forms of subjectivity and perform an explicitly engaged and communicative strategy of intervention. Using the telenovela, a mainstay of Latin American pop culture, the producers of *Sexto Sentido* were immensely successful in capturing the attention of large sectors of the Nicaraguan population. For the activists who produced, directed, and wrote *Sexto Sentido*, normalizing lesbian and gay characters and making them familiar and appealing to the viewing audience was a way (literally) to produce a viable sexual subject on Nicaraguan television screens. However, normalizing gay and lesbian characters also meant consigning other sexual subjects, such as the cochón and cochona, to the margins. Activist producers promoted a very particular homosexual habitus that featured properly gendered, and declared, lesbian and gay subjects. The formulation of a gay man as (an) Angel and Vicki's feminine trappings are intentionally crafted "preferred readings," a set of intended values or messages that may or may not be read as their authors intend (Hall 1997). The call-in radio program *Sin Máscaras* and the lesbian magazine *Humanas* also promoted positive messages about homosexuality and lesbian identity. For the activists who initiated these projects, radio and print media have offered ways to create more *visibilidad* for sexual rights. However, this visibility occurs through the somewhat ironic turn of making contributors (on the phone and in print) anonymous, disembodied, and largely invisible. In a carefully constructed [reiterates this fact] space of confidentiality, lesbian poets using pseudonyms and unidentified radio show callers are able to give voice and visibility to the cause of sexual rights without endangering themselves. On television and radio airwaves as well as in print, activists have produced carefully calculated degrees of anonymity and visibility. Their message—to promote equality, visibility, and rights—is clear, but it is also always conditioned by the medium that they employ.

Nicaraguan sexual rights activists have intentionally mobilized media as eliciting devices, hoping to create a conversation between themselves and their audiences. Their commitment to this kind of dialogic engagement, even in the notoriously unidirectional realm of television and radio broadcasts, is significant; it demonstrates important overlaps between media production and consumption. How media is produced—whether in the hands of indigenous peoples or among elite media professionals—is necessarily determined by how particular media will be consumed.[17] However, the relationship between (so-called) spheres of production and consumption has often proved difficult to analyze, partly because audiences may receive much more, or much less, than the producers hope to convey. In other words, it is very hard to know what audiences are "getting" from the dialogue, images, and affective dimensions of producers' messages.[18] In an attempt to understand media and the social relationships that it embodies in more complex terms, anthropologists have shown that ongoing and reciprocal processes of mediation operate within larger contexts that cannot simply be reduced to production and consumption.[19] New genres of media—such as digital networks and new communications technology—have been useful in illustrating a post-production and post-consumption paradigm. In this view, circulation and exchange are foundational to how media operate, as well as to how "users" (as opposed to audiences) experience and engage with them. The dialogic model that Nicaraguan sexual rights activists attempted to establish, encouraging conversations between activists and the people they are hoping to reach, explicitly encouraged responsiveness. The Nicaraguan case does not fully depart from the binary model of production and consumption, because ultimately activist producers had to determine whether and how they would use input from the audience. However, activists were clearly invested in a politics of elicitation and dialogue. They actively sought ways to use the channels of television, print, and radio to speak to, and hear from, their audience and interlocutors. By establishing this kind of communicational landscape in their media activism, sexual rights advocates incorporated, and hoped to realize, the democratic and nonhierarchical principles that are foundational to their politics. Activists have sought to create intermediated activist projects in which a premium is placed on the cocreation of knowledge. In this sense, their work parallels the audience-involved modes of communication and interaction found in contemporary digital platforms and circulatory media models.[20] Activists' dialogic model—even in light of the technological limits imposed by broadcast and print media—was, one might argue, communicationally ahead of its time, foreshadowing the contemporary, social-mediated moment.

CONCLUSION

=

Getting the Word Out

Truth and Testimony

The attorney and I have already been through several hours of
what she calls "practice testimony." It is ironic to me that one
needs to practice telling "the truth, the whole truth, and noth-
ing but the truth." But the law is fastidious and aspires to pre-
cision, so the attorney and I dutifully focus my narrative on the
pertinent elements of the asylum case that will be presented
in the coming weeks. I am serving as an expert witness; thus,
the attorney's questions always begin with the same phrase:
"In your research and experience in Nicaragua . . ." The constant repetition of the phrase is like a liturgical device. But, of
course, this is also an illocutionary act meant to establish and
reestablish my credentials for the judge and for the record. I
will be a "country conditions expert" on behalf of Rafael Vega
Maltez (a pseudonym), a Nicaraguan man who has filed for
asylum in the United States. Rafael has brought the asylum
claim because he is convinced that, because of his sexuality,
he will face abuse, torture, and possibly death if he is deported
back to his native Nicaragua. Part of my task in this juridi-

cal project is to help establish that the Nicaraguan government is "un-willing or unable" to protect Rafael from the harm that he might face. The attorney and I are working pro bono, and we have each invested a substantial amount of time and energy on Rafael's behalf. We both want him to win his case. If he receives asylum, Rafael is likely to have a more secure future, both financially and physically. However, in an ironic way, if he wins his case, it will also mean that sexual rights activists in Nicaragua and the government that overturned the antisodomy law will, in one instance, have lost in the court of global public opinion. Nicaragua will have been deemed a place that is intolerant and dangerous for people like Rafael—precisely the opposite of what sexual rights advocates have worked so hard to change.

Whether sexual rights activists have been able to transform the values, life conditions, and culture in Nicaragua in the ways they have hoped to faces a transnational challenge in cases like Rafael's. Such asylum cases effectively test, in a legal and symbolic way, whether sexual rights activists and the Nicaraguan government have been able to ensure that certain lives are "worthy of protection" (Butler 2004: 32). I have read the description in Rafael's application for asylum of how he has suffered as a "very feminine homosexual" in Nicaragua. He recounts being raped at six by a young man who broke into the house where he and his mother lived in a Miskito village on the Atlantic coast. He testifies to having been sexually assaulted several times by older male family members when he was shipped off to Managua at eleven. He describes how he was beaten and raped by a group of police officers when he was a high school student and later when he was a young man on the streets of the capital city. Rafael has not had contact with his family for years. He does not know where any of them are or whether they are alive or dead. Leaving Nicaragua for what he felt were much more tolerant conditions in Mexico and, finally, the United States, Rafael was ultimately apprehended and detained by La Migra (U.S. immigration enforcement). Rafael and I have never met, but during his incarceration, we spoke on the phone, and the desperate tone of his voice made his story all the more troubling. I believe Rafael is telling the truth about what he has experienced. I have heard similar stories from other Nicaraguans, especially from those who do not follow the conventions of gender and are therefore particularly vulnerable on the street and within their families. Rafael's attorney will argue that, because he is a very visible "member of a particular social group" (homosexuals), his safety cannot be ensured. My testimony will support that position and add that because of his sexuality, his gender presentation, his lack of family networks, and the impossibility of his finding work in a place such as Nicaragua, where there are few jobs for people dubbed "normal," Rafael will indeed be forced to return to street prostitution in Managua, where he will invariably face harm.

Rafael's testimony, however, will be heard by a judge who disapproves 75 percent of the asylum cases he adjudicates. It will also take place in a context in which there has been a recent spate of media on sexual asylum cases in the United States. In Washington State, a heterosexual couple was prosecuted for peddling coaching sessions to undocumented immigrants that instructed them how to pass as gay to receive asylum protection in the United States. On the U.S. East Coast, media outlets have documented judges who have granted asylum more readily to male applicants who appear flamboyant and feminine, their queer appearance apparently proving that they are truly gay. This kind of juridical reductionism fails to register the particular vulnerabilities and dangers that individuals face. And while quotients of vulnerability ought to be the calculus in all of these cases, reality rarely matches the ideal. After several weeks of deliberation, the judge eventually ruled that Rafael should be deported to Nicaragua. As soon as the news was announced, Rafael's attorney was already at work on the appeal.

A Postscript in the Present

This book began with an assertion that it would be more than a celebratory reflection on a hard-won victory. It is, however, important to underscore that Nicaraguan sexual rights activists were instrumental in helping to create the conditions that would lead to the overturning of their country's antisodomy law. Article 204 posed a legal threat not only to individuals who were, or were thought to be, involved in same-sex sexual and affective relationships, but also to those who were thought to be "propagandizing or promoting" same-sex sexuality. The legal codification of discrimination that Article 204 embodied created a climate in which anti-gay and anti-lesbian sentiments found legal refuge. The existence of Article 204 may have fostered individual acts of discrimination, violence, and antipathy, even if the law itself was rarely used to prosecute individuals. Eradicating this element of the Nicaraguan criminal code is an unquestionable milestone for sexually marginalized people in Nicaragua—and, perhaps by extension, elsewhere. It is nevertheless a victory situated in a particular political, discursive, and moral moment in Nicaragua and in the world. The Nicaraguan National Assembly's decision, at least nominally, showed a commitment to the ethical principles of human rights. At the same time, the law was overturned in the context of a fraught dispute over abortion and reproductive rights. These debates themselves were conditioned by wider political shifts in Latin America. Leftist populism has had a resurgence — in the spread of the "Bolivarian Revolution," for example, and the election of Left-leaning heads of state in many Latin American countries. Decades of LGBT activism in other Latin American states, such as Argentina, Brazil, and Mexico (which have each legalized same-sex marriage either fully or in certain areas of the country), have had a cumulative and multiplying effect, as well. Abolishing Article 204, then, is clearly a move toward greater legal tolerance in Nicaragua. But as with all things juridical, it does not capture the entirety of the dynamics at work. Overturning the antisodomy law, as activists themselves have told me many times now, is not the end of the story. For them, the struggle for sexual rights needs to continue. Although they have brought about a dramatic change in policy, changing Nicaraguan "culture" remains an unfinished project.

Legal recognition does not always, or immediately, transform *la vida cotidiana* (daily life), and many Nicaraguan lesbians and gay men continue to face ridicule, employment discrimination, and mistreatment. In the report "A Look at Sexual Diversity in Nicaragua" (2010), the Nicaraguan Grupo Estratégico por los Derechos Humanos de la Diversidad Sexual (GEDDS), a consortium of NGOs, activist groups, and individuals funded by the Norwegian Embassy, documented the contemporary conditions for sexual minorities in Nicaragua.[1] The GEDDS project surveyed 1,300 lesbians, homosexual/gay men, *travestis*, and transgender and intersex people in every region of Nicaragua using surveys, focus groups, and in-depth interviews. The report confirmed high rates of unemployment and underemployment among sexual minorities. In a country where stable and adequate employment is scarce for everyone, employment discrimination against gays, lesbians, and trans-people often means it will be nearly impossible for many of them to obtain secure, remunerative work. All of the respondents in the GEDDS survey reported harassment, bullying, and discrimination in the Nicaraguan school system, from elementary school to the university level. More than half spoke about disapproval and discrimination within their families, primarily by male kin. Several respondents, particularly *travestis*, pointed out that they are victims of violent attacks on the street by both police and street gangs.

The incidences of violence that the survey documents may be a function of better reportage: as the *lucha* gains visibility and viability, individuals may be more willing to come forward with their stories of discrimination and harm, whether within the family or on the street. However, among many of the activists with whom I have stayed in contact, it is more than this. They believe that there actually is *more* violence against sexual minorities now than there was in the past. With their new legal status, Nicaraguan *homosexuales/gays, lesbianas,* and trans- people have a new identity and greater recognition in the public imagination. This sanctioned subjectivity has meant that they are a step closer to achieving equal rights, but it also appears to have exacerbated attacks and abuse. In the first nine months of 2012, for example, five murders and six physical and sexual assaults were attributed to homophobic violence in Nicaragua. This represents a fifty percent increase from the prior year. Claims for equal rights are often followed by aggressive backlashes, as was the case in the U.S. Civil Rights Movement and innumerable other such movements. For the authors of the GEDDS report, "This violence is directly proportional to the degree of visibility of our sexual identity."[2] Visibility, for the lucha and for individuals, entails the risk of increased violence and discrimination. This is one critical reason, as I argued in chapter 3, that activists have been cautious and deliberative about how the lucha should come "out." It is why activists have interrogated whether the lucha ought to focus on a Sexuality Free from Prejudice or Lesbian and Gay Pride, whether *declaración* is imperative, and whether there are other ways to establish subjectivity and maintain satisfying relationships that do not necessarily live under the signs of lesbian and gay identity.

Many of the people and organizations that have appeared throughout this book continue their work in Nicaragua. New organizations, coalitions, and groups of grassroots activists have also arisen, including Grupo Safo, the Iniciativa desde La Diversidad Sexual por los Derechos Humanos (Sexual Diversity Initiative for Human Rights), and the Asociación Nicaragüense de Transgénera (Nicaraguan Transgender Association), which campaign to bring sexual diversity and human rights into greater public dialogue. In 2009, these organizations, along with others, hosted the first "sexual diversity" parade, with approximately forty participants marching through the streets of Managua carrying rainbow flags and banners declaring their newly obtained rights. In December 2009, the Nicaraguan government created an Ombudsperson's Office for the Defense of Sexual Diversity Rights, directed by a young lesbian attorney who has been active in sexual rights activism in the country. Omar Cabezas, a well-known author and revolutionary and the human rights ombudsman for Nicaragua, explained that the new office was necessary to "recognize the constitutional rights and duties of all citizens, whatever their sexual orientation, as universal rights which must be respected."[3] Following the opening of the Office for the Defense of Sexual Diversity Rights, congregants at Sunday mass in several Catholic churches in Nicaragua were implored to reject "sodomite practices." The National Council of Evangelical Pastors of Nicaragua, which represents the second largest religious community in the country after the Catholic church, submitted an official pastoral letter outlining its concerns about the establishment of the office, fearing it would give "free rein to immorality."[4] The Catholic church and Protestant denominations continue to wield influence in Nicaragua, in the pews and in the press. Although they may articulate the issue in different terms, with the state opting for a discourse of rights and religious leaders choosing a discourse of morality, the fact is that the Nicaraguan government and the country's largest religious communities are now divided on the issue of sexual diversity.

In the course of their struggle, as we have seen throughout this book, activists have engaged with many categories, strategies, and conceptual frameworks to shape their advocacy practices. The prevailing logic that best captures activists' work, I have argued, is the rubric of "sexual rights," in which rights operate as a political *method* and sexuality represents a political *object* of intervention. Contemporary claims for sexual rights in Nicaragua appear to follow these contours of dissent. Among Nicaragua's new generation of sexual rights activists, there are many young people. Some of them participated in lesbian and homosexual discussion groups, where they were trained in the pedagogies of identity and consciousness; some of them grew up in the era of sexuality free from prejudice. However, many of those involved in sexual rights advocacy in Nicaragua are the same people with whom I worked a decade ago, some of them now occupying leadership positions. A network of engaged feminists and others continue to support sexual rights, just as they did in earlier times. Activists are persevering in their efforts on the legal front, including lobbying for the Office for the Defense of Sexual Diversity Rights. They also continue on the "cultural" front by, for example, hosting lesbian film nights and marching for sexual diversity in the streets of Managua. Sexual rights activists, young and old, are also making use of the Internet, allowing them to have a global digital presence and provide informational resources to other Nicaraguans.[5] The current generation of activists has been reared in an era of rights discourses. They remain committed to human rights as a key trope and tactic in their struggle, and their activist messages, online and on the street, continue to emphasize rights as fundamental. The lucha itself also seems to have come of age. Activists now say that they are "working toward the formation of a social movement," surpassing the stage of struggle and becoming a larger "movement" with greater impact.[6] The same sexual rights activists who assured me in 1999 that "there is no gay movement here in Nicaragua" now say, "Sí hay" (Yes there is).

Sexual vocabularies have also changed in Nicaragua. Sexual Categories have clearly expanded and now include terms that are very new to the Nicaraguan context: transgénera/o (transgendered), transexual (transsexual), and intersexual (intersex). Sexual rights activism also designates travestí and bisexual more explicitly within the rubric of sexual diversity, a multiplying "logic of enumeration" (Boellstorff 2007: 27).[7] Activists, however, are aware of both the possibilities and the limitations of the classificatory system of sexual identity. In the GEDDS report, they note that, "in reality, there are many sexual identities because each person is unique. We have used these categories to enable analysis, not because they are the only classifications possible."[8] In earlier generations of sexual rights activism, the concept of heterosexismo often prevailed. Now, the concepts of homofobia, transfobia, and homo-lesbo-transfobia appear more readily across activists' discourses and far more frequently than they did in the past. A "fear" of homosexual people or the idea that interacting with a queer person might conjure latent desires in an unsuspecting straight person (and thereby potentially cause a "gay panic") historically has not been an operative logic in Nicaragua. The concept of homofobia previously was far more diagnostic of Northern forms of gay and lesbian antipathy, but this seems to have shifted, as well. While multiculturalist forms of diversity are increasing and fobias seem to have taken hold, Nicaragua's legacy of communitarian politics continues to influence contemporary iterations of sexual rights. As one young woman at the sexual diversity parade in Managua in 2009 put it, "I have the right to live my sexuality free from prejudice." Marching for "sexual diversity" rather than for "pride" per se indicates that although specific sexual and gender categories may be more resonant in their current work, many activists continue to frame their project as an opportunity to be free from prejudice, and sexual categories, as they imagine them, continue to be broadly conceived.

Throughout this book, I have paid close attention to the ways in which sexual rights activists pedagogically craft, intellectually engineer, and dialogically engage with audiences and with other activists. As I showed in chapter 3, producing specific knowledge regimes—the ideological foundations of the lucha—has been an integral and vital element in activists' work. In the intimate pedagogies of lesbian discussion groups (chapter 2), activist facilitators were committed to designing an inclusive set of principles that would capture the complexities of sexual identity; in turn, these were meant to be comprehensive and clear to participants seeking to find their own experiences represented in the unfolding dialogues of the groups. Within these advocacy frameworks, activists have grappled with the intimacies of local and global categories of sexuality and sought to shape the language that is used, and that will be used, to describe same-sex sexuality. In this process, sexual rights activists have been involved in both constructive and deconstructive exercises, mobilizing the terms of subjectivity through different media forms and levels of engagement. Many scholars working with communities that are marked by sexual or gender difference have voiced concern about the homogenizing potential of sexual identity categories. The fear is that a "global gay" identity—one that strictly adheres to a reified, putatively modern and egalitarian sexual selfhood—will erase local forms of sexuality. Autochthonous sexual subjectivities will, by this logic, be replaced with hegemonic, and homogenous, forms of sexuality that have been disseminated through the channels of media, tourism, and human rights campaigns originating in the global North. However, as other scholars have found—and as I hope I have demonstrated—while many of the terms that circulate in contemporary sexual rights movements may appear hegemonic, they are not necessarily monological. Nor are they equivalent in the global North and the global South. Without question, discourses and identities do travel. However, they are taken up, disputed, and creatively reappropriated within local contexts. Or, as the authors of the GEDDS report accurately put it, "Sexual identity" is a term *por ahora* (for the time being) because "we understand that these concepts are in the process of being constructed and their meaning(s) are a point of debate."[9]

Ethnographies of Activism

Nicaraguans, like people everywhere, like to talk for many different reasons: to share stories, to communicate their perspective on the world, to complain and to compliment, to lament losses, and to revel in the good moments of life. Among the Nicaraguan activists with whom I spent many of my days and nights, one thing often became very clear, usually within our first conversation about this research project. And that is that they wanted the results of this project to be published in English and in el Norte. As many activists put it, they wanted me to be sure to "tell the gringos what we are doing here" and to "get the word out." Getting the word out has been, and continues to be, a critical yet complicated project for anthropologists. Anthropology has a long tradition of advocacy, beginning with Franz Boas's critique of racist assumptions both within and outside the discipline in the early twentieth century (Baker 1998; Boas 1995 [1940]). Salvage anthropology and many of the midcentury approaches to ethnographic research attempted to speak "for" marginalized populations in some way. Now, most, if not all, cultural anthropologists would describe ethical and methodological commitments to speaking "with" the communities with whom they work. While anthropology at times has sought to insulate its analytic purity from a putatively instrumental world of politics, the more recent consensus is that anthropology is, and always has been, deeply affected by its social and political milieu; it has never been free from politics. As David Valentine (2007: 276, n. 4) has described it, anthropologists historically have demonstrated an "ongoing spirit of advocacy within the discipline." Having recognized that distanced objectivity cannot, or should not, be the ultimate purpose of ethnographic research, many anthropologists have become committed to more explicitly public, engaged, and activist anthropology. Engaged and public approaches to anthropology call for ethnographic analysis and an interpretive lens that prioritize ethical considerations (Faubion 2011). Ultimately, this may produce a kind of ethnographic engagement that can contribute to redressing social inequalities or prove useful in changing public policy (Scheper-Hughes 1995). By advocating on behalf of the social justice issues that are important to the people with whom they work, many anthropologists have become increasingly out about their activist identities and practices.[10]

Ethnographies of activism that are based on and *within* activist communities involve particular kinds of contingencies and, potentially, pitfalls. The intimate union between anthropology and advocacy challenges us to balance interpretation, and sometimes critique, of activists' work while simultaneously striving to support the cause. As Jean Jackson and Kay Warren (2005: 557) have rightly noted, "Ethnographic practice that bridges inquiry, activism, and participatory approaches to the production of cultural knowledge raises complex questions, epistemological and ethical, answers to which are not exactly around the corner."[11] Participants in social struggles, as well as observers and analysts of those struggles, are often vulnerable to utopian portrayals of their goals, motives, and techniques. Social scientists—and perhaps particularly anthropologists, who often work with, and within, marginalized populations—must be cautious about romanticizing the politics of subalterns, particularly when a movement (or, for that matter, a struggle) is the object of analysis. David Graeber (2009: 13) echoes this sentiment when he writes that his intention, as an anthropologist and an avowed activist, is "to avoid both the temptation to idealize the movement, or the (equally annoying) habit many activists have of only talking about its problems." Invariably, contradictions and conflicts arise when worthy political causes are placed under the painstaking microscope of ethnographic analysis. Moments of tension are not incommensurable, however; indeed, these tensions can provide an opportunity for the "open question" that leads to others (Valentine 2007). I believe, along with other anthropologists who identify themselves as "engaged," "collaborative," or "public" researchers, that scholarly rigor does not exclude, nor should it eclipse, political commitments to resolving injustices; these are instead "mutually enriching" practices (Hale 2008: 2). The anthropology of rights in fact demands a careful consideration of how to combine activism and cultural critique (Hale 2006a; Speed 2006). By documenting and analyzing the mediational work of activists, as this book does, we are able to illuminate both the ideals and the idiosyncrasies of political action. But perhaps more important, we can render a more nuanced and complex view of the frictions that impede, or compel, activists' political interventions. Empirical and theoretical studies of social justice struggles, ethnographies of activism, have the potential to elucidate both the troubles and the triumphs of social justice struggles and, ideally, move the agenda forward.

Ethnographies of activism are also, I would argue, a doubly reflexive and reflective project for anthropologists and others who are involved in community-based research. Activist cultures bear a resemblance to the cultures of ethnographic research in several ways. Each of them depends on close and collaborative conversations; each demands grappling with the social issues of the time and translating aspects of social life into terms that engage a broader public (Speed and Reyes 2002). As I showed in chapter 4, activists use distinct strategies of representation for different constituencies, but it is only through a dialogic engagement with one's audience—or, in the case of ethnographic fieldwork, a dialogic engagement with communities—that a synthetic result is created. Furthermore, the structural inequalities and injustices that have incited many anthropologists to pursue certain lines of inquiry are similar, and sometimes coeval with, the social inequities that activists are committed to resolving. A good ethnographer must find a balance between analytic representation and observed social practices. Activists must also be adept at communication and skilled at representing their cause in transparent terms while continuing to focus on the larger goals they hope to reach. Finally, there seems to be a very clear affinity of practice between those who are attempting to "transform culture" (to use the terms of Nicaraguan sexual rights activists) and the discipline that, for better or worse, has popularized the culture concept. The bounded "Culture" of anthropology's past no longer appears in contemporary ethnographic work because its static order no longer corresponds well to the empirical realities of globalization, migration, media dissemination, and transnational networks.[12] It is precisely these latter dynamics, as I have shown throughout this book, that Nicaraguan activists engage; for their politics, as for contemporary anthropology, the local and the global have become, to a degree, indivisible.

This book has been about a relatively small group of activists in a relatively small country. However, the story of sexual rights in Nicaragua is an important one not simply because activists have contributed to overturning their country's antisodomy law, but also because sexual rights, in and of themselves, have proven to be a significant part of our contemporary global episteme. The United Nations Decade for Women (1976–1985), in part, opened new arenas for activist intervention around the world, including lesbian and gay rights; HIV/AIDS prevention; adolescent sexuality; the right to bodily integrity; and the prevention of systematic rape, forced pregnancy, sexual slavery, and trafficking (Petchesky 2000: 83).[13] For many policymakers, activists, and health-promotion professionals, there is a new urgency to intervene in cases of sexual exploitation and in the politics of sexuality more broadly (Duggan 2004).[14] Although struggles to establish equality for sexual minorities are not new to Latin America or other regions of the global South, the global interconnectivity of activist projects has added new dimensions and dynamics to the possibilities for sexual rights. Transnational organizations (such as Amnesty International, the International Gay and Lesbian Human Rights Commission, and the International Lesbian and Gay Association) continue to exert political pressure on countries that have not decriminalized homosexuality. The legalization of same-sex partnerships in Latin American, African, and European countries, as well as some states in the United States, indicates shifting social conditions and modifications to policy that have come, at least in part, through the efforts of activists. Together, movements for LGBTQ rights, campaigns against sex trafficking, development projects to *[in relation to intimate labors]* promote sexual health and HIV prevention, and the ongoing debates about reproductive rights around the world demonstrate how a putatively "private" or "personal" realm of experience has become increasingly politicized and publicized. Or, as Jean Comaroff (2007: 200) has plainly put it, "Ever more assertively, sex is seen, for good and ill, to hold the key to life."

Finally, let me end with good news about one particular life. Following a successful appeal made by his attorney, Rafael was, after almost a year, freed from the jail cell in central Texas where he had been incarcerated. He was granted asylum in the United States. I imagine he was thrilled; I know his attorney and I were delighted. I also imagine that one day Rafael and I may pass each other on the street, never knowing the small role each of us had in the story of sexual rights, and of a new kind of revolution, in Nicaragua.

NOTES

=

Introduction

1. Following the abolition of Article 204, which took place several years after my field research, I have had many conversations with Nicaraguan activists, political commentators, journalists, and academics about why the antisodomy law was overturned when it was. None of them has a precise answer. However, I offer some of their speculations at the end of chapter 1.

2. For discussions of the uneven transnationalization of sexual rights, identity politics, and sexual subjectivity, see, e.g., de la Dehesa 2010; Hirsch 1999; Ghaziani 2008; Grewal and Kaplan 2001; Howe and Rigi 2009; Jackson 2009; Massad 2002; Ong and Collier 2004; Povinelli and Chauncey 1999; Puar 2005, 2007.

3. She defines the "liberal diaspora" as "the colonial and postcolonial subjective, institutional, and discursive identifications, dispersions, and elaborations of the enlightenment idea that society should be organized on the basis of rational mutual understanding" (Povinelli 2004: 6).

4. For discussions on the global variability of sexual subjectivity, practice, and desire, historically and in the present, see, e.g., Babb 2003, 2009; Balderston and Guy 1997; Binnie 2004; Blackwood 1999, 2010; Blackwood and Wieringa 1999; Boellstorff 2005; Cantú 2002; Carrier 1995; Carrillo 2001; De la Dehesa 2010; Donham 1998; Elliston 1995; Foucault 1979, 1985; González-Lopez 2005; Herdt 1987; Howe 2001, 2008a, 2008b, 2009; Jacobs et al. 1997; Leap and Boellstorff 2003; Lewin and Leap 2002; Luibhéid and Cantú 2005; Lumsden 1996; Manalansan 2003; Manalansan and Cruz-Malavé 2002; McLelland 2000; McLelland and Dasgupta 2005; Montoya 2002; Murray and Roscoe 1997, 1998; Parker 1991, 1999; Robertson 1998, 2004; Rofel 1999; Sang 2003; Sinnott 2004; Sullivan and Jackson 1999, 2001; Wilson 2004.

5. Or as one of my very close friends put it (riffing on "fag hag"), "You are a 'dyke denizen.'"

6. I intentionally alternate between the terms sexual rights "activist" and sexual rights "advocate" throughout this book in order to avoid creating a sharp distinction between paid advocates and grassroots activists. Reifying these differences could result in the romanticization of the unpaid labor of grassroots activists and dismiss the deeply held convictions that professional advocates attribute to their social justice work.

7. The great majority of the activists and others represented here are Nicaraguan, however. I will indicate when I refer to a foreign national or an expatriate living in Nicaragua.

8. Throughout the text, I have maintained the terms that people used in our conversations (e.g., "gay," "lesbiana," "homosexual," "cochona" or "cochón"). "Bisexual," "transgénero" (transgender), and "transsexual" were incipient terms in the Nicaraguan sexual rights community during the time of my research. Although some activists were aware of them, these terms were not commonly discussed, nor were they a priority of activists' work. In my recent conversations with activists, "transgénero" and "bisexual" are more frequently included when activists talk about sexual rights. "Travestis" (biological men who wear women's clothing and who are presumed to take a passive role in sexual encounters with more masculine men) is a term that was familiar to most Nicaraguans with whom I interacted. However, the English-language term "queer" was not in wide circulation during my fieldwork; only one activist used it, once, in reference to North American sexual politics.

9. As several scholars have pointed out, the category of "civil society" can be problematic in that it presumes a liberal trajectory of development and social welfare: see, e.g., Edelman 1999; Gill 2000; Paley 2002. Likewise in Nicaragua, civil society is not a singular entity but a network of overlapping agencies, institutes, and organizations that are often interconnected with state projects.

10. Les Field (1999: 12) writes that "thousands of foreigners, especially North Americans and Western Europeans, flocked to Nicaragua following the triumph of the Sandinista Front on July 19, 1979, [and these] foreigners were officially accorded a semi-insider status as *internacionalistas* [foreigners in solidarity with the revolutionary process]." These international allies were also sometimes referred to as *sandalistas*.

11. Although I have provided pseudonyms for individuals throughout the text, I have maintained the actual names of organizations and collective groups. The NGOs Fundación Xochiquetzal and Puntos de Encuentro (Common Ground), both based in Managua, have been very public (and published) about their work for sexual rights. Other organizations, such as the Center for Education and the Prevention of AIDS and the Fundación Nimehuatzin, also have been transparent about their advocacy for sexual health and opposition to discrimination. Several organizations have produced materials that are clearly marked as theirs, including magazines, radio productions, pamphlets, informational materials, and, in the case of Puntos de Encuentro, a television show. I have also preserved the true name of smaller activist groups, such as Shomos and Amigas Juntas, because the naming process itself illustrates important elements of their identity. Because individuals who are, or have been, involved with the groups are protected with anonymity, there is no clear risk involved in using the names of grassroots activist groups.

12. For discussions of the successes and failures of the Sandinista Revolutionary state, see Belli 2003; Bretlinger 1995; Chuchryk 1991; Close and Deonandan 2004; Field 1999; Hale 1994; Hoyt 1997; Lancaster 1988, 1992; Prevost and Vanden 1997; Randall 1981, 1994; Rushdie 1987; Vilas 1989, 1992; Walker 1991, 2003; Zimmermann 2000.

13. "Fiscal terrorism" was a term activists used to describe the government's repeated, politically motivated financial audits of particular organizations and clinics. Many sexual rights advocates believed that politically controversial organizations, such as those dedicated to sexual or reproductive health, were singled out and subjected to an inordinate number of audits by government agents in an effort to disrupt their work and, implicitly, to remind members of civil society of the state's disciplinary power.

14. Rather than focusing on how religious institutions have contributed to the "socially conservative" atmosphere that Nicaraguan activists describe, I am concerned with the ways that activists, in a secular vein, have attempted to address this moral and political context: for further analysis of the role of religion in Nicaraguan politics and society, see Dodson 1990; Lancaster 1988; Williams 1989.

15. Feature articles in *Salud y Sexualidad* have covered a wide range of sexual topics, including "Sexo joven: Entre presiones, machistas y homosexualismo" (Youth sex: Between the pressures of machismo and homosexuality), "Fantasía sexual: Cual es la tuya" (Sexual fantasy: What's yours?), "Descubrí que mi esposo es gay" (I discovered that my husband is gay), and "Juego lésbico, el nuevo fenómeno adolescente" (Lesbian games, the new adolescent phenomenon).

16. While I have schematized a particular trajectory here, one could safely say that Nicaraguans have been engaged with social theories of various kinds since the advent of the managerial and extractive mandates of colonialism. For an extended discussion of conservative ("right-wing") Nicaraguan women's engagements with social theory before the revolutionary period, see González-Rivera 2011.

17. The form of human rights that has predominated in Nicaraguan politics reflects many of the principles and language of the Universal Declaration of Human Rights. However, similar sentiments can be found in the texts and works of Father Antonio Valdivieso, an important historical figure in Nicaragua, who was renowned for his protests against the mistreatment and bondage of indigenous peoples while he served as bishop beginning in 1544 (Bancroft 1886: 179–83).

18. Grounded in the values of the Enlightenment and the French Revolution, human rights have inherited liberal notions of autonomy and the individual as the preeminent rights-bearing subject. Anthropologists and others have been concerned with how the putatively universal quality of human rights may be used to trump cultural particularities. At the same time, many anthropologists have questioned the misuse (or abuse) of one of the discipline's signature concepts, cultural relativism, when it is applied in defense of inhumane practices. For discussions of anthropology and human rights, see, e.g., Ahmed An-Na'im 1992; Balfour and Cadava 2004; Bunch 1990; Claude and Weston 1992; Englund 2006; Goodale 2006a, 2006b; Goodale and Merry 2007; Lazarus-Black and Merry 2003; Merry 2006a, 2006b; Peters and Wolper 1995; Riles 2000. Studies that document the intersection of sexuality and human rights are in Brown 1999; Edelman 2001; Howe 2009; Teunis and Herdt 2007; Wright 2000.

19. María Josefina Saldaña-Portillo (2003) similarly argues that Sandinista revolutionary discourses and political practices (along with other Marxian and anti-

imperialist projects) have depended on developmentalist narratives of progress, discipline, maturity, and consciousness.

20. I have limited the abbreviation here to LGBTQ (lesbian, gay, bisexual, transgender, and queer) with the understanding that other categories of selfhood might be "enumerated" (Boellstorff 2007) or omitted—including Q (for "questioning"), I (intersex), T (transvestite or travesti), A (asexual) and A (ally).

21. In much of the scholarship, sexual rights movements in Latin America have not received the same degree of attention given to other movements (Brown 1999), though this is being remediated as more research and publications become available. Social-science studies of new social movements have provided important insights into ethnic, gender, class-based, and labor movements, particularly in the wake of Latin America's transition from authoritarian regimes to a more democratic era: see, e.g., Alvarez et al. 1998; Edelman 1999, 2001; Field 1998, 1999; Fox and Starn 1997; Hale 2006b; Lamphere, Ragoné, and Zavella 1997; Nelson 1999; Paley 2001; Smith 2000; Starn 1999; Stephen 1997; Warren 1997.

22. For discussions of the distinctions between the "new" and "old" variants of social movements, particularly the intersections of political goals and cultural aspirations, see Alvarez et al. 1998; Eder 1985; Laclau and Mouffe 1985; McCarthy and Zald 1977; Melucci 1989; Offe 1985; Rabasa 1997; Ribiero 1998; Tarrow 1994; Touraine 1981. Critiques of social movements as linear and developmental are in Edelman 2001; Gamson 1991; Gledhill 1994.

23. It is worth noting that President Barack Obama came out in support of same-sex marriage in a speech in May 2012. According to a Gallup poll from 2011, for the first time ever, the majority of Americans showed support for marriage equality and same-sex marriage rights.

24. Of course, the fact that there are no documented hate crimes against sexual minorities may be because of under-reporting to authorities. In the concluding chapter of the book, I return to the question of violence against those who are, or are believed to be, homosexual. I describe violence against a "very effeminate" Nicaraguan man and provide more recent statistics gathered on the issue of violence against lesbians and gay men in contemporary Nicaragua.

25. While some Nicaraguans with whom I spoke did say that they had been targets of physical harassment by some of their peers, particularly in school or by family members, they were also clear that most of the discrimination they faced was in the form of mockery and taunting and employment discrimination. Roger Lancaster (1992: 247) notes that during his fieldwork in Nicaragua, his informants "could not imagine a Nicaraguan equivalent of gay-bashing" and his discussion demonstrates how the relative lack of hate crimes against sexual minorities in Nicaragua follows the logic of a gendered system that distributes power and privilege in particular ways (Lancaster 1992: 235–78). He underscores that cochones have not provoked violent sentiments precisely because they are a pitiable figure and, not incidentally, a subject with whom "masculine" men may have sex without risking damage to their own heterosexual status.

26. Nicaragua's antisodomy law can be described as a legal threat rather than aggressively prosecutorial. Article 204 was used to imprison people who were seen to

have violated the law, as in the highly publicized case of Aura Rosa Pavón Pavón, who was incarcerated for "sodomy" because of her relationship with her girlfriend (see Howe 2009). However, the antisodomy law has not been a policing priority. For the Nicaraguan government actively to have persecuted *lesbianas* and *gays* would have been a risky political move that very likely would have provoked international condemnation, as happened when the law went into effect. The antisodomy law functioned primarily as a warning and intimidation tactic against the "promotion" of same-sex sexuality. But its existence, as every sexual rights advocate would agree, has been an affront to equality.

27. The notion that "in the North sexual rights are more developed" might be attributed to a hegemonic presumption (or mythos) about the North and sexual rights struggles. However, Nicaraguan activists also are not naïve in their estimation of sexual politics in the United States and Europe. In fact, they are quite astute about the state of sexual rights in the United States, including recent developments such as same-sex marriage legislation and other liberal projects to establish particular forms of equality. Since the issue of Northern hegemony, particularly in the register of rights, is so salient in Nicaragua, I return to these questions in different ways throughout this book.

28. For discussions of how sexuality and sexual identity have been variously emplaced, appropriated, and negotiated, see Babb 2003, 2009; Bell and Binnie 2000; Blasius 2001; Duggan 2000; Faiman-Silva 2004; Gopinath 2005; Howe 2007; Lancaster 2003; Leap and Boellstorff 2003; Manalansan 2003; Manalansan and Cruz-Malave 2002; Phelan 1997; Phelan and Blasius 1997; Plummer 2003; Provencher 2007; Puar 2005, 2007; Rubin 1984, 2002, Seidman 2002; Stychin 2001; Weismantel 2001; Weston 1991; Wilson 2004.

29. Discussions of the problematic implementation of universal (sexual) categories are in Adam et al. 1999; Boellstorff 2003a, 2003b; Brennan 2004; Cantú 2009; Carrier 1995; Carrillo 2001; Chernoff 2003; Constable 2003; Dave 2012; Gopinath 1998, 2005; Herdt and Howe 2007; Howe 2002; Howe and Rigi 2009; Kulick 1998; Lancaster 1997b; Lewin 2009; Luibheid and Cantú 2005; Manalansan 2003; Manalansan and Cruz-Malave 2002; Martin 2000; Massad 2002; Newton 2000; Padilla 2007; Parker 1997, 1999; Patel 2004; Patton 2000; Phelan 1997; Povinelli 2006; Povinelli and Chauncey 1999; Puar 2007; Quiroga 2000; Reddy 2005; Rofel 2007; Sánchez-Eppler and Patton 2000; Sang 2003; Sinnott 2004; Wekker 2006.

30. As Matthew Gutmann (1996: 227) and others have observed, designating someone "macho" (or *machista*) is problematic partly because of racist stereotypes in the United States; these behaviors are too easily interpreted as antiquated performances of masculinity and sexist aggression by (all) "Latin men." In his discussion of machismo in Nicaragua, Roger Lancaster (1992) describes how machismo is a set of behaviors that are both valorized and deplored. It indicates an important category of distinction, separating women from men and men from cochones. In this tripartite gender system, machismo exaggerates the dramatic differences between (putative) femininity and masculinity. In chapter 2, I discuss how, when the question of machismo and "proper" masculine and feminine behaviors arise in lesbian discussion groups, Nicaraguan stereotypes of femininity and masculinity

(and men's and women's social behaviors and expectations) must be understood within changing interpretations of sexual identity and gendered status.

31. Often used to account for same-sex sexual practices between men in Latin America and the Middle East (among other places), the Mediterranean model has drawn on concepts of honor and shame, activity and passivity, and masculine and feminine gender roles. The Mediterranean model has been critiqued because, as with many models, it cannot fully account for the actual diversity of sexual practices and perceptions of those practices in different settings. Further, given that what goes on behind closed doors often remains elusive to the gaze of social science, it is difficult to know how accurate the model is or ever was. For more on the Mediterranean model, see, e.g., Cantú 2009; Carrier 1995; Kulick 1998; Murray 1995; Parker 1999; Prieur 1998.

32. According to several scholars, and among Nicaraguans with whom I have spoken, this configuration of men's same-sex sexual encounters has predominated historically in Nicaragua. While a postcolonial version of the Mediterranean model has prevailed, concepts of sexuality in Nicaragua, as everywhere, are shifting. Beginning in the early 1990s, I had several discussions with men who had engaged in various forms of "active" sexual behavior with cochones. These men, who called themselves "hombres hombres," did not claim that their encounters with cochones enhanced their masculinity or sexual status; instead, they described their sexual encounters with cochones by saying, "Era joven" (I was young) or "Era emborrachado" (I was drunk). These men did not see themselves as "gay," but neither were they shy about discussing the fact that they had engaged in sex, multiple times, with other men. The covers of "I was young" or "I was drunk" does indicate some hedging about their agency in these encounters; this is likely evidence that stigma is becoming attached to the act itself, not only to one's gendered performance or activo versus pasivo role in the encounter.

33. The egalitarian model of homosexuality is often associated with the global North where, in the popular imagination, both male (or female) partners in a same-sex relationship would be stigmatized as gay or lesbian. As with the Mediterranean model, the egalitarian model is less than fully adequate. While an egalitarian model may predominate in any given social context, this does not result in a strict adherence to its ethos. In the United States, for instance, "Down Low" behavior, when men engage with clandestine sex with other men, has been the subject of much controversy and speculation because many of the men on the Down Low have refused the designation "bisexual" or "homosexual."

34. John Gagnon's "sexual scripts" are similar to the work of Erving Goffman (1959) on the performance of everyday life, where, like actors on a stage, social roles and behaviors are implicitly understood by those undertaking them. Gagnon's formulation follows a psychological developmental framework suggesting that sexual interactions are socially organized through various stages of scripting (according to age and cultural location) wherein (sexual) actors apprehend their "lines" and "roles" as if they were performers on stage.

35. Many times I have been told, "Here in Nicaragua, every barrio has its cochón," a comment that has been made with no (perceptible) guile. Cochones are teased,

and their "tan afeminado" (so effeminate) presentation is often parodied. But they have also been recognized and spoken about in positive terms for their hairdressing talent or their skill as vendors in local open air markets. However, neutral or positive interpretations of cochones seem to be on the decline (as I address in the final chapter).

36. The terms "cochona" and "marimacha" are commonly used to designate dykes in Nicaraguan popular parlance in reference to the *macha* or *masculina* partner in a women's same-sex relationship. "Marimacha," a term used in other Latin American settings, though less so in Nicaragua, refers to a tomboy or a masculine dyke. I have also heard the term "tortillera"—again familiar in other parts of Latin America—used to designate homosexual women in Nicaragua. *Tortillera* literally means a female tortilla maker. But it also, metaphorically, calls attention to various beliefs about women's same-sex sexuality, including questions about how two women actually "do it." As many Nicaraguans described it, two women, lacking penetrative genitals, could only ever be two flat planes pressed against each other, like two tortillas in the hands of the tortillera. "Tortillera" may further refer to women's genitalia in general as that which is doubled over and in need of "filling."

37. "Hombruna" is a colloquial term to designate mannish or butch qualities. The term can be used in a derogatory fashion, suggesting that this form of masculine behavior is inappropriate for a woman. But it was also a term I heard within lesbian communities in Managua in a more positive sense, indicating simply that someone was butch in her gendered presentation.

Because of the extraordinary heat and humidity in Managua, it is striking that anyone would choose to wear long-sleeve shirts. However, many women with whom I worked placed emphasis on the semiotic value of their long-sleeve "men's" shirts (Oxford style buttoned shirts made of lightweight material). As I will describe in further detail in the ensuing chapters, *mangas largas* (long-sleeve) shirts are intentionally selected as a way to mark one's female masculinity and engendering a sense of masculinity for one's self and others.

38. It would be incorrect to say that femenina women do not become involved with other femeninas (or that masculinas do not become involved with other masculinas), but this has not been part of the socially understood repertoire. Beliefs about gender—in Nicaragua, as elsewhere—are central to how sexuality is defined and marked. For instance, the Nicaraguan term "cochonera" designates, literally, a woman who "drives," or directs, the cochona (*ella que manda la cochona*). The gender-"appropriate" feminine partner is seen as wielding more power in the relationship partly because she escapes stigma via her (socially normative) gender presentation. This suggests that, as with cochones and hombres hombres, the gender-normative partner is in the "driver's seat" of the relationship. A productive parallel might be made here with discussions of butch and femme in U.S. lesbian and gay communities (Halberstam 1998; Kennedy and Davis 1993; Nestle 1992), for example, as well as the politics of gender performance (Brett et al. 1995; Butler 1990, 1993; Case 2009).

39. "Cochona" has also been a term, however, that seems to have some neutrality. I was struck, for example, when in the politically progressive and "gay-friendly"

Nicaraguan households in which I lived during my field research, several visitors were rather nonchalantly and without any apparent animosity announced in this way: "There is a cochona here to see you." Dora María Tellez, heroine of the Sandinista Revolution and arguably Nicaragua's most famous *guerrillera*, is also often referred to as "la cochona." For some Sandinistas, this designation seemed to have a rather affectionate spin, as when one older woman wondered out loud one day during the 2001 campaign season, "Por qué no podemos tener nuestro cochona como presidenta?" (Why can't we have our dyke for president?).

40. For studies of women's same-sex sexuality in Nicaragua, see Bolt González 1996a, 1996b; Ferguson 1991; Randall 1993; van Gijsel 2003.

41. Studies of Latin American men's homoerotic practices, "gay" identity, and same-sex sexual behavior have been important for understanding some of the contingencies of gender, desire, and identity. Analyses of Latin American women's and feminist activism have also been relatively well studied, although lesbian groups, when they appear as low-profile "tendencies" in gender rights movements, have been less well documented. Studies that focus ethnographic attention on men's same-sex sexuality in Latin America and the Caribbean include Carrier 1995; Carrillo 2001; Kulick 1998; Lancaster 1992, 1997b; Lumsden 1996; Murray 1995; Padilla 2007; Parker 1999; Prieur 1998. For women's activism in Latin America, see Bouvard 2002; González and Kampwirth 2001; Jacquette 1989; Kampwirth 2004b, 2006, 2010; Randall 1994; Stephen 1997. On lesbians and women's same-sex sexualities in the global North, see Esterberg 1997; Faiman-Silva 2004; Gray 2009; Hennessy 2000; Kennedy and Davis 1993; Lang 1998; Lewin 1996, 1998; Mogrovejo 1999, 2000; Stein 1997; Sullivan 2004; Weston 1996.

42. For ethnographic studies of women's same-sex sexuality in the global South, see, e.g., Blackwood 2010; Blackwood and Wieringa 1999; Dave 2012; Kantsa 2002; Martin 2010; Sang 2003; Sinnott 2004; Wekker 2006; Wieringa et al. 2007; Wilson 2004.

43. Analyses of lesbian rights and activism among self-identified lesbian Nicaraguan women are in Chuchryk 1991; Collinson 1990; Ferguson 1991; Howe 2009; Montenegro 2000; Randall 1993, 1994; Thayer 1997.

One: A History of Sexuality

1. For further accounts of how women were incorporated into the Sandinista Revolutionary project and became, as Les W. Field (1999: 132) has put it, "articulatory" intellectuals, see, e.g., Chavez Metoyer 1997; Chinchilla 1990, 1994; Collinson 1990; Fernández Poncela 2001; Field 1999; Kampwirth 1996a; Molyneux 1985a, 1985b.

2. For an excellent account of women's political participation and role in Nicaraguan politics and social life before the Sandinista Revolution, see González-Rivera 2011.

3. This expression is also familiar in Mexico, where it may have its origins.

4. At this juncture, the political power grabs between the conservatives and the liberals had effectively balkanized the country. "Conservatives" and "liberals" were associated with particular geographic regions, as well as with distinct economic

orientations. Conservatives were based in the city of Granada, linked to the Catholic church, and inclined toward *latifundia-* or *hacienda*-based production systems (self-sufficient large estates held by wealthy landowners employing large numbers of often underpaid laborers) as an economic model. Liberals, based in León, were committed to professionalizing, "modernizing," and liberalizing the Nicaraguan economy.

5. Anastasio Somoza García, the father, served as president from 1937 to 1947 and from 1950 to 1956. Luis Somoza Debayle, his eldest son, ruled from 1956 to 1963 (although he effectively maintained political control over the country until his death in 1967). Anastasio Somoza Debayle, Somoza García's second son, was in office from 1967 to 1972 and from 1974 to 1979.

6. The most famous of the putative prostitutes within Somocismo was Nicolasa Sevilla, who worked closely with the Somozas and was the founder and leader of the feared Somocista Popular Front. Although many questions remain about Sevilla's sexual life—including whether she was in fact ever engaged with prostitution or was simply a serial monogamist connected to politically powerful men—is in some ways beside the point. What remains of Sevilla's legacy is her political and sexual reputation. To this day, to call someone a "Nicolasa" is to accuse them of fomenting working-class political violence and, in a more subtle fashion, a way to gesture to sexual deviance for the sake of political power: see González-Rivera 2011: 113–34; Sequeira 1995.

7. The rapes perpetrated in El Cua are also critically memorialized in at least one well-known poem by Ernesto Cardenal, a prominent anti-Somoza priest.

8. For a discussion of how birds often operate as a metaphor for homosexuality, see La Fountain-Stokes 2007.

9. Ricardo Sánchez Ramírez, "Puntos de referencia en la vieja Managua," *La Prensa* (Managua), 25 July 2005, http://archivo.laprensa.com.ni/archivo/2005/julio/25/nacionales/nacionales-20050725-01.html (accessed 17 January 2013).

10. Carmen Aguirre was a biological woman who dressed primarily in men's clothes and preferred to go publicly by the name Carmelo. As is clear in her widow's recounting of their relationship, Carmelo replicated macho behavior in many ways, including womanizing, fighting, and drinking. Although Carmelo at times identified in a masculine register, her partner uses the feminine pronoun to describe her in her narrative. Indeed, her widow refers to her as "Carmen." Here, I will switch between the gendered pronouns "he" and "she."

11. The FSLN was founded in July 1961 by Carlos Fonseca, Tomas Bórge, and Silvio Mayorga. In the ensuing months, other young would-be revolutionaries became involved, many of whom were students disenchanted with Nicaragua's more traditional socialist left. Fonseca was considered the primary architect of Sandinismo, as he re-crafted Sandino's original discourse for a new generation of revolutionaries (Palmer 1988). The FSLN faced internal debates about military strategies and ideological priorities before it successfully launched the cross-class and rural–urban coalition necessary to overthrow the Somoza dictatorship. A number of books examine the evolution of Sandinismo over time from analytical and first-

person perspectives: see Field 1999; Hoyt 1997; Lancaster 1988; Pastor 2002; Randall 1981; Rossett and Vandermeer 1986; Rushdie 1987; Spalding 1987; Vilas 1989; Walker 2003; Zimmerman 2000.

12. At this time, Nicaragua also became a much written about place. The U.S.-backed counterinsurgency war against Nicaragua throughout the 1980s inspired leftist activism, rightist reactions, and a raft of journalistic and scholarly analyses in the global North. Travelers' tales and personal accounts of revolution (Bretlinger 1995; Cabezas 1985; Cortazar 1979; Rich 1986; Rushdie 1987) and literary works (Belli 1995; Cortazar 1990; De la Campa 1999) were produced in and about Nicaragua. Political scientific analyses (Hoyt 1997; Kampwirth 1996; Prevost and Vanden 1997; Smith 1993; Spalding 1987, 1994, 1997; Stahler-Sholk 1995; Vilas 1989; Walker 1991, 1997, 2000, 2003), historical readings (González 2001; Gould 1990, 1998; Zimmerman 2000), and anthropological assessments (Babb 2001; Bourgois 1981; Field 1999; Hale 1994; Higgins and Coen 1992; Lancaster 1988, 1992) all added to the extensive literature on Nicaragua's revolutionary experience.

13. In addition to the internal divisions familiar in many countries, including those of class, rural–urban distinctions, and political party affiliations, Nicaragua is starkly divided between its western (Pacifico) and eastern (Costa Atlantica) regions. Bisected by what many deem "impenetrable rainforest" (the second largest in the Americas), the Pacifico and Costa Atlantica regions vary greatly in terms of colonial history, language, ethnic identities, and religious affiliations. Arguably, the Costa Atlantica, a former British colony with creole, African-descended, and indigenous populations and influenced by the Moravian church, has more in common with the Caribbean region than with Nicaragua's Pacifico region (Dozier 1985; Montenegro 1985). The Pacifico, with its Spanish colonial history and language, is generally understood as an ethnically *mestizo* region, and the vast majority of the population claim Catholicism as their religious affiliation. Indigenous people continue to live in the Pacifico. However, as Jeffrey Gould (1998) has documented, a national narrative of cultural homogeneity and *mestizaje* has prevailed historically there, partly because of the systematic erasure of indigenous identity since the nineteenth century.

14. The FSLN's difficulty with the "Indian question" and its inability to adequately address the concerns of Costa Atlantica minorities and the indigenous populations in the Pacifico (see, e.g., Field 1999; Gould 1998) prefigures the political and ideological tensions the party faced with regard to women and sexual minorities. On the Atlantic coast, indigenous people made alliances with the U.S.-based American Indian Movement in an early example of transnational political networking between new social movements. At the same time, the Reagan regime seized a political opportunity to accuse the Sandinistas of human rights violations. The FSLN's displacement of indigenous people in the Costa Atlantica region was used as a means of justifying the continuation of Contra military actions (Americas Watch Committee 1985) under the auspices of protecting the human rights of native peoples.

15. While the preservation of human rights in Sandinista Nicaragua was certainly not perfect, it was better than in Guatemala and El Salvador, where the United

States was deeply involved in political and military matters. Sandinista Nicaragua also boasts a better human rights record than Cuba during the same era (Walker 2000).

16. According to Helen Collinson (1990: 154) and Margaret Randall (1981: 216–17), women made up 30 percent of Sandinista combatants in the late 1970s. Others estimate that women made up only 6 percent of combatants (Vilas 1986: 108) and were represented more within support functions such as providing safe houses, delivering messages and arms, and providing clandestine medical care and meals.

17. The Sandinista era also hosted a cultural renaissance, particularly among women, born of Nicaragua's long-standing poetic tradition. Literature and poetry by Nicaraguan women, drawing from their revolutionary experiences and their gendered perspectives, gained global popularity in the 1980s, and some female Nicaraguan authors continue to find a global readership: see, e.g., Belli 2004, 2007; Zamora 1992.

18. Daniel Ortega, then the president, demonstrated a more cautious approach to the question of sexual rights at the Women and Law Conference in Managua in 1988. Responding to a question about whether Nicaragua had a policy of discriminating against homosexuals or denying them human rights, Ortega simply answered, "No."

19. Women were sometimes re-"feminized" as they were channeled into certain kinds of reproductive labor in accord with what many Nicaraguans would consider traditional gender roles. Women's sewing and food-processing cooperatives flourished across the country with support from the FSLN. While these projects focused on traditional women's work, the cooperatives also fostered solidarity and networking among women, and they served to politicize and bring together women from diverse class backgrounds. The FSLN opened centers across the country for the revolution's "heroes and martyrs," and groups for the mothers of heroes and martyrs held a prominent place in the minds of many Nicaraguans (Bayard de Volo 2001).

20. According to the FSLN directive on the status of women, "We reject tendencies that promote the emancipation of women as the outcome of a struggle against men, or as an activity exclusively of women, for this type of position is divisive and distracts the people from their fundamental tasks. It is the work of the FSLN and all revolutionaries, of all the advanced sectors of society, men and women together, to lead the ideological, political and socioeconomic battles that will result in the elimination of all forms of oppression and discrimination in Nicaragua, including those which women endure" (quoted in Field 1999: 127).

21. While traces of the terms "gay" and "lesbian" can be found in documents and conversations from the 1980s—as with the controversy in AMNLAE and in the Nicaraguan Gay Movement—for many, if not most, Nicaraguans at this time, these terms were largely associated with North Americans and Europeans. The autochthonous categories cochona and cochón continued to be used in common parlance.

22. An editorial published in 1987 in *El Nuevo Diario*, one of the national dailies, illustrates this anxiety. The author writes, "You claim to be intelligent, conscious and

revolutionary. When will you stop imitating this lesbian song of European women and let the voice of Nicaraguan women be heard?": Carlos Ivan Torres Meza, *El Nuevo Diario*, 15 January 1987.

23. From a public health point of view, CEP-SIDA was extremely forward thinking in its preventative impulse. There were no known cases of AIDS in Nicaragua when CEP-SIDA began, but by January 1989, three deaths from AIDS and sixteen cases of HIV had been reported. If the Nicaraguan state was less than exemplary in allowing political dissent of sexual minorities within its ranks, Nicaraguan officials' response to the threat of AIDS stands in stark contrast to the silence surrounding the epidemic in the United States under the Reagan administration in the 1980s.

24. The organization Shomos (We Are Homos), which is described in more detail in chapter 3, originated at this time and participated in CEP-SIDA's outreach campaigns.

25. Although the Sandinistas had attempted to rid the streets of prostitution, sex work by both men and women (unsurprisingly) continued during the Sandinista era.

26. Cuba purged homosexuals in the mid-1960s on the grounds that their sexuality was a symptom of bourgeois decadence. Further, early AIDS policy in Cuba mandated that those infected with HIV be quarantined. Policies of homosexual exclusion and persecution in revolutionary Cuba have been critiqued by the international community, often by North American lesbian and gay activists (Rich and Arguelles 1984; Lumsden 1996).

27. The term "revuelta," derived from the verb *revolver* (to stir, toss, or mix), is defined as a civil uprising or social revolt. Several of the people with whom I worked described the Sandinista Revolution as a revuelta in which society was turned upside down in a time of social turbulence and mixed up in relation to the social order that had prevailed.

    Nicaragua never saw a blossoming of gay ghettos in urban neighborhoods. The sort of lesbian and gay enclave communities that appeared in San José, Costa Rica, during the 1980s and in the United States in the 1950s, for example, had no analogue in Nicaragua (Chauncey 1995; D'Emilio 1993; D'Emilio and Freedman 1997; Kennedy and Davis 1993). For those marked as cochón or cochona, especially those who transgressed gender norms, securing steady employment was very difficult. This financial instability caused many same-sex-attracted Nicaraguans to be less likely to move away from their families of origin. From a less economically deterministic standpoint, some Nicaraguan lesbians and gay men stayed in their natal homes because of strong familial obligations. The Sandinista Revolution, for some, did offer an opportunity for more personal autonomy and distance from intolerant families as young people were able to leave natal families and participate in the revolutionary endeavor (Babb 2003).

28. Consisting of fourteen parties of disparate political orientation, Chamorro's Unified National Opposition (UNO) Party cannot be described as anything other than a concerted effort to disassemble Sandinista rule with the help of powerful allies.

29. As Kampwirth (1996) has described, Chamorro's campaign relied on antifeminist rhetoric and a maternalist discourse. During her term as president, Chamorro was often clad in white, evoking both the Virgin Mary and a brand of feminine purity.

Chamorro's political platform centered on the role she would play as a reconciling mother, loyal wife, and widow of the well-known Nicaraguan martyr Pedro Joaquin Chamorro. With her political support from the United States, Chamorro promised to end the war and normalize relations with the United States. Her regime also increased neoliberal economic reforms and external-debt-management schemes. Chamorro's objective to "mother" the nation was apparent in her promise to end the conflicts between Nicaragua's two most prominent political parties, the Liberal Party and the Sandinistas. While reconciliation and an end to the Contra war were certainly a high priority for most, if not all, Nicaraguans voting that year, Chamorro's attempts to be a peacemaker can also be understood as an explicitly antifeminist stance, as her rhetoric relied on traditional perceptions of women as naturally inclined to domestic pacification. Her electoral victory, according to Roger Lancaster (1992: 293), was both a feminist triumph (because most of the electorate voted for a woman) and a "perversion of feminism" (because her campaign was developed around un-feminist rhetoric and values).

30. The complete text of the code is: "Comete delito de sodomía el que induzca, promueva, propagandice o practique en forma escandalosa el concúbito entre personas del mismo sexo. Sufrirá la pena de uno a tres años de prisión. Cuando uno de los que lo practican, aun en privado tuviere sobre el otro poder disciplinario o de mando, como ascendiente, guardador, maestro, jefe, guardian, o en cualquier otro concepto que implique influencia de autoridad o de dirección moral, se le aplicará la pena de la seducción ilegítima, como unico responsable."

31. For a description of the National Assembly's voting process and the issues raised, see the interview with Doris Tijerino in Randall 1994: 226–27.

32. Hazel Fonseca, quoted in "Nicaragua: Forum on Women's Issues," Agence-France Presse, 1998, available online at http://ladb.unm.edu/cgibin/SFgate (accessed 12 October 1998).

33. Deborah Tyroler, "Nicaragua: Controversial Reforms to Penal Code Ratified by President," 28 August 1992, NotiCen, available online at http://ladb.unm.edu /noticen/1992/08/28-059747 (accessed 18 January 2013).

34. The founding of the Sandinista Renovation Movement in 1995 marked a significant rupture for the Sandinista party because several founding members, including Dora María Téllez and Sergio Ramírez, Luis Carrión, and Mirna Cunningham, chose to abandon the political party that they had been so instrumental in building and maintaining. The decision to break away from the Sandinista party was initiated by Ramírez following the vote by the Sandinista National Assembly to remove the well-respected editor of the pro-Sandinista daily *Barricada*. Dissatisfaction had been growing, particularly about the continued dominance of Daniel Ortega and the party's failure to address ethical issues and remedy political mechanisms that were vulnerable to corruption and manipulation.

35. Transparency International, "Corruption Perception Index, 2001," available online at www.transparency.org (accessed 28 March 2012).

36. Ministerio de Educación y Deporte, Managua, n.d.

37. Victoria González-Rivera (2011: 170) points out that, although the original accusations and scandals surrounding Narváez may have been conditioned partly by

Monicagate (as Kipnis notes), the more salient national history to invoke here is the fact that the Sandinistas could be said to have invented the so-called sexual-abuse narrative in Nicaragua in response to the sexual chaos and rape associated with Somocismo. This narrative, as González-Rivera puts it, would "boomerang decades later against [the Sandinista] party leader, albeit in a reconstituted feminist form."

38. "A Test of Ethics for a Society in Crisis," *Envio*, March 1998, 6.

39. *La Prensa*, 14 July 2001, 4.

40. Because of a five-year statute of limitations for rape and sexual abuse, and Ortega's immunity from prosecution as a member of the National Assembly (a right granted to all former presidents in Nicaragua; see note 41), Narváez took her complaint to the Inter American Human Rights Commission (IACHR) in 2001. After reviewing the file and hearing testimony from both Narváez and a representative of the Nicaraguan state, the IACHR recommended a "friendly settlement" between the Nicaraguan government and Narváez. For many observers, the commission's recommendation and the Nicaraguan government's agreeing to it was tacit acceptance of the fact that Narváez's allegations were indeed true: "Caso 12,230: Zoilamérica Narváez contra el Estado de Nicaragua," *Envio*, no. 240, March 2002, available online at http://www.envio.org.ni/articulo/1130 (accessed 14 September 2011). However, no amicable agreement was ever reached, and the IACHR continued to receive communications and materials. In 2009, Narváez communicated to the commission that she intended to end the lawsuit amicably and to officially close the file. She requested confidentiality in regard to her reasons for closing the file and withdrawing the lawsuit, which the IACHR did, officially, in November 2009: Organization of American States, Inter-American Commission on Human Rights, "Decision to Archive Zoilamérica Narváez Murillo, Nicaragua, November 12, 2009," report no. 131/09, case 12.230, available online at http://www.cidh.oas.org/annualrep/2009eng/Nicaragua12230eng.htm (accessed 13 December 2011).

41. The pacto devised between Alemán and Ortega and certified by the National Assembly in 1999 is a startling collection of political machinations, amendments to the Nicaraguan constitution, and changes to electoral law. The formation of a political agreement of this scale and profundity was possible only, as Katherine Hoyt (2004) argues, because of the relatively equal vulnerability and caudillo power of each of these party leaders. The pact has many dimensions, but a central motivation for Ortega (and the Sandinistas) to enter into the pact with his political enemy, Alemán, was that it would preserve Ortega's parliamentary immunity and prevent him from standing trial in Narváez's sexual abuse case. Among other things, the pact gave lifetime seats in the National Assembly to outgoing presidents and vice-presidents (hence, parliamentary immunity); it reduced the proportion of votes needed to win the presidency from 45 percent to 40 percent (and to just 35 percent of the popular vote if the second candidate's total percentage of votes was 5 points (or more) fewer than the leading candidate's); and more severely restricted the ability of electoral alliances and competing parties to gain a place on the ballot. Overall, the pacto instituted dramatic changes in Nicaraguan

politics and electoral law and for many Nicaraguans was a throwback to Somocismo in its nearly authoritarian exercise to ensure a two-party political system
and provide legal immunity for powerful political leaders.

42. Amnesty International further condemned the potential firing of lesbian and gay
government officials, noting that such high-level homophobia gave official sanction
to acts of violence committed against LGBT people: see "The Americas: Nicaragua," *Amnesty International Report 2007*, available online at http://archive.amnesty
.org/report2007/eng/Regions/Americas/Nicaragua/default.htm (accessed 14 September 2011).

43. Under Ortega, Nicaragua also joined the Bolivarian Alliance for the Peoples of
Our America, a fair trade alliance intended as an antidote to global capitalism,
neoliberalism, and other international trade agreements (such as the Central
America Free Trade Agreement and the North American Free Trade Agreement).

44. World Health Organization, "Country Cooperation Strategy at a Glance, Nicaragua," 2006, available online at http://www.who.int/countryfocus/cooperation
_strategy/ccsbrief_nic_en.pdf (accessed 4 May 2012).

45. Rosario Murillo, "FSLN con Dios y contra el aborto," 21 August 2006, available
online at http://www.izquierda.info/modules.php?name=News&file=article&sid
=1498 (accessed 6 May 2012).

46. Kampwirth (2010: 174) also notes that although the feminist movement in Nicaragua was larger than the antifeminist movement that had enjoyed the support of
sympathetic governments over the previous fifteen years, the feminist movement
was somewhat divided in 2006, a fact that may have limited its collective political
power at a crucial moment.

47. See also Tania Sirias and Edgar Barbarena, "Más voces internacionales en defensa
del aborto terapéutico, *El Nuevo Diario*, 18 November 2006, available online at
http://www.elnuevodiario.com.ni (accessed 18 December 2006).

48. According to the Center for Reproductive Rights, among countries for which
legislative information is available, Nicaragua is one of only four in the world
that prohibit all forms of abortion for any reason and for which the "availability
of defense of necessity [is] highly unlikely": Center for Reproductive Rights,
"The World's Abortion Laws Map," September 2011, available online at http://
worldabortionlaws.com/map (accessed 7 May 2012).

In other words, there is a scant possibility that a woman could legally justify
an abortion under any conditions according to the current legislation. While the
law applies to all women in Nicaragua, this kind of legislation, no matter where it
is instituted, tends to affect poor women more dramatically than affluent women,
as poor women are less likely to have access to regular birth control and, unlike
some middle-class and upper-middle-class women, do not have the ability to leave
the country to have the procedure.

49. Irma Franco, Róger Olivas, and Melvin Martinez, "Otra embarazada bajo grave
riesgo." *El Nuevo Diario*, 9 November 2006, available online at http://www.elnuevo
diario.com.ni (accessed 22 December 2006).

50. Kampwirth (2011: 37, n. 22) notes that while the issue of therapeutic abortion

received nearly constant attention in the press and popular media from August–November 2006, Article 204 and its potential to be overturned was hardly mentioned in the Nicaraguan public sphere.

Two: Intimate Pedagogies

1. Given the reach of Nicaragua's antisodomy law, the fact that lesbian and homosexual men's discussion groups have existed at all is rather remarkable. However, persecuting relatively small grassroots groups (and the amount of potential national and international negative publicity this would generate), as well as aggravating the leadership of Nicaraguan NGOs (many of whom have foreign allies and funding), are likely reasons the state has not interfered with the discussion groups. Larger threats to discussion groups have been their fiscal instability and the attrition of motivated leaders. Groups supported by NGOs have been more stable because they have access to more consistent sources of funding and locations in which to meet. Groups that I describe here as "grassroots"—those without institutional support—have often depended on charismatic, motivated leaders (and usually someone's living room for meeting space). Over the course of three years, I participated in five different lesbian discussion groups, two of which were supported by NGOs and three that were self-organizing.

2. Strictly defined, the term "bien educado/a" is the quality of being polite, well-mannered, and courteous. These manners are also indicative, in many cases, of one's socioeconomic status and the association between being bien educáda and middle (or upper middle) class is significant. In the discussion that follows, I will elaborate on how this particular "distinction," as Bourdieu might put it, surfaces in discussions of sexual rights, self-esteem, and identity ascription.

3. For a discussion of Managua's influence and role in Nicaragua more broadly see, e.g., Babb 1999.

4. *Empoderamiento de mujeres Lesbianas* [Empowerment of lesbian women] (Managua: Fundación Xochiquetzal, n.d.), 4–5.

5. "Elisabet" was the youngest of the three facilitators and worked for the foundation as a public relations coordinator. "Sonia" was an anthropology student from the Netherlands.

6. Some participants did have pink-collar professions, often as secretaries or receptionists, but the great majority were unemployed, partially employed, or working in the informal economy.

7. Some Nicaraguans, including some of the participants in the group, used mobile phones at the time. However, the technology was not ubiquitous, as it is now, in Nicaragua. In any case, facilitators and staff of the organization were cautious and conscientious about the information they disclosed in phone messages, whether on cell phones or land lines.

8. Nancy Fraser has described the importance of "subaltern counterpublics," including consciousness-raising groups, as fundamental to the constitution of oppositional identities, particularly those that challenge racial, class, and gender hierarchies. Subaltern counterpublics also serve as a venue to elaborate novel ways of imagining and enacting social justice.

9. For a critical theory of recognition, see Fraser 1995.

10. Although Brandon Teena was biologically female, I follow his desired gender identity and refer to him as "him" rather than "her." I also refer to Brandon Teena as "Brandon" rather than following the convention of using a surname, again to better preserve his gender identity.

11. The film had been shown in some Nicaraguan theaters the year before, with little public fanfare. At a screening I attended in Granada in 2000, a large group of young people (in apparently heterosexual pairs) stood in unison and marched from the theater as the scene in which Brandon Teena and his girlfriend first kiss came onto the screen. It was very apparent that the eight people who left—and who did not return—did so to protest what they saw as inappropriate homoerotic visibility.

12. None of the women in the group used any of "Cony's" drawings depicting women, often together in romantic and erotic scenes. However, Cony's drawings were the most authentically Nicaraguan, as well as the most contemporary images, among those from which we could choose. The notable absence of Cony's work could have been a teachable moment to elaborate on contemporary lesbian (and gay) activism, as well as the quotidian contingencies of living one's same-sex sexual desire in Nicaragua.

13. Matagalpa is Nicaragua's fifth-largest city, with a population of approximately 110,000 in the city proper. Because of the vast rural area surrounding the city and the agricultural work that sustains the region, Matagalpa is seen as a more rural locale than Managua and its environs.

14. Chinandega is on Nicaragua's northern border with Honduras. Partly because it is a hub of transnational traffic and trade, the city has faced higher rates of HIV transmission (particularly among sex workers) than other parts of the country.

15. Because she was a schoolteacher, Berta's gender presentation was keenly calibrated to Nicaraguan norms of femininity. This was no accident, Berta explained, "because it is very hard to get work in the public sector if you do not look like a woman."

16. According to Freire, this "authentic" approach to education allows people to become more fully human by uncovering the ways in which they are incomplete or barred from full human participation (by virtue of being a member of an oppressed group). Freire coined the term "conscientization" to indicate an educational process in which both society and individuals are encouraged to consciously question and evaluate the inequalities, as well as the opportunities, within their social world.

    Popular education was a key strategy of the revolutionary regime as a way to raise political consciousness among the disenfranchised populace and promote the ethos of Sandinismo (Prevost and Vanden 1997; Walker and Armony 2000).

17. Povinelli (2007: 570) defines autological discourse as "discourses, practices, and fantasies of self-making, self-sovereignty, and the value of individual freedom," which she juxtaposes against "genealogical" forms that comprise the "discourses, practices, and fantasies of inheritances of various sorts as constraints on the self-actualizing subject."

Three: Pride and Prejudice

1. The party I am describing was held in 2001. It was hosted at a local restaurant by a man whom one attendee described as "sympathetic to homosexuals and lesbians." This fiesta was one of three SFFP closing parties I attended between 1999 and 2001.

2. In addition to standard political definitions of solidarity, I agree with Deborah Gould that solidarity must also be understood as an affective condition and set of practices. As Gould (2009: 328) puts it, the affective dimension of solidarity is an "inclination toward and perhaps identification with" a group of people, and activist practices of solidarity are rendered through "mutual assistance and support."

3. Several ethnographic and theoretical pursuits have emphasized the role of intellectuals in crafting public knowledge, culture, and schemata of identity (Boyer and Lomnitz 2005; Herzfeld 1997).

4. The name of the magazine appears to be bilingual, using the Spanish term "fuera del" (outside of) and the English term "closet." While this might be an example of the global diffusion of the concept of the closet in LGBT politics and discourse, it may actually be less hegemonic than it seems, since most Nicaraguans use the English-language term "closet" rather than the Spanish term "armario" for all closets.

5. The Metropolitan Community Church, a transnational Protestant denomination that originated in the United States (Howe 2007; Perry and Swicegood 1990; Warner 1995), has a congregation in Managua.

6. Erick Blandón (2003: 198–99) notes that, following the Sandinista Revolution, many lesbians dissolved heterosexual marriages they had maintained for appearances.

7. Of course, less than a decade earlier, the Nicaraguan state had criminalized same-sex sexuality more virulently than it ever had in the past, suggesting not only that repression was still present but also that recollections that the past was less tolerant, at least from a legal point of view, are not accurate. However, the students seem to be articulating an awareness of a new era in Nicaragua in which sexual rights campaigns have more visibility than they did formerly.

8. Rubén Darío is credited as the father of the Spanish and American *modernismo* literary movement, particularly with his book of poetry *Azul* (Darío 1968 [1888]).

9. This issue of ordering the terms in a particular way (e.g. GLBTQ versus LGBTQ) is reminiscent of similar discussions in the United States.

10. In my conversations with them, advocates of Lesbian and Gay Pride primarily used the term "gay" rather than "homosexual" or "cochón." Use of the term "*gay*" suggests a further affinity between the Nicaraguan form of pride and that seen in other countries.

11. Sexuality Free from Prejudice shares the vision of broad social change indicative of liberationist approaches. However, it is dissimilar to the classic formulations of gay liberation because SFFP does not make the claim that "everyone is a little bit gay" or that there is a continuum of homoerotic desire that would emerge, were it not for oppressive prohibitions against it. Rather, SFFP imagines a society "free

from prejudice," indexing a tolerance for difference in a multiculturalist vein instead of drawing attention to the presence or absence of homoerotic desire (see Altman 1993 [1971]; Blasius and Phelan 1997; Hocquenghem 1993 [1978]; Lancaster 2003).

12. See, e.g., Butler 1990; Johnson and Henderson 2005; Muñoz 1999; Rubin 1984; Sedgwick 1990; Seidman 1996; Vaid 1995; Warner 1993.

13. Clearly, normative values regarding status and socioeconomic class are being evoked and performed in these events. It is in fact very rare for average Nicaraguans to wear the kind of flamboyant and almost fantastical clothing that is seen in the travesti shows. As in other settings (e.g., the drag balls made famous in the film *Paris Is Burning*), the ability to mimetically perform these class distinctions and corporeal performance are important elements of the overall effect of each contestant's presentation. In this sense, the travesti concursos indicate two sorts of transgressive aspirations: toward femininity and toward the embodiment of global glamour and upper-class status.

14. The contestants did not talk about experiences with plastic surgery, silicone injections, or hormones. This contrasts with other Latin American countries, where some biological or transgendered males create a more feminine appearance through these practices (Kulick 1998; Prieur 1998).

15. The travestis I have encountered in Nicaragua prefer to use feminine pronouns, especially when they are dressed in women's clothing. They may use women's names in place of their given names. However, more complex questions remain about how they perceive themselves, as well as how they are perceived by others: as women, men, both, or neither. The answer to this question would require further research and is likely to depend on context. For further discussion on the complexities of transvestics in Nicaragua, see Borland 2006; Lancaster 1997a.

16. Erick Blandón, "El torovenado, lugar para la diferencia en un espacio no letrado," *Istmo*, 2004, available online at http://istmo.denison.edu/no8/articulos/torovenado .html (accessed 7 December 2011).

17. Ibid., 2.

18. For an in-depth discussion of how masculine boyfriends provide gender legitimacy (and femininity) for travestis, see Kulick 1998.

19. For ethnographic accounts of more campy, comedic cabaret and how this coincides with political goals, see Newton 1979, 1993; Rupp and Taylor 2003.

20. See, however, Besnier 2002; Brubach and O'Brien 1999; Halberstam 1998; Newton 1979, 1993; Robertson 1998; Rupp and Taylor 2003; Valentine 2007.

21. "Shomos" is a neologism that blends the verb "*ser* (to be)" with "*homos* (homosexual)." The pronunciation of the initial "sh" in "Shomos" also evokes the lisp that is stereotypically associated with cochones in Nicaragua. Federico never commented on this, but other Nicaraguan advocates did tell me that the group's name served to reinforce some of the stereotypes about effeminacy and overly dramatized speech that is often attributed to cochones.

22. Other lesbian and gay Nicaraguans echoed that they share Federico's challenge. It can be very difficult for cochones and cochonas to get jobs, especially when they do not conform to gender norms. When this is coupled with Nicaragua's unem-

ployment and underemployment rate, which often hovers near 50 percent, people may go without work for long stretches of time.

23. Colectivo Somos, "Quienes Somos," Managua, n.d., 2.

24. Federico's comments about providing capacitación and uplifting self-esteem mirrors much of the contemporary discourse in discussion groups (as shown in the previous chapter 2). The fact that he is describing work undertaken in the 1980s further links these discourses to the revolutionary era.

25. It is worth noting that in 1990, a very prominent HIV/AIDS-prevention organization (one that received a commendation from the United Nations) was founded by three people, including two lesbian women.

26. Latin American feminists often have been accused of lesbianism (Mogrovejo 2000), as has been the case in the United States (Phelan 1989, 1993).

27. In the competitive terrain of international funding, lesbians, who are seen as twice marginalized—as women and as sexual minorities—may constitute a more attractive constituency. In the case of Guatemala, for instance, development funding has often been funneled to those who appear "more Indian" or "more traditional," or those who more closely fit the stereotypes of development agencies' imagined indigenous subject (Smith 1990).

28. Federico, like Miguel in a previous chapter, used the term "homosexual rights" to describe the lucha. Since the term *"homosexual"* is largely gendered male in Nicaragua, selecting it further suggests some gender bias on Federico's part.

29. Timothy Wright (2000), for example, documents how a program developed by the Bolivian government that attempted to stop the spread of HIV failed to attract many men who have sex with men, partly because the outreach center that it established was designated *"gay."*

30. In this sense, the epistemic work of activists is not dissimilar to the representational conundrums that anthropology has faced since its origins—namely, what are the epistemological grounds of ethnographic interventions, and "whose knowledge" and "what sort of knowledge" is being represented?

31. Warren (1998) argues that identities and identity politics are often shaped by the tensions between different generations of activists (and their critics). This parallels the Nicaraguan case in some aspects where generational divisions are also apparent between those activists who were involved with the revolutionary struggle and a younger generation of advocates who have gained their political experience through human rights and civil society activism.

Four: Mediating Sexual Subjectivities

1. Funding agencies and programs that provided financial support for the show are Agencia Sueca para el Desarrollo Internacional, the Ford Foundation, Hivos, Instituto Austriaco Norte Sur, the Moriah Fund, NDC/USAID, Novib, the Shaler Adams Foundation, and the Summit Foundation.

2. The residents of Nicaragua's Atlantic coast are often referred to as costeños. Many costeños are of African and/or indigenous descent and face prejudice and racism.

3. The media has played important, if uneasy, roles in the political cultures of many Latin American countries. Brazilian television, for example, was crucial to main-

taining the military dictatorship (Skidmore 1999: 171), while in Cuba, a flourishing film industry became emblematic of a revolutionary aesthetic and ethos (Chanan 2004). In Mexico, multiple forms of media, from films to comic books, have codified tropes of national identity (Lomnitz 2001; Rubenstein 1998). More recently, accusations of media censorship haunted Hugo Chavez's regime in Venezuela.

4. The use of media to advance sexual rights is not limited to the Nicaraguan case, of course (see, e.g., Gross 2001).

5. During the Somoza dictatorship, support from the U.S. government paved the way for U.S. media interests in Nicaragua and promoted a climate in which Hollywood productions and U.S. television shows would be the dominant fare (Whisnant 1995). Until recently, Nicaragua had little cinematic culture, very few theaters, and virtually no native filmmakers. During the revolutionary era, the Sandinista state sponsored the development of the Nicaraguan Institute of Cinema, which was partially inspired by Cuba's revolutionary filmmaking and anti-imperialist Latin American cinema.

6. This national constituency is an "imagined community" (Anderson 1983) in the sense that the Nicaraguan population is putatively linked by media (though only partially in "print capital" form) and may understand itself in terms that are consonant with the nation.

7. Movie and television stars are often associated with Hollywood and the U.S. film and television industries. However, the notion of the TV or movie "star" has traveled far beyond Hollywood, as Bollywood celebrity, for one, attests. While the actors on *Sexto Sentido* may not have the same degree of stardom as popular movie icons, in Nicaragua they are seen as minor celebrities. They are often recognized on the street and asked for autographs.

8. The producers of *Sexto Sentido* were conscious of how they represented class differences in the show and included characters from a wide range of socioeconomic backgrounds. Some characters were poor (though not destitute), and others were clearly upper middle class (though not among the very elite). Most of the show's characters were middle class and working class (based on their resources and levels of education and employment). By highlighting this segment of Nicaraguan society, the producers hoped that a wide swath of the population would identify with the characters.

9. "Edu-tainment" was made famous by *Sesame Street*, the children's show produced by the U.S. Public Broadcasting Service that debuted in 1969. Combining pedagogical lessons with entertainment, edu-tainment has since become a multibillion-dollar industry in the United States (Barnett 1999; Buckingham and Scanlon 2005; Rodríguez 2001). In a trailer for the series *Puerto Azul*, the follow-up to *Sexto Sentido* (it was not nearly as successful), the narrator notes that the show comes "from the same people who brought you *Sexto Sentido*," who "revolutionized educational entertainment" in Latin America.

10. Puntos de Encuentro received hundreds of responses describing how much viewers appreciated the gay characters and their unfolding identities. The winners of the contest were invited to a party, where they mingled with the stars of the show.

11. For instance, the movie *The Bird Cage*, starring Robin Williams, was shown at least five times on Nicaraguan TV between April and September 2001. While U.S. television featured network and cable shows with lesbian characters (*The L Word*) or hosts (*Ellen*), neither show had yet been screened in Nicaragua.

12. This scene is foreshadowed when Sofía, another protagonist, has a job interview at a human rights organization, and Gabriel taunts, "Human rights—I got better things to do, like washing underwear." That is, Gabriel would rather do anything—even the cochón-like task of washing underwear—than undertake human rights work.

13. Angel's greater degree of unimpeachability could be attributed to an ethic of machismo that finds male homosexuality more disturbing than female homosexuality (thus mandating an idealized character). However, the reasoning the producers employed was that because Angel was introduced first as a central character, they needed to err on the side of caution, making him unquestionably affable and wholesome. Once viewers had come to accept Angel, the producers were willing to attempt to further challenge negative stereotypes with Vicki's character.

14. Erick Blandón, "El torovenado, lugar para la diferencia en un espacio no letrado," *Istmo*, 2004, available online at http://istmo.denison.edu/n08/articulos/torovenado .html (accessed 7 December 2011).

15. The development schema voiced by the USAID director, taken at face value, resonates with the analysis in *The Antipolitics Machine* (Ferguson 1990), in which "development" is primarily an apparatus of knowledge and power rather than singularly technical or instrumental in its effect.

16. Unfortunately, for reasons that are not clear, the video clips were removed, possibly by Puntos de Encuentro to preserve the value of the program for syndication.

17. For perspectives on media and indigenous peoples see, e.g., Ginsburg 1993, 1997; Singer 2001; Turner 1992, 2002. For anthropological work on media professionals see, e.g., Bourdieu 1999; Boyer 2005, 2013; Dávila 1997, 2001; Dornfeld 1998; Hannerz 2004; Mazzarella 2003; Pedelty 1995.

18. Indeed, theorizing mass media has been a tendentious project in the social sciences and humanities, even beyond the debates about production and consumption. The Frankfurt School famously warned against mass media as a tool of mass deception likely to "fetter consciousness" (Adorno 1997: 29) and render the public supplicants to a grand ideological regime. Guy Debord (1995 [1967]) had similar suspicions about the "society of the spectacle," in which media would dissolve collective consciousness and political commitments. Alternatively, Jürgen Habermas's (1992) "public sphere" took a more utopian view of the possibility of public dialogue emerging through the medium of media. Also see, e.g., Abu-Lughod 1993, 2002, 2004; Ang 1985, 1995; Mankekar 1999.

19. For discussions of media, mediational processes, and post–Cold War information flows, see Appadurai 1996; Askew 2002; Bourdieu 1999; Boyer 2007, 2011; Downing 1987, 2001; Friedman 2006; Ganti 2002; Ginsburg et al. 2002; Mazzarella 2003, 2004; McLuhan 1964; Rodríguez 2001; Schein 2002; Spitulnik 1993; Weiner 1997; Williams 1974.

20. For ethnographic studies of audience-involved modes of communication and anal-

yses of the communicative dynamics of contemporary digital platforms, see, e.g., Boellstorff 2010; Boyer 2013; Coleman 2012; Gershon 2012; Kelty 2008; Schiller 2009; Shipley 2009.

Conclusion

1. Grupo Estratégico por los Derechos Humanos de la Diversidad Sexual, "Una mirada a la diversidad sexual en Nicaragua," Managua, 2010; available online at http://idsdh.org/?page_id=268 (accessed January 17, 2013).

2. Ibid., 2.

3. José Adán Silva, "An Ombudswoman for Sexual Diversity," Inter Press Service, 2009, available online at http://ipsnews.net/print.asp?idnews=49692 (accessed 11 January 2011), 1.

4. Ibid., 2.

5. See, e.g., the website of GEDDS (Grupo Estratégico por los Derechos Humanos de la Diversidad Sex): http://www.gedds2010.blogspot.mx (accessed 17 January 2013).

6. Grupo Estratégico por los Derechos Humanos de la Diversidad Sexual, "Una mirada a la diversidad sexual en Nicaragua," 6.

7. The addition of newer categories of identification, and intervention, also coincides with what Don Kulick (2000: 244) has called the "affective appeal of acronyms," an ever expanding representation of gender and sexual categories—from GL, for gay and lesbian, to LGBTTIQQAA, for lesbian, gay, bisexual, transgender, *transvesti*, intersex, queer, questioning, (queer) ally, and asexual—with, potentially, an infinite enumeration of identities. The affective appeal, in part, is the representational recognition that comes with these kinds of acronymics.

8. Grupo Estratégico por los Derechos Humanos de la Diversidad Sexual, "Una mirada a la diversidad sexual en Nicaragua," 10.

9. Ibid., n. 4.

10. See, e.g., Borofsky 2005; Farmer 2003, 2005; Field and Fox 2007; Fortun 2001; Graeber 2004, 2009; Johnston and Slyomovics 2009; Hale and Calhoun 2008; Lewin and Leap 2009; Manz 2004; Maskovsky 2002; Messer 2003; Nagengast and Turner 1997; Pine 2008; Razsa and Kurnik 2012; Sanford 2004; Sanford and Angel-Ajani 2006; Sawyer 2004; Scheper-Hughes 1995; Speed 2007; Starn 1999; Tate 2007; Turner 1997; Valentine 2007; Vine 2009.

11. See, e.g., Field 2009; Field and Fox 2007; Hale and Calhoun 2008; Jackson 1999; Razsa and Kurnik 2012.

12. See, e.g., Appadurai 1996; Clifford and Marcus 1986; Faubion and Marcus 2009; Marcus 1995.

13. Sexual rights also have been influenced and shaped partly by the United Nation Decade for Women, which worked to establish a specific focus on "women's rights as human rights" (Bunch 1990; Rosenbloom 1996). The World Conference on Human Rights held in 1993 in Vienna called on countries to "eliminate gender based violence and all forms of sexual harassment and exploitation," including trafficking in women (Petchesky 2000: 83). The International Conference on Population and Development held in 1994 in Cairo saw embattled debate over

birth control, abortion, and the right to sexual and reproductive health. The Program of Action that resulted described sexuality as a positive aspect of human life, explicitly stating that "sexual health" is integral to reproductive health and fertility control as well as a requirement for a "satisfying and safe sexual life." While the Program of Action managed to include sexual health needs within the purview of sexual rights, it did not mention sexual pleasure or freedom of sexual expression or sexual orientation (Parker 1997).

14. For many people, this burgeoning interest in sexual health and behavior is unsurprising. It is simply evidence of a further proliferation of biopolitical discourse and the transnational expansion of modes of managing life (Agamben 1998; Foucault 1979, 1980).

REFERENCES

Abu-Lughod, Lila. 1993. "Finding a Place for Islam: Egyptian Television Serials and the National Interest." *Public Culture* 5(3): 493–513.

———. 2002. "Egyptian Melodrama—Technology of the Modern Subject?" *Media Worlds: Anthropology on New Terrain*, ed. Faye D. Ginsburg, Lila Abu-Lughod, and Brian Larkin, 115–33. Berkeley: University of California Press.

———. 2004. *Dramas of Nationhood: The Politics of Television in Egypt*. Chicago: University of Chicago Press.

Adam, Barry D. 1993. "In Nicaragua: Homosexuality without a Gay World." *Journal of Homosexuality* 24: 171–81.

Adam, Barry D., Jan Willem Duyvendak, and André Krouwel, eds. 1999. *The Global Emergence of Gay and Lesbian Politics: National Imprints of a Worldwide Movement*. Philadelphia: Temple University Press.

Adorno, Theodor. 1997. "Culture Industry Reconsidered." *Media Studies: A Reader*, ed. Paul Marris and Sue Thornham, 24–29. Edinburgh: Edinburgh University Press.

Agamben, Giorgio. 1993. *The Coming Community*. Minneapolis: University of Minnesota Press.

———. 1998. *Homo Sacer: Sovereign Power and Bare Life*, trans. Daniel Heller-Roazin. Stanford: Stanford University Press.

Ahmed An-Na'im, Abdullahi. 1992. *Toward an Islamic Reformation: Civil Liberties, Human Rights and International Law*. Syracuse: Syracuse University Press.

Alcoff, Linda Martín, Michael Hames-García, Satya P. Mohanty, and Paula M. L. Moya, eds. 2005. *Identity Politics Reconsidered*. New York: Palgrave Macmillan.

Allen, Chadwick. 2002. *Blood Narrative: Indigenous Identity in Native American and Maori Literary and Activist Texts*. Durham: Duke University Press.

Altman, Dennis. 1993 (1971). *Homosexual Oppression and Liberation*. New York: New York University Press.

———. 2001. *Global Sex*. Chicago: University of Chicago Press.

Alvarez, Sonia, Evelina Dagnino, and Arturo Escobar, eds. 1998. *Cultures of Politics / Politics of Cultures: Re-visioning Latin American Social Movements*. Boulder, Colo.: Westview.

Americas Watch Committee. 1985. "Human Rights in Nicaragua: Reagan, Rhetoric, and Reality." *Nicaragua, Unfinished Revolution: The New Nicaragua Reader*, ed. Peter Rosset and John Vandermeer, 122–29. New York: Grove.

Amnesty International. 2006. "Lesbian, Gay, Bisexual and Transgender People at Risk in Nicaragua." April.

———. 2009. "The Total Abortion Ban in Nicaragua: Women's Lives and Health Endangered, Medical Professionals Criminalized." London: Amnesty International Publications.

Amnistía Internacional. 1999. *El derecho a la propia identidad: La acción en favor de los derechos humanos de gays y lesbianas*. Madrid: Amnesty International.

Anderson, Benedict. 1983. *Imagined Communities: Reflections on the Origin and Spread of Nationalism*. New York: Verso.

Ang, Ien. 1985. *Watching Dallas: Soap Opera and the Melodramatic Imagination*. London: Methuen.

———. 1995. *Living Room Wars: Rethinking Media for a Postmodern World*. London: Routledge.

Appadurai, Arjun. 1996. *Modernity at Large: Cultural Dimensions of Globalization*. Minneapolis: University of Minnesota Press.

Arendt, Hannah. 1958. *The Human Condition*. Chicago: University of Chicago Press.

Askew, Kelly. 2002. "Introduction." *The Anthropology of Media: A Reader*, ed. Kelly Askew and Richard R. Wilk, 1–14. Oxford: Blackwell.

Babb, Florence E. 1999. "Managua Is Nicaragua: The Making of a Neoliberal City." *City and Society* 11(1–2): 27–48.

———. 2001. *After Revolution: Mapping Gender and Cultural Politics in Neoliberal Nicaragua*. Austin: University of Texas Press.

———. 2003. "Out in Nicaragua: Local and Transnational Desires after the Revolution." *Cultural Anthropology* 18(3): 304–32.

———. 2009. "Neither in the Closet nor on the Balcony." *Out in Public: Reinventing Lesbian/Gay Anthropology in a Globalizing World*, ed. Ellen Lewin and William Leap, 240–55. Malden, Mass.: Wiley-Blackwell.

Badiou, Alain. 2012. *Philosophy for Militants*. London: Verso.

Baker, Lee D. 1998. *From Savage to Negro: Anthropology and the Construction of Race, 1896–1954*. Berkeley: University of California Press.

Bakhtin, Mikhail. 2009 (1968). *Rabelais and His World*. Bloomington: University of Indiana Press.

Balderston, Daniel, and Donna Guy, eds. 1997. *Sex and Sexuality in Latin America*. New York: New York University Press.

Balfour, Ian, and Eduardo Cadava. 2004. "The Claims of Human Rights: An Introduction." *South Atlantic Quarterly* 103(2): 277–96.

Bancroft, Hubert Howe. 1886. *History of Central America, Volume 2: 1530–1880*. San Francisco: A. L. Bancroft.

Barnett, Clive. 1999. "The Limits of Media Democratization in South Africa: Politics, Privatization, and Regulation." *Media, Culture, and Society* 21(5): 649–71.

Bayard de Volo, Lorraine. 2001. *Mothers of Heroes and Martyrs: Gender Identity Politics in Nicaragua, 1979–1999*. Baltimore: Johns Hopkins University Press.

Bell, David, and Jon Binnie. 2000. *The Sexual Citizen: Queer Politics and Beyond*. Malden, Mass.: Polity.

Belli, Gioconda. 1995. *La mujer habitada / The Inhabited Woman*, trans. Kathleen March. New York: Warner Books.

———. 2003. *The Country under My Skin: A Memoir of Love and War.* New York: Alfred A. Knopf.

———. 2004. *The Inhabited Woman.* Madison: University of Wisconsin Press.

———. 2007. *The Scroll of Seduction: A Novel of Power, Madness, and Royalty.* New York: Harper.

Benavides, O. Hugo. 2008. *Drugs, Thugs, and Divas: Telenovelas and Narco-dramas in Latin America.* Austin: University of Texas Press.

Besnier, Niko. 2002. "Transgenderism, Locality, and the Miss Galaxy Beauty Pageant in Tonga." *American Ethnologist* 29:534–66.

Binnie, Jon. 2004. *The Globalization of Sexuality.* London: Sage.

Blackwood, Evelyn. 1999. "Tombois in West Sumatra: Constructing Masculinity and Erotic Desire." *Female Desires: Same-Sex Relations and Transgender Practices across Cultures*, ed. Evelyn Blackwood and Saskia Wieringa, 181–205. New York: Columbia University Press.

———. 2005. "The Specter of the Patriarchal Man." *American Ethnologist* 32(1): 42–45.

———. 2010. *Falling into the Lesbi World: Desire and Difference in Indonesia.* Honolulu: University of Hawai'i Press.

Blackwood, Evelyn, and Saskia Wieringa, eds. 1999. *Female Desires: Same-Sex Relations and Transgender Practices across Cultures.* New York: Columbia University Press.

Blandón, Erick. 2003. *Barroco descalzo: Colonialidad, sexualidad, genero y raza en la construccion de la hegemonia cultural en Nicaragua.* Managua: Universidad de las Regiones Autonomas de la Costa Caribe Nicaragüense.

Blasius, Mark. 2001. *Sexual Identities, Queer Politics.* Princeton: Princeton University Press.

Blasius, Mark, and Shane Phelan. 1997. *We Are Everywhere: A Historical Sourcebook of Gay and Lesbian Politics.* London: Routledge.

Boas, Franz. 1995 (1940). *Race, Language, and Culture.* Chicago: University of Chicago Press.

Boellstorff, Tom. 2003a. "I Knew It Was Me: Mass Media, 'Globalization,' and Lesbian and Gay Indonesians." *Mobile Cultures: New Media in Queer Asia*, ed. Chris Berry, Fran Martin, and Audrey Yue, 21–51. Durham: Duke University Press.

———. 2003b. "Dubbing Culture: Indonesian *Gay* and *Lesbi* Subjectivities and Ethnography in an Already Globalized World." *American Ethnologist* 30(2): 225–42.

———. 2005. *The Gay Archipelago: Sexuality and Nation in Indonesia.* Princeton: Princeton University Press.

———. 2007. "Queer Studies in the House of Anthropology." *Annual Review of Anthropology* 36:17–35.

———. 2010. *Coming of Age in Second Life: An Anthropologist Explores the Virtually Human.* Princeton: Princeton University Press.

Bolt González, Mary. 1996a. "Nicaragua." *Unspoken Rules: Sexual Orientation and Women's Human Rights*, ed. Rachel Rosenbloom, 121–37. London: Cassell.

———. 1996b. *Sencillamente diferentes: La autoestima de las mujeres lesbianas en los sectores urbanos de Nicaragua.* Managua: Fundación Xochiquetzal.

Borland, Katherine. 2006. *Unmasking Class, Gender, and Sexuality in Nicaraguan Festival.* Tucson: University of Arizona Press.

Borofsky, Rob. 2005. *Yanomami: The Fierce Controversy and What We Can Learn from It.* Berkeley: University of California Press.

Bourdieu, Pierre. 1984. *Distinction: A Social Critique of Judgment of Taste*, trans. Richard Nice. Cambridge: Harvard University Press.

———. 1999. *On Television.* New York: New Press.

Bourgois, Philippe. 1981. "Class, Ethnicity, and the State among the Miskitu Amerindians of Northeastern Nicaragua." *Latin American Perspectives* 8(2): 22–39.

Bouvard, Margarite Guzman. 2002. *Revolutionizing Motherhood: The Mothers of the Plaza de Mayo.* Wilmington, Del.: Scholarly Resources.

Boyer, Dominic. 2005. *Spirit and System: Media, Intellectuals, and the Dialectic in Modern German Culture.* Chicago: University of Chicago Press.

———. 2007. *Understanding Media: A Popular Philosophy.* Chicago: Prickly Paradigm.

———. 2011. "Media Anthropology and the Anthropology of Mediation." *The ASA Handbook of Social Anthropology*, ed. Richard Fardon and John Gledhill, 411–22. London: Sage.

———. 2013. *The Life Informatic: Newsmaking in the Digital Era.* Ithaca: Cornell University Press.

Boyer, Dominic, and Claudio Lomnitz. 2005. "Intellectuals and Nationalism: Anthropological Engagements." *Annual Review of Anthropology* 34:105–20.

Brennan, Denise. 2004. *What's Love Got to Do with It? Transnational Desires and Sex Tourism in the Dominican Republic.* Durham: Duke University Press.

Bretlinger, John. 1995. *The Best of What We Are: Reflections on the Nicaraguan Revolution.* Amherst: University of Massachusetts Press.

Brett, Philip, Sue-Ellen Case, and Susan Leigh Foster, eds. 1995. *Cruising the Performative: Interventions into the Representation of Ethnicity, Nationality, and Sexuality.* Bloomington: Indiana University Press.

Brown, Stephen. 1999. "Democracy and Sexual Difference: The Lesbian and Gay Movement in Argentina." *Global Emergence of Gay and Lesbian Politics: National Imprints of a Worldwide Movement*, ed. Barry D. Adam, Jan Willem Duyvendak, and André Krouwel, 110–32. Philadelphia: Temple University Press.

Brown, Wendy. 1995. *States of Injury: Power and Freedom in Late Modernity.* Princeton: Princeton University Press.

———. 2005. *Edgework: Critical Essays on Knowledge and Politics.* Princeton: Princeton University Press.

Brubach, Holly, and Michael James O'Brien. 1999. *Girlfriend: Men, Women, and Drag.* New York: Random House.

Buchsbaum, Jonathan. 2003. *Cinema and the Sandinistas: Filmmaking in Revolutionary Nicaragua.* Austin: University of Texas Press.

Buckingham, David, and Margaret Scanlon. 2005. "Selling Learning: Towards a Political Economy of Edutainment Media." *Media, Culture and Society* 27(1): 41–58.

Bunch, Charlotte. 1990. "Women's Rights as Human Rights: Toward a Re-vision of Human Rights." *Human Rights Quarterly* 12:486–98.

Butler, Judith. 1988. "Performative Acts and Gender Constitution: An Essay in Phenomenology and Feminist Theory." *Theatre Journal* 40(4): 519–31.

———. 1990. *Gender Trouble: Feminism and the Subversion of Identity.* New York: Routledge.

———. 1993. *Bodies That Matter: On the Discursive Limits of "Sex."* New York: Routledge.

———. 2004. *Undoing Gender.* New York: Routledge.

Cabezas, Omar. 1985. *Fire from the Mountain: The Making of a Sandinista*, trans. Kathleen Weaver. New York: Crown.

Cantú, Lionel. 2002. "De Ambiente: Queer Tourism and the Shifting Boundaries of Mexican Male Sexualities." GLQ 8:139–66.

———. 2009. *The Sexuality of Migration: Border Crossings and Mexican Immigrant Men*, ed. Nancy Naples, and Salvador Vidal-Ortiz. New York: New York University Press.

Carrier, Joseph. 1995. *De Los Otros: Intimacy and Homosexuality among Mexican Men.* New York: Columbia University Press.

Carrillo, Héctor. 2001. *The Night Is Young: Sexuality in Mexico in the Time of AIDS.* Chicago: University of Chicago Press.

Case, Sue-Ellen. 2009. *Feminist and Queer Performance: Critical Strategies.* New York: Palgrave Macmillan.

Chanan, Michael. 2004. *Cuban Cinema.* Minneapolis: University of Minnesota Press.

Chauncey, George. 1995. *Gay New York: Gender, Urban Culture, and the Making of the Gay Male World, 1890–1940.* New York: Basic Books.

Chavez Metoyer, Cynthia. 1997. "Nicaragua's Transition of State Power: Through Feminist Lenses." *The Undermining of the Sandinista Revolution*, ed. Gary Prevost and Harry E. Vanden, 114–40. New York: St. Martin's.

Chernoff, John. 2003. *Hustling Is Not Stealing: Stories of an African Bar Girl.* Chicago: University of Chicago Press.

Chinchilla, Norma. 1990. "Revolutionary Popular Feminism in Nicaragua: Articulating Class, Gender and National Sovereignty." *Gender and Society* 4(3): 370–97.

———. 1994. "Feminism, Revolution, and Democratic Transitions in Nicaragua." *The Women's Movement in Latin America*, ed. Jane Jaquette, 1–12. Boulder, Colo.: Westview.

Chuchryk, Patricia. 1991. "Women in the Revolution." *Revolution and Counterrevolution in Nicaragua*, ed. Thomas Walker, 143–65. Boulder, Colo.: Westview.

Claude, Richard Pierre, and Burns H. Weston. 1992. *Human Rights in the World Community: Issues and Action.* Philadelphia: University of Pennsylvania Press.

Clifford, James, and George E. Marcus, eds. 1986. *Writing Culture: The Poetics and Politics of Ethnography.* Berkeley: University of California Press.

Close, David, and Kalowatie Deonandan, eds. 2004. *Undoing Democracy: The Politics of Electoral Cuadillismo.* Lanham, Md.: Lexington Books.

Coleman, E. Gabriella. 2012. *Coding Freedom: The Ethics and Aesthetics of Hacking.* Princeton: Princeton University Press.

Collinson, Helen. 1990. *Women and Revolution.* London: Zed Books.

Comaroff, Jean. 2007. "Beyond Bare Life: AIDS, (Bio)Politics, and the Neoliberal Order." *Public Culture* 19(1): 197–219.

Comaroff, Jean, and John Comaroff. 1997. "Postcolonial Politics and Discourses of Democracy in Southern Africa." *Journal of Anthropological Research* 53(2): 123–46.

Constable, Nicole. 2003. *Romance on a Global Stage: Pen Pals, Virtual Ethnography, and "Mail Order" Marriages.* Berkeley: University of California Press.

Corrales, Javier, and Mario Pecheny, eds. 2010. *The Politics of Sexuality in Latin America.* Pittsburgh: University of Pittsburgh Press.

Cortazar, Julio. 1979. *Nicaragua in Perspective.* New York: St. Martin's.

———. 1990. *Nicaraguan Sketches*, trans. Kathleen Weaver. New York: W. W. Norton.

Craske, Nikki. 1999. *Women and Politics in Latin America.* New York: St. Martin's.

Darío, Rubén. 1968 (1888). *Azul.* Madrid: Espasa-Calpe.

Dave, Naisargi. 2012. *Queer Activism in India: A Story in the Anthropology of Ethics.* Durham: Duke University Press.

Dávila, Arlene. 1997. *Sponsored Identities: Cultural Politics in Puerto Rico.* Philadelphia: Temple University Press.

———. 2001. *Latinos, Inc.: The Marketing and Making of a People.* Berkeley: University of California Press.

Dávila Bolaños, Alejandro. 1973. *Teatro popular colonial revolucionario: El Güegüense o Macho-Ratón; Drama épico indígena.* Estelí: Tipografía Geminis.

Debord, Guy. 1995 (1967). *The Society of the Spectacle*, trans. Donald Nicholson-Smith. New York: Zone Books.

Decena, Carlos Ulises. 2011. *Tacit Subjects: Belonging and Same-Sex Desire among Dominican Immigrant Men.* Durham: Duke University Press.

D'Emilio, John. 1983. *Sexual Politics, Sexual Communities: The Making of a Homosexual Minority in the United States, 1940–1970.* Chicago: University of Chicago Press.

———. 1993. "Capitalism and Gay Identity." *The Lesbian and Gay Studies Reader*, ed. Michèle Aina Barale and Henry Abelove, 467–76. London: Routledge.

D'Emilio, John, and Estelle B. Freedman. 1997. *Intimate Matters: A History of Sexuality in America.* Chicago: University of Chicago Press.

De la Campa, Román. 1999. *Latin Americanism.* Minneapolis: University of Minnesota Press.

de la Dehesa, Rafael. 2010. *Queering the Public Sphere in Mexico and Brazil: Sexual Rights Movements in Emerging Democracies.* Durham: Duke University Press.

Dinshaw, Carolyn, Lee Edelman, Roderick A. Ferguson, Carla Freccero, Elizabeth Freeman, Judith Halberstam, Annamarie Jagose, Christopher Nealon, and Nguyen Tan Hoang. 2007. "Theorizing Queer Temporalities: A Roundtable Discussion." GLQ 13:177–95.

Dodson, Michael. 1990. *Nicaragua's Other Revolution: Religious Faith and Political Struggle.* Chapel Hill: University of North Carolina Press.

Donham, Donald D. 1998. "Freeing South Africa: The 'Modernization' of Male–Male Sexuality in Soweto." *Cultural Anthropology* 13(1): 3–21.

Dornfeld, Barry. 1998. *Producing Public Television: Producing Public Culture.* Princeton: Princeton University Press.

Downing, John. 1987. *Film and Politics in the Third World.* New York: Praeger.

———. 2001. *Radical Media: Rebellious Communication and Social Movements.* London: Sage.

Dozier, Craig L. 1985. *Nicaragua's Mosquito Shore: The Years of British and American Presence*. Tuscaloosa: University of Alabama Press.

Duggan, Lisa. 2000. *Sapphic Slashers: Sex, Violence, and American Modernity*. Durham: Duke University Press.

———. 2004. *The Twilight of Equality? Neoliberalism, Cultural Politics and the Attack on Democracy*. Boston: Beacon.

Dye, David R., and David Close. 2004. "Partrimonialism and Economic Policy in the Alemán Administration." *Undoing Democracy: The Politics of Electoral Cuadillismo*, ed. David Close and Kalowatie Deonandan, 119–42. Lanham, Md.: Lexington Books.

Edelman, Marc. 1999. *Peasants against Globalization: Rural Social Movements in Costa Rica*. Stanford: Stanford University Press.

———. 2001. "Social Movements: Changing Paradigms and Forms of Politics." *Annual Review of Anthropology* 30:285–317.

Eder, Klaus. 1985. "The 'New' Social Movements: Moral Crusades, Political Pressure Groups, or Social Movements?" *Sociological Research* 52:869–901.

Elias, Norbert. 2000 (1994). *The Civilizing Process: Sociogenic and Psychogenic Investigations*, 2nd ed. Oxford: Wiley-Blackwell.

Elliston, Deborah. 1995. "Erotic Anthropology: 'Ritualized Homosexuality' in Melanesia and Beyond." *American Ethnologist* 22(4): 848–67.

Englund, Harri. 2006. *Prisoners of Freedom: Human Rights and the African Poor*. Berkeley: University of California Press.

Epstein, Steven. 1999a. "Gay and Lesbian Movements in the United States: Dilemmas of Identity, Diversity, and Political Strategy." *The Global Emergence of Gay and Lesbian Politics: National Imprints of a Worldwide Movement*, ed. Barry D. Adam, Jan Willem Duyvendak, and André Krouwel, 30–90. Philadelphia: Temple University Press.

———. 1999b. "Gay Politics, Ethnic Identity: The Limits of Social Constructionism." *Socialist Review* 93/94:9–54.

Esterberg, Kristin. 1997. *Lesbian and Bisexual Identities: Constructing Communities, Constructing Selves*. Philadelphia: Temple University Press.

Faiman-Silva, Sandra. 2004. *The Courage to Connect: Sexuality, Citizenship, and Community in Provincetown*. Urbana: University of Illinois Press.

Farmer, Paul. 2003. *Pathologies of Power: Health, Human Rights, and the New War on the Poor*. Berkeley: University of California Press.

———. 2005. *The Uses of Haiti*, 2nd ed. Monroe, Maine: Common Courage.

Fassin, Didier. 2011. *Humanitarian Reason: A Moral History of the Present*. Berkeley: University of California Press.

Faubion, James. 2011. *An Anthropology of Ethics*. Cambridge: Cambridge University Press.

Faubion, James, and George E. Marcus, eds. 2009. *Ethnography Is Not What It Used to Be: Learning Anthropology's Method in a Time of Transition*. Ithaca: Cornell University Press.

Ferguson, Ann. 1991. "Lesbianism, Feminism, and Empowerment in Nicaragua." *Social Review* 21(3): 75–97.

Ferguson, James. 1990. *The Anti-politics Machine: "Development," Depoliticization, and Bureaucratic Power in Lesotho*. Cambridge: Cambridge University Press.

Ferguson, Roderick A. 2004. *Aberrations in Black: Toward a Queer of Color Critique*. Minneapolis: University of Minnesota Press.

Fernández Poncela, Anna M. 2001. *Mujeres, revolución y cambio cultural: Transformaciones sociales versus modelos culturales persistentes*. Mexico City: Anthropos Research and Publications.

Field, Les W. 1998. "Post-Sandinista Ethnic Identities in Western Nicaragua." *American Anthropologist* 100(2): 431–43.

———. 1999. *The Grimace of Macho Ratón: Artisans, Identity and Nation in Late-Twentieth-Century Western Nicaragua*. Durham: Duke University Press.

———. 2009. *Abalone Tales: Collaborative Explorations of Sovereignty and Identity in Native California*. Durham: Duke University Press.

Field, Les W., and Richard G. Fox, eds. 2007. *Anthropology Put to Work*. Oxford: Berg.

Firestone, Shulamith. 1970. *The Dialectic of Sex: The Case for Feminist Revolution*. New York: W. W. Norton.

Fisher, William F. 1997. "Doing Good? The Politics and Antipolitics of NGO Practices." *Annual Review of Anthropology* 26:439–64.

Fortun, Kim. 2001. *Advocacy after Bhopal: Environmentalism, Disaster, New Global Orders*. Chicago: University of Chicago Press.

Foucault, Michel. 1979. *The History of Sexuality, Volume 1: An Introduction*. New York: Pantheon Books.

———. 1980. *Power/Knowledge: Selected Interviews and Other Writings, 1972–1977*, ed. Colin Gordon. New York: Pantheon Books.

———. 1985. *The History of Sexuality, Volume 2: The Use of Pleasure*, trans. Robert Hurley. New York: Pantheon Books.

Fox, Richard G., and Orin Starn, eds. 1997. *Between Resistance and Revolution: Cultural Politics and Social Protest*. New Brunswick: Rutgers University Press.

Fraser, Nancy. 1989. *Unruly Practices: Power, Discourse, and Gender in Contemporary Social Theory*. Minneapolis: University of Minnesota Press.

———. 1994. "Rethinking the Public Sphere: A Contribution to the Critique of Actually Existing Democracy." *Habermas and the Public Sphere*, ed. Craig Calhoun, 109–42. Cambridge: MIT Press.

———. 1995. "From Redistribution to Recognition? Dilemmas of Justice in a 'Post-Socialist' Age," *New Left Review* 212:68–93.

———. 2005. "Reframing Justice in a Globalizing World." *New Left Review* 36:69–88.

Freire, Paulo. 1973. *Pedagogy of the Oppressed*. New York: Seabury.

Friedman, Sara L. 2006. "Watching *Twin Bracelets* in China: The Role of Spectatorship and Identification in an Ethnographic Analysis of Film Reception." *Cultural Anthropology* 21(4): 603–32.

Gagnon, John H. 2004. *An Interpretation of Desire: Essays in the Study of Sexuality*. Chicago: University of Chicago Press.

Gal, Susan, and Gail Kligman. 2000. *The Politics of Gender after Socialism: A Comparative-Historical Essay*. Princeton: Princeton University Press.

Gamson, Joshua. 1991. *Freaks Talk Back: Tabloid Talk Shows and Sexual Nonconformity.* Chicago: University of Chicago Press.

Ganti, Tejaswini. 2002. "'And Yet My Heart Is Still Indian': The Bombay Film Industry and the (H)Indianization of Hollywood." *Media Worlds: Anthropology on New Terrain,* ed. Faye D. Ginsburg, Lila Abu-Lughod, and Brian Larkin, 281–300. Berkeley: University of California Press.

Garber, Marjorie. 1997. *Vested Interests: Cross-Dressing and Cultural Anxiety.* New York: Routledge.

Geertz, Clifford. 1973. *Interpretation of Cultures.* New York: Basic Books.

Gershon, Ilana. 2012. *The Breakup 2.0: Disconnecting over New Media.* Ithaca: Cornell University Press.

Gevisser, Mark. 2000. "Mandela's Stepchildren: Homosexual Identity in Post-Apartheid South Africa." *Different Rainbows,* ed. Peter Drucker, 111–36. New York: Gay Men's Press.

Ghaziani, Amin. 2008. *The Dividends of Dissent: How Conflict and Culture Work in Lesbian and Gay Marches on Washington.* Chicago: University of Chicago Press.

Gill, Lesley. 2000. *Teetering on the Rim: Global Restructuring, Daily Life and the Armed Retreat of the Bolivian State.* New York: Columbia University Press.

Ginsburg, Faye D. 1993. "Aboriginal Media and the Australian Imaginary." *Public Culture* 5(3): 557–78.

———. 1997. "'From Little Things, Big Things Grow': Indigenous Media and Cultural Activism." *Between Resistance and Revolution: Cultural Politics and Social Protest,* ed. Richard G. Fox and Orin Starn, 118–44. New Brunswick: Rutgers University Press.

Ginsburg, Faye D., Lila Abu-Lughod, and Brian Larkin. 2002. *Media Worlds: Anthropology on New Terrain.* Berkeley: University of California Press.

Gitlin, Todd. 1995. *The Twilight of Common Dreams: Why America Is Wracked by Culture Wars.* New York: Henry Holt.

Gledhill, John. 1994. *Power and Its Disguises: Anthropological Perspectives on Politics.* Boulder, Colo.: Pluto.

Goffman, Erving. 1959. *The Presentation of Self in Everyday Life.* New York: Doubleday.

González, Victoria. 2001. "Somocista Women, Right-Wing Politics, and Feminism in Nicaragua, 1936–1979." *Radical Women in Latin America: Left and Right,* ed. Victoria González and Karen Kampwirth, 41–78. University Park: Pennsylvania State University Press.

González, Victoria, and Karen Kampwirth, eds. 2001. *Radical Women in Latin America: Left and Right.* University Park: Pennsylvania State University Press.

González-Lopez, Gloria. 2005. *Erotic Journeys: Mexican Immigrants and Their Sex Lives.* Berkeley: University of California Press.

González-Rivera, Victoria. 2010. "Gender, Clientelistic Populism, and Memory: Somocista and Neo-Somocista Women's Narratives in Neo-liberal Nicaragua." *Gender and Populism in Latin America: Passionate Politics,* ed. Karen Kampwirth, 67–90. University Park: Pennsylvania State University Press.

———. 2011. *Before the Revolution: Women's Rights and Right-Wing Politics in Nicaragua, 1821–1979.* University Park: Pennsylvania State University Press.

Goodale, Mark. 2006a. "Introduction to 'Anthropology and Human Rights in a New Key.'" *American Anthropologist* 108(1): 1–8.

———. 2006b. "Toward a Critical Anthropology of Human Rights." *Current Anthropology* 47:485–511.

Goodale, Mark, and Sally Engle Merry, eds. 2007. *The Practice of Human Rights: Tracking Law between the Global and the Local*. Cambridge: Cambridge University Press.

Gopinath, Gayatri. 1998. "On Fire." GLQ 4(4): 631–36.

———. 2005. *Impossible Desires: Queer Diasporas and South Asian Public Cultures*. Durham: Duke University Press.

Gould, Deborah B. 2009. *Moving Politics: Emotion and ACT UP's Fight against AIDS*. Chicago: University of Chicago Press.

Gould, Jeffrey L. 1990. *To Lead as Equals: Rural Protest and Political Consciousness in Chinandega, Nicaragua, 1912–1979*. Chapel Hill: University of North Carolina Press.

———. 1998. *To Die in This Way: Nicaraguan Indians and the Myth of Mestizaje, 1880–1965*. Durham: Duke University Press.

Graeber, David. 2004. *Fragments of an Anarchist Anthropology*. Chicago: Prickly Paradigm.

———. 2009. *Direct Action: An Ethnography*. Edinburgh: AK Press.

Gramsci, Antonio. 1971. *Selections from the Prison Notebooks of Antonio Gramsci*, ed. and trans. Quintin Hoare and Geoffrey Nowell Smith. New York: International.

———. 1992. *Prison Notebooks, Volumes 1 and 2*, ed. and trans. Joseph Buttigieg. New York: Columbia University Press.

Gray, Mary. 2009. *Out in the Country: Youth, Media, and Queer Visibility in Rural America*. New York: New York University Press.

Grewal, Inderpal, and Caren Kaplan. 2001. "Global Identities: Theorizing Transnational Studies of Sexuality." GLQ 7(4): 663–79.

Gross, Larry. 2001. *Up from Invisibility: Lesbians, Gay Men, and the Media in America*. New York: Columbia University Press.

Gutmann, Matthew C. 1996. *The Meanings of Macho: Being a Man in Mexico City*. Berkeley: University of California Press.

Habermas, Jürgen. 1992. *The Structural Transformation of the Public Sphere*. New York: Polity.

Halberstam, Judith. 1998. *Female Masculinity*. Durham: Duke University Press.

Hale, Charles R. 1996. *Resistance and Contradiction: Miskitu Indians and the Nicaraguan State, 1894–1987*. Stanford: Stanford University Press.

———. 2006a. "Activist Research v. Cultural Critique: Indigenous Land Rights and the Contradictions of Politically Engaged Anthropology." *Cultural Anthropology* 21(1): 96–120.

———. 2006b. *Más Que un Indio (More Than an Indian): Racial Ambivalence and the Paradox of Neoliberal Multiculturalism in Guatemala*. Santa Fe: School for Advanced Research Press.

———. 2008. "Introduction." *Engaging Contradictions: Theory, Politics, and Methods of Activist Scholarship*, ed. Charles R. Hale and Craig Calhoun, 1–30. Berkeley: University of California Press.

Hale, Charles R., and Craig Calhoun, eds. 2008. *Engaging Contradictions: Theory, Politics, and Methods of Activist Scholarship.* Berkeley: University of California Press.

Hall, Radclyffe. 1990 (1928). *The Well of Loneliness.* New York: Anchor Books.

Hall, Stuart S. 1997. "The Work of Representation." *Representation: Cultural Representation and Signifying Practices,* ed. Stuart Hall, 13–64. London: Sage.

Halperin, David M. 2002. *How to Do the History of Homosexuality.* Chicago: University of Chicago Press.

Hannerz, Ulf. 2004. *Foreign News: Exploring the World of Foreign Correspondents.* Chicago: University of Chicago Press.

Hennessy, Rosemary. 2000. *Profit and Pleasure: Sexual Identities in Late Capitalism.* New York: Routledge.

Herdt, Gilbert. 1987. *The Sambia: Ritual and Gender in New Guinea.* New York: Holt, Rinehart and Winston.

Herdt, Gilbert, ed. 2009. *Moral Panics, Sex Panics: Fear and the Fight Over Sexual Rights.* New York: New York University Press.

Herdt, Gilbert, and Cymene Howe, eds. 2007. *21st Century Sexualities: Contemporary Issues in Health, Education and Rights.* New York: Routledge.

Herzfeld, Michael. 1997. *Cultural Intimacy: Social Poetics in the Nation-State.* New York: Routledge.

Heyck, Denis L. D. 1990. *Life Stories of the Nicaraguan Revolution.* London: Routledge.

Higgins, Michael James, and Tanya Leigh Coen. 1992. *Oigame! Oigame! Struggle and Social Change in a Nicaraguan Urban Community.* Boulder, Colo.: Westview.

Hirsch, Jennifer S. 1999. "En el Norte la Mujer Manda: Gender, Generation, and Geography in a Mexican Transnational Community." *American Behavioral Scientist* 42(9): 1332–49.

Hocquenghem, Guy. 1993 (1978). *Homosexual Desire,* trans. Diniella Dangoor. Durham: Duke University Press.

Howe, Cymene. 2001. "Queer Pilgrimage: The San Francisco Homeland and Identity Tourism." *Cultural Anthropology* 16(1): 35–61.

———. 2002. "Undressing the Universal Queer Subject: Nicaraguan Activism and Transnational Identity." *City and Society* 1(2): 237–79.

———. 2007. "Sexual Borderlands: Lesbian and Gay Migration, Human Rights, and the Metropolitan Community Church." *Sexuality Research and Social Policy* 4(2): 88–106.

———. 2008a. "Spectacles of Sexuality: Televisionary Activism in Nicaragua." *Cultural Anthropology* 23(1): 48–84.

———. 2008b. "Transgender Sex Workers and Sexual Transmigration." With Susanna Zaraysky and Lois Lorentzen. *Latin American Perspectives* 35(1): 31–50.

———. 2009. "The Legible Lesbian: Crimes of Passion in Nicaragua." *Ethnos* 74(3): 361–78.

Howe, Cymene, and Jakob Rigi. 2009. "Transnationalizing Desire: Sexualizing Culture and Commodifying Sexualities." *Ethnos* 74(3): 297–306.

Hoyt, Katherine. 1996. *Thirty Years of Memories: Dictatorship, Revolution, and Nicaraguan Solidarity.* Washington, D.C.: Nicaragua Network Education Fund.

———. 1997. *The Many Faces of Sandinista Democracy.* Athens: Ohio University Press.

————. 2004. "Parties and Pacts in Contemporary Nicaragua." *Undoing Democracy: The Politics of Electoral Cuadillismo*, ed. David Close and Kalowatie Deonandan, 219–30. Lanham, Md.: Lexington Books.

Jackson, Jean E. 1999. "The Politics of Ethnographic Practice in the Colombian Vaupés." *Identities* 6(2–3): 281–317.

Jackson, Jean E., and Kay B. Warren. 2005. "Indigenous Movements in Latin America, 1992–2004: Controversies, Ironies, New Directions." *Annual Review of Anthropology* 34:549–73.

Jackson, Peter. 2009. "Capitalism and Global Queering: National Markets, Parallels among Sexual Cultures, and Multiple Queer Modernities." GLQ 15(3): 357–95.

Jacobs, Sue-Ellen, Wesley Thomas, and Sabine Lang, eds. 1997. *Two-Spirit People: Native American Gender Identity, Sexuality, and Spirituality*. Urbana: University of Illinois Press.

Jacquette, Jane. 1989. *The Women's Movement in Latin America: Feminism and the Transition to Democracy*. Boston: Unwin Hyman.

Johnson, E. Patrick, and Mae G. Henderson. 2005. *Black Queer Studies: A Critical Anthology*. Durham: Duke University Press.

Johnston, Barbara Rose, and Susan Slyomovics, eds. 2009. *Waging War, Making Peace: Reparations and Human Rights*. Walnut Creek, Calif.: Left Coast.

Jones, Adam. 2002. *Beyond the Barricades: Nicaragua and the Struggle for the Sandinista Press, 1979–1998*. Athens: Ohio University Press.

Kampwirth, Karen. 1996a. "Confronting Adversity with Experience: The Emergence of Feminism in Nicaragua." *Social Politics* 3(2–3): 136–58.

————. 1996b. "The Mother of the Nicaraguans: Doña Violeta and the UNO's Gender Agenda." *Latin American Perspectives* 23(1): 67–86.

————. 2004a. "Alemán's War on the NGO Community." *Undoing Democracy: The Politics of Electoral Cuadillismo*, ed. David Close and Kalowatie Deonandan, 65–86. Lanham, Md.: Lexington Books.

————. 2004b. *Feminism and the Legacy of Revolution: Nicaragua, El Salvador, Chiapas*. Athens: Ohio University Press.

————. 2006. "Resisting the Feminist Threat: Antifeminist Politics in Post-Sandinista Nicaragua." *NWSA Journal* 18(2): 73–101.

————. 2010. "Populism and the Feminist Challenge in Nicaragua: The Return of Daniel Ortega." *Gender and Populism in Latin America: Passionate Politics*, ed. Karen Kampwirth, 162–79. University Park: Pennsylvania State University Press.

————. 2011. *Latin America's New Left and the Politics of Gender: Lessons from Nicaragua*. London: Springer.

Kantsa, Venetia. 2002. "Certain Places Have Different Energy": Spatial Transformations in Eresos, Lesvos." GLQ 8(1–2): 35–55.

Keck, Margaret E., and Kathryn Sikkink. 1998. *Activists beyond Borders: Advocacy Networks in International Politics*. Ithaca: Cornell University Press.

Kelty, Christopher. 2008. *Two Bits: The Cultural Significance of Free Software*. Durham: Duke University Press.

Kennedy, Elizabeth Lapovsky, and Madeline D. Davis. 1993. *Boots of Leather, Slippers of Gold: The History of a Lesbian Community*. New York: Routledge.

Kettering, Sharon. 1988. "The Historical Development of Political Clientalism." *Journal of Interdisciplinary History* 18(3): 419–47.

Kimmel, Michael, ed. 2007. *The Sexual Self: The Development of Sexual Scripts.* Nashville: Vanderbilt University Press.

Kipnis, Laura. 1999. "The Stepdaughter's Story: Scandals National and Transnational." *Social Text* 58:59–73.

Kulick, Don. 1998. *Travesti: Sex, Gender, and Culture among Brazilian Transgendered Prostitutes.* Chicago: University of Chicago Press.

———. 2000. "Gay and Lesbian Language." *Annual Review of Anthropology* 29:243–85.

Laclau, Ernesto, and Chantal Mouffe. 1985. *Hegemony and Socialist Struggle: Towards a Radical Democratic Politics.* London: Verso.

La Fountain-Stokes, Lawrence. 2007. "Queer Ducks, Puerto Rican Patos, and Jewish-American Feygelekh: Birds and the Cultural Representation of Homosexuality." *Centro Journal* 19(1): 192–229.

Lamphere, Louise, Helena Ragoné, and Patricia Zavella, eds. 1997. *Situated Lives: Gender and Culture in Everyday Life.* New York: Routledge.

Lancaster, Roger. 1987. "Subject Honor and Object Shame: The Construction of Male Homosexuality and Stigma in Nicaragua." *Ethnology* 27(2): 111–25.

———. 1988. *Thanks to God and the Revolution: Popular Religion and Class Consciousness in the New Nicaragua.* New York: Columbia University Press.

———. 1992. *Life Is Hard: Machismo, Danger, and the Intimacy of Power in Nicaragua.* Berkeley: University of California Press.

———. 1997a. "Guto's Performance: Notes on the Transvestism of Everyday Life." *Sex and Sexuality in Latin America,* ed. Daniel Balderston and Donna J. Guy, 9–32. New York: New York University Press.

———. 1997b. "On Homosexualities in Latin America (and Other Places)." *American Ethnologist* 24(1): 193–202.

———. 2003. *The Trouble with Nature: Sex in Science and Popular Culture.* Berkeley: University of California Press.

Lancaster, Roger N., and Micaela di Leonardo. 1997. "Introduction: Carnal Meanings, Embodied Practices." *The Gender/Sexuality Reader: Culture, History, Political Economy,* ed. Roger N. Lancaster and Micaela di Leonardo. New York: Routledge.

Lang, Sabine. 1998. *Men as Women, Women as Men: Changing Gender in Native American Cultures,* trans. John L. Vantine. Austin: University of Texas Press.

La Pastina, Antonio C. 2004. "Telenovela Reception in Rural Brazil: Gendered Readings and Sexual Mores." *Critical Studies in Media Communication* 21(2): 162–81.

Lazarus-Black, Mindie, and Sally Engle Merry. 2003. "The Politics of Gender Violence: Law Reform in Local and Global Places." *Law and Social Inquiry* 28(4): 931–39.

Leap, William L., and Tom Boellstorff, eds. 2003. *Speaking in Queer Tongues: Globalization and Gay Language.* Urbana: University of Illinois Press.

Lewin, Ellen, ed. 1996. *Inventing Lesbian Cultures in America.* Boston: Beacon.

———. 1998. *Recognizing Ourselves: Ceremonies of Lesbian and Gay Commitment.* New York: Columbia University Press.

———. 2009. *Gay Fatherhood: Narratives of Family and Citizenship in America.* Chicago: University of Chicago Press.

Lewin, Ellen, and William L. Leap, eds. 2002. *Out in Theory: The Emergence of Lesbian and Gay Anthropology*. Urbana: University of Illinois Press.

———. 2009. *Out in Public: Reinventing Lesbian/Gay Anthropology in a Globalizing World*. Malden, Mass.: Wiley-Blackwell.

Lomnitz, Claudio. 2001. *Deep Mexico, Silent Mexico: An Anthropology of Nationalism*. Minneapolis: University of Minnesota Press.

Long, Scott. 1999. "Gay and Lesbian Movements in Eastern Europe: Romania, Hungary, and the Czech Republic." *The Global Emergence of Gay and Lesbian Politics*, ed. Barry D. Adam, Jan Willem Duyvendak, and André Krouwel, 242–65. Philadelphia: Temple University Press.

López, Ana M. 1995. "Our Welcomed Guests: *Telenovelas* in Latin America." *To Be Continued . . . : Soap Operas around the World*, ed. Robert C. Allen, 256–75. New York: Routledge.

Lorde, Audre. 1984. *Sister Outsider: Essays and Speeches*. Trumansburg, N.Y.: Crossing.

Luibheid, Eithne, and Lionel Cantú, eds. 2005. *Queer Migrations: Sexuality, U.S. Citizenship, and Border Crossings*. Minneapolis: University of Minnesota Press.

Lumsden, Ian. 1996. *Machos, Maricones, and Gays: Cuba and Homosexuality*. Philadelphia: Temple University Press.

Manalansan, Martin F., IV. 1997. "In the Shadows of Stonewall: Examining Gay Transnational Politics and the Diasporic Dilemma." *The Politics of Culture in the Shadow of Capital*, ed. Lisa Lowe and David Lloyd, 485–505. Durham: Duke University Press.

———. 2003. *Global Divas: Filipino Men in the Diaspora*. Durham: Duke University Press.

Manalansan, Martin F., IV, and Arnaldo Cruz-Malavé. 2002. *Queer Globalizations: Citizenship and the Afterlife of Colonialism*. New York: New York University Press.

Mankekar, Purnima. 1999. *Screening Culture, Viewing Politics: An Ethnography of Television, Womanhood, and Nation in Postcolonial India*. Durham: Duke University Press.

Manz, Beatriz. 2004. *Paradise in Ashes: A Guatemalan Journey of Courage, Terror, and Hope*. Berkeley: University of California Press.

Marcus, Eric. 1993. *Making History: The Struggle for Gay and Lesbian Equal Rights, 1945–1990*. New York: HarperCollins.

Marcus, George E. "Ethnography in/of the World System: The Emergence of Multisited Ethnography." *Annual Review of Anthropology* 24:95–117.

Martin, Fran. 2000. "Surface Tensions: Reading Productions of Tongzhi in Contemporary Taiwan." GLQ 6(1): 61–86.

———. 2010. *Backward Glances: Contemporary Chinese Cultures and the Female Homoerotic Imaginary*. Durham: Duke University Press.

Martín-Barbero, Jesús. 1995. "Memory and Form in the Latin American Soap Opera." *To Be Continued . . . : Soap Operas around the World*, ed. Robert C. Allen, 276–84. London: Routledge.

Maskovsky, Jeff. 2002. "Do We All 'Reek of the Commodity'? Consumption and the Erasure of Poverty in Gay and Lesbian Studies." *Out in Theory: The Emergence of Lesbian and Gay Anthropology*, ed. Ellen Lewin and William Leap, 264–86. Urbana: University of Illinois Press.

Massad, Joseph. 2002. "Re-orienting Desire: The Gay International and the Arab World." *Public Culture* 14(2): 361–85.

———. 2008. *Desiring Arabs*. Chicago: University of Chicago Press.

Mazzarella, William. 2003. *Shoveling Smoke: Advertising and Globalization in Contemporary India*. Durham: Duke University Press.

———. 2004. "Culture, Globalization, Mediation." *Annual Review of Anthropology* 33:345–67.

McCarthy, John D., and Mayer N. Zald. 1977. "Resource Mobilization and Social Movements: A Partial Theory." *American Journal of Sociology* 82:1212–41.

McLelland, Mark. 2000. *Male Homosexuality in Modern Japan: Cultural Myths and Social Realities*. Richmond, Va.: Curzon.

McLelland, Mark, and Romit Dasgupta, eds. 2005. *Genders, Transgenders, and Sexualities in Japan*. New York: Routledge.

McLuhan, Marshall. 1964. *Understanding Media: The Extensions of Man*. New York: McGraw-Hill.

Melucci, Alberto. 1989. *Nomads of the Present: Social Movements and Individual Needs in Contemporary Society*. Philadelphia: Temple University Press.

Merry, Sally Engle. 2006a. *Human Rights and Gender Violence: Translating International Law into Local Justice*. Chicago: University of Chicago Press.

———. 2006b. "Transnational Human Rights and Local Activism: Mapping the Middle." *American Anthropologist* 108(1): 38–51.

Messer, Ellen. 2003. "Anthropologists in a World with and without Human Rights." *Exotic No More: Anthropology on the Front Lines*, ed. Jeremy MacClancy, 319–37. Chicago: University of Chicago Press.

Miller, Liz, dir. 2002. *Novela, Novela*, 30 mins. Frameline.

Mogrovejo, Norma. 1999. "Sexual Preference, the Ugly Duckling of Feminist Demands: The Lesbian Movement in Mexico." *Female Desires*, ed. Evelyn Blackwood and Saskia Wieringa, 308–35. New York: Columbia University Press.

———. 2000. *Un amor que se atrevió a decir su nombre: La lucha de las lesbianas y su relación con los movimientos homosexual y feminista en América Latina*. Mexico City: Centro Documentación y Archivo Histórico Lésbico de México, América Latina y El Caribe and Plaza y Valdés.

Molyneux, Maxine. 1985a. "Mobilization without Emancipation? Women's Interests, the State, and Revolution in Nicaragua." *Feminist Studies* 11(2): 227–54.

———. 1985b. "Women." *Nicaragua: The First Five Years*, ed. Thomas W. Walker, 145–62. New York: Praeger.

———. 2000. "Twentieth-Century State Formations in Latin America." *Hidden Histories of Gender and the State in Latin America*, ed. Elizabeth Dore and Maxine Molyneux, 33–82. Durham: Duke University Press.

———. 2003. *Doing the Rights Thing: Rights-Based Development and Latin American NGOs*. London: ITDG.

Montenegro, Sofia. 1985. *Memorias del Atlántico*. Managua: Editorial El Amancer.

———. 2000. *La cultura sexual en Nicaragua*. Managua: Centro de Investigaciones para la Comunicación.

Montoya, Rosario. 2002. "Women's Sexuality, Knowledge, and Agency in Rural Nicaragua." *Gender's Place: Feminist Anthropologies of Latin America*, ed. Rosario Montoya, Lessie Jo Frazier, and Janise Hurtig, 65–88. New York: Palgrave Macmillan.

Morales Henríquez, Viktor. 1980 *De Mrs. Hanna a la Dinorah principio y fin de la dictadura somocista: Historia de medio siglo de corrupción*. Managua: s.n.

Morgan, Robin. 1977. *Going Too Far: The Personal Chronicle of a Feminist*. New York: Random House.

Morris, Rosalind C. 1995. "All Made Up: Performance Theory and the New Anthropology of Sex and Gender." *Annual Review of Anthropology* 24:567–92.

Mosse, George L. 1985. *Nationalism and Sexuality: Middle-Class Morality and Sexual Norms in Modern Europe*. Madison: University of Wisconsin Press.

Muñoz, José Esteban. 1999. *Disidentifications: Queers of Color and the Performance of Politics*. Minneapolis: University of Minnesota Press.

Murray, Stephen O. 1995. *Latin American Male Homosexualities*. Albuquerque: University of New Mexico Press.

Murray, Stephen O., and Will Roscoe, eds. 1997. *Islamic Homosexualities: Culture, History, and Literature*. New York: New York University Press.

———, eds. 1998. *Boy-Wives and Female Husbands: Studies of African Homosexualities*. New York: St. Martin's.

Nagengast, Carole, and Terence Turner. 1997. "Introduction: Universal Human Rights versus Cultural Relativity." *Journal of Anthropological Research* 53(3): 269–72.

Nelson, Diane. 1999. *A Finger in the Wound: Body Politics in Quincentennial Guatemala*. Berkeley: University of California Press.

Nestle, Joan. 1992. *The Persistent Desire: A Femme–Butch Reader*. New York: Alyson.

Newton, Ester. 1979. *Mother Camp: Female Impersonators in America*. Chicago: University of Chicago Press.

———. 1993. *Cherry Grove, Fire Island: Sixty Years in America's First Gay and Lesbian Town*. Boston: Beacon.

———. 2000. *Margaret Mead Made Me Gay: Personal Essays, Public Ideas*. Durham: Duke University Press.

Offe, Clause. 1985. "New Social Movements: Challenging the Boundaries of Institutional Politics." *Social Research* 52:816–68.

Ong, Aihwa, and Stephen J. Collier, eds. 2004. *Global Assemblages: Technology, Politics and Ethics as Anthropological Problems*. Malden, Mass.: Blackwell.

Padilla, Mark. 2007. *Caribbean Pleasure Industry: Tourism, Sexuality, and AIDS in the Dominican Republic*. Chicago: University of Chicago Press.

Padilla, Martha Luz, Clara Murguialday, and Ana Criquillon. 1987. "Impact of the Sandinista Agrarian Reform on Rural Women's Subordination." *Rural Women and State Policy: Feminist Perspectives on Latin American Agricultural Development*, ed. Carmen Diana Deere and Magdalena Leon, 124–41. Boulder, Colo.: Westview.

Paley, Julia. 2001. *Marketing Democracy: Power and Social Movements in Post-dictatorship Chile*. Berkeley: University of California Press.

———. 2002. "Toward an Anthropology of Democracy." *Annual Review of Anthropology* 31:469–96.

———, ed. 2008. *Democracy: Anthropological Approaches*. Santa Fe: School for Advanced Research Press.

Palmberg, Mai. 1999. "Emerging Visibility of Gays and Lesbians in Southern Africa: Contrasting Contexts." *The Global Emergence of Gay and Lesbian Politics*, ed. Barry D. Adam, Jan Willem Duyvendak, and André Krouwel, 266–92. Philadelphia: Temple University Press.

Palmer, Steven. 1988. "Carlos Fonseca and the Construction of Sandinismo in Nicaragua." *Latin American Research Review* 23(1): 92–121.

Parker, Richard. 1991. *Bodies, Pleasures and Passions: Sexual Culture in Contemporary Brazil*. Boston: Beacon.

———. 1997. "Sexual Rights: Concepts and Actions." *Health and Human Rights* 2(3): 31–37.

———. 1999. *Beneath the Equator: Cultures of Desire, Male Homosexuality, and Emerging Gay Communities in Brazil*. New York: Routledge.

Pastor, Robert. 2002. *Not Condemned to Repetition*, 2nd ed. Boulder, Colo.: Westview.

Patel, Geeta. 2004. "Homely Housewives Run Amok: Lesbians in Marital Fixes." *Public Culture* 16(1): 131–58.

Patton, Cindy. 2000. "Migratory Vices." *Queer Diasporas*, ed. Beningo Sanchez-Eppler and Cindy Patton, 15–37. Durham: Duke University Press.

Pedelty, Mark. 1995. *War Stories: The Culture of Foreign Correspondents*. New York: Routledge.

Peirce, Kimberly, dir. 1999. *Boys Don't Cry*, 118 mins. Harp-Sharp Entertainment.

Pérez-Baltodano, Andrés. 2004. "Unholy Alliance: Church and the State in Nicaragua (1996–2002)." *Undoing Democracy: The Politics of Electoral Cuadillismo*, ed. David Close and Kalowatie Deonandan, 87–102. Lanham, Md.: Lexington Books.

Perry, Troy D., and Thomas L. P. Swicegood. 1990. *Don't Be Afraid Anymore: The Story of Reverend Troy Perry and the Metropolitan Community Churches*. New York: St. Martin's.

Petchesky, Rosalind P. 2000. "Sexual Rights: Inventing a Concept, Mapping an International Practice." *Framing the Sexual Subject: The Politics of Gender, Sexuality, and Power*, ed. Richard Parker, Regina Maria Barbosa, and Peter Aggleton, 81–103. Berkeley: University of California Press.

Peters, Julie, and Andrea Wolper, eds. 1995. *Women's Rights, Human Rights: International Feminist Perspectives*. New York: Routledge.

Phelan, Shane. 1989. *Identity Politics: Lesbian Feminism and the Limits of Community*. Philadelphia: Temple University Press.

———. 1993. "(Be)Coming out: Lesbian Identity and Politics." *Signs* 18(4): 765–90.

———. 1997. *Playing with Fire: Queer Politics, Queer Theories*. New York: Routledge.

Phelan, Shane, and Mark Blasius, eds. 1997. *We Are Everywhere: A Historical Sourcebook of Lesbian and Gay Politics*. New York: Routledge.

Pine, Adrienne. 2008. *Working Hard, Drinking Hard: On Violence and Survival in Honduras*. Berkeley: University of California Press.

Plummer, Kenneth. 1992. *Modern Homosexualities: Fragments of Lesbian and Gay Experience*. New York: Routledge.

————. 2003. *Intimate Citizenship: Private Decisions and Public Dialogues.* Seattle: University of Washington Press.

Povinelli, Elizabeth A. 2004. *The Cunning of Recognition.* Durham: Duke University Press.

————. 2006. *The Empire of Love: Toward a Theory of Intimacy, Genealogy, and Carnality.* Durham: Duke University Press.

————. 2007. "Disturbing Sexuality." *South Atlantic Quarterly* 106(3): 565–76.

Povinelli, Elizabeth A., and George Chauncey. 1999. "Thinking Sexuality Transnationally: An Introduction." *GLQ* 5(4): 439–50.

Prevost, Gary, and Harry E. Vanden, eds. 1997. *The Undermining of the Sandinista Revolution.* New York: St. Martin's.

Prieur, Annick. 1998. *Mema's House, Mexico City: On Transvestites, Queens, and Machos.* Chicago: University of Chicago Press.

Provencher, Denis. 2007. *Queer French: Globalization, Language, and Sexual Citizenship in France.* Burlington, Vt.: Ashgate.

Puar, Jasbir. 2005. "Queer Times, Queer Assemblages." *Social Text* 23(3–4): 121–39.

————. 2007. *Terrorist Assemblages: Homonationalism in Queer Times.* Durham: Duke University Press.

Puig, Salvador Marti. 2004. "The External Debt of Nicaragua and the Alemán Liberal Administration." *Undoing Democracy: The Politics of Electoral Cuadillismo*, ed. David Close and Kalowatie Deonandan, 143–66. Lanham, Md.: Lexington Books.

Quiroga, José. 2000. *Tropics of Desire: Interventions from Queer Latino America.* New York: New York University Press.

Rabasa, José. 1997. "Of Zapatismo: Reflections on the Folkloric and the Impossible in a Subaltern Insurrection." *The Politics of Culture in the Shadow of Capital*, ed. Lisa Lowe and David Lloyd, 399–431. Durham: Duke University Press.

Ramírez, Sergio, ed. 1981. *El pensamiento de Sandino.* Managua: Editorial Nueva.

Ramírez, Sergio, and Robert E. Conrad. 1990. *Sandino: Testimony of a Nicaraguan Patriot, 1921–1934.* Princeton: Princeton University Press.

Randall, Margaret. 1981. *Sandino's Daughters: Testimonies of Nicaraguan Women in Struggle.* Vancouver: New Star Books.

————. 1993. "To Change Our Own Reality and the World: A Conversation with Lesbians in Nicaragua." *Signs* 18(4): 907–24.

————. 1994. *Sandino's Daughters Revisited: Feminism in Nicaragua.* New Brunswick: Rutgers University Press.

Razsa, Maple J., and Andrej Kurnik. 2012. "The Occupy Movement in Žižek's Hometown: Direct Democracy and a Politics of Becoming." *American Ethnologist* 39(2): 238–58.

Reddy, Gayatri. 2005. *With Respect to Sex: Negotiating Hijra Identity in South India.* Chicago: University of Chicago Press.

Ribiero, Gustavo Lins. 1998. "Cybercultural Politics: Political Activism at a Distance in a Transnational World." *Cultures of Politics / Politics of Cultures: Re-visioning Latin American Social Movements*, ed. Sonia Alvarez, Evelina Dagnino, and Arturo Escobar, 325–52. Boulder, Colo.: Westview.

Rich, Adrienne. 1980. *On Lies, Secrets, and Silence: Selected Prose, 1966–1978*. New York: W. W. Norton.

———. 1986. "Notes toward a Politics of Location." *Blood, Bread, and Poetry: Selected Prose, 1979–1985*. New York: W. W. Norton.

Rich, B. Ruby, and Lourdes Arguelles. 1984. "Homosexuality, Homophobia, and Revolution: Notes toward an Understanding of the Cuban Lesbian and Gay Male Experience." Parts I and II, *Signs* 9(4): 683–99 and 11(1): 120–36.

Riles, Annelise. 2000. *The Network Inside Out*. Ann Arbor: University of Michigan Press.

Robertson, Jennifer. 1998. *Takarazuka: Sexual Politics and Modern Culture in Modern Japan*. Berkeley: University of California Press.

———, ed. 2004. *Same-Sex Cultures and Sexualities: An Anthropological Reader*. Malden, Mass.: Wiley-Blackwell.

Rodríguez, Clemencia. 2001. *Fissures in the Mediascape: An International Study of Citizens' Media*. Creskill, N.J.: Hampton.

Rofel, Lisa. 1999. *Other Modernities: Gendered Yearnings in China after Socialism*. Berkeley: University of California Press.

———. 2007. *Desiring China: Experiments in Neoliberalism, Sexuality, and Public Culture*. Durham: Duke University Press.

Rosenbloom, Rachel, ed. 1996. *Unspoken Rules: Sexual Orientation and Women's Human Rights*. London: Cassell.

Rossett, Peter, and John Vandermeer, eds. 1986. *Nicaragua, Unfinished Revolution: The New Nicaragua Reader*. New York: Grove.

Rubenstein, Anne. 1998. *Bad Language, Naked Ladies, and Other Threats to the Nation: A Political History of Comic Books in Mexico*. Durham: Duke University Press.

Rubin, Gayle. 1984. "Thinking Sex: Notes for a Radical Theory of the Politics of Sexuality." *Pleasure and Danger*, ed. Carole Vance, 267–319. New York: Routledge.

———. 2002. "Studying Sexual Subcultures: Excavating the Ethnography of Gay Communities in Urban North America." *Out in Theory: The Emergence of Lesbian and Gay Anthropology*, ed. Ellen Lewin and William Leap, 17–68. Urbana: University of Illinois Press.

Rupp, Leila J., and Verta A. Taylor. 2003. *Drag Queens at the 801 Cabaret*. Chicago: University of Chicago Press.

Rushdie, Salman. 1987. *The Jaguar Smile: A Nicaraguan Journey*. New York: Viking.

Saldaña-Portillo, María Josefina. 2003. *The Revolutionary Imagination in the Age of Development*. Durham: Duke University Press.

Sánchez-Eppler, Benigno, and Cindy Patton, eds. 2000. *Queer Diasporas*. Durham: Duke University Press.

Sandoval, María Adelia. 2004. "La Caimana: La primera lesbiana declarada." *7 Días*, no. 419: 3–7.

Sanford, Victoria. 2004. *Buried Secrets: Truth and Human Rights in Guatemala*. New York: Palgrave Macmillan.

Sanford, Victoria, and Asale Angel-Ajani, eds. 2006. *Engaged Observer: Anthropology, Advocacy, and Activism*. New Brunswick: Rutgers University Press.

Sang, Tze-Lan Deborah. 2003. *The Emerging Lesbian: Female Same-Sex Desire in Modern China*. Chicago: University of Chicago Press.

Saporta Sternbach, Nancy, Marysa Navarro-Aranguren, Patricia Chuchryk, and Sonia E. Alvarez. 1992. "Feminisms in Latin America: From Bogota to San Bernardo." *Signs* 17(21): 393–434.

Sawyer, Suzana. 2004. *Crude Chronicles: Indigenous Politics, Multinational Oil, and Neoliberalism in Ecuador*. Durham: Duke University Press.

Schein, Louisa. 2002. "Mapping Hmong Media in Diasporic Space." *Media Worlds: Anthropology on New Terrain*, ed. Faye D. Ginsburg, Lila Abu-Lughod, and Brian Larkin, 229–46. Berkeley: University of California Press.

Scheper-Hughes, Nancy. 1995. "The Primacy of the Ethical: Propositions for a Militant Anthropology." *Current Anthropology* 36(3): 409–20.

Schiller, Naomi. 2009. "Framing the Revolution: Circulation and Meaning of 'The Revolution Will Not Be Televised.'" *Mass Communication and Society* 4:478–502.

Sedgwick, Eve Kosofsky. 1990. *Epistemology of the Closet*. Berkeley: University of California Press.

Seidman, Steven. 1996. *Queer Theory Sociology*. London: Wiley Blackwell.

———. 2002. *Beyond the Closet: The Transformation of Gay and Lesbian Life*. New York: Routledge.

Sequeira, Consuelo Cruz. 1995. "Mistrust and Violence in Nicaragua: Ideology and Politics." *Latin American Research Review* 30(1): 212–25.

Shipley, Jesse Weaver. 2009. "Aesthetic of the Entrepreneur: Afro-cosmopolitan Rap and Moral Circulation in Accra, Ghana." *Anthropological Quarterly* 82(3): 631–68.

Sinclair, John. 1999. *Latin American Television: A Global View*. New York: Oxford University Press.

Singer, Beverly. 2001. *Wiping the War Paint off the Lens: Native American Film and Video*. Minneapolis: University of Minnesota Press.

Sinnott, Megan. 2004. *Toms and Dees: Transgender Identity and Female Same-Sex Relationships in Thailand*. Honolulu: University of Hawai'i Press.

Skidmore, Thomas E. 1999. *Brazil: Five Centuries of Change*. New York: Oxford University Press.

Smith, Carol. 1990. *Guatemalan Indians and the State, 1540–1988*. Austin: University of Texas Press.

———. 2000. "The Militarization of Civil Society in Guatemala: Economic Reorganization as a Continuation of War." *Latin American Perspectives* 17(4): 8–41.

Smith, Hazel. 1993. *Nicaragua: Self-Determination and Survival*. London: Pluto.

Spalding, Rose J. 1987. *The Political Economy of Revolutionary Nicaragua*. Boulder, Colo.: Westview.

———. 1994. *Capitalists and Revolution in Nicaragua: Opposition and Accommodation, 1979–1993*. Chapel Hill: University of North Carolina Press.

———. 1997. "The Economic Elite." *Nicaragua without Illusions: Regime Transition and Structural Adjustment in the 1990s*, ed. Thomas W. Walker, 249–64. Lanham, Md.: Rowman and Littlefield.

Speed, Shannon. 2006. "At the Crossroads of Human Rights and Anthropology: Toward a Critically Engaged Activist Research." *American Anthropologist* 108(1): 66–76.

———. 2007. *Rights in Rebellion: Indigenous Struggle and Human Rights in Chiapas*. Stanford: Stanford University Press.

Speed, Shannon, and Alvaro Reyes. 2002. "'In Our Own Defense': Rights and Resistance in Chiapas." *Political and Legal Anthropology Review* 25(1): 69–89.

Spitulnik, Deborah. 1993. "Anthropology and Mass Media." *Annual Review of Anthropology* (22): 293–315.

Stahler-Sholk, Richard. 1995. "Sandinista Social and Economic Policy: The Mixed Blessings of Hindsight." *Latin American Research Review* 30(2): 235–50.

Starn, Orin. 1999. *Nightwatch: The Politics of Protest in the Andes*. Durham: Duke University Press.

Stein, Arlene. 1997. *Sex and Sensibility: Stories of a Lesbian Generation*. Berkeley: University of California Press.

Stephen, Lynn. 1997. *Women and Social Movements in Latin America: Power from Below*. Austin: University of Texas Press.

Stoler, Ann L. 1995. *Race and the Education of Desire*. Durham: Duke University Press.

Stychin, Carl. 2001. *Law and Sexuality: The Global Arena*. Minneapolis: University of Minnesota Press.

Sullivan, Gerard, and Peter A. Jackson, eds. 1999. *Lady Boys, Tom Boys, Rent Boys: Male and Female Homosexualities in Contemporary Thailand*. Binghamton, N.Y.: Haworth.

———. 2001. *Gay and Lesbian Asia: Culture, Identity, Community*. New York: Harrington Park.

Sullivan, Maureen. 2004. *The Family of Woman: Lesbian Mothers, Their Children, and the Undoing of Gender*. Berkeley: University of California Press.

Tarrow, Sidney. 1994. *Power in Movement: Social Movements, Collective Action, and Politics*. Cambridge: Cambridge University Press.

Tate, Winifred. 2007. *Counting the Dead: The Culture and Politics of Human Rights Activism in Colombia*. Berkeley: University of California Press.

Taylor, Charles. 1992. *Multiculturalism and the Politics of Recognition: An Essay*. Princeton: Princeton University Press.

Teunis, Niels, and Gilbert Herdt, eds. 2007. *Sexual Inequalities and Social Justice*. Berkeley: University of California Press.

Thayer, Millie. 1997. "Identity, Revolution, and Democracy: Lesbian Movements in Central America." *Social Problems* 44(3): 386–406.

Touraine, Alain. 1981. *The Voice and the Eye*. Cambridge: Cambridge University Press.

Tsing, Anna Lowenhaupt. 2004. *Friction: An Ethnography of Global Connection*. Princeton: Princeton University Press.

Turner, Terence. 1992. "Defiant Images: The Kayapo Appropriation of Video." *Anthropology Today* 8(6): 5–16.

———. 1997. "Human Rights, Human Difference: Anthropology's Contribution to an Emancipatory Cultural Politics." *Journal of Anthropological Research* 53(3): 273–91.

———. 2002. "Representation, Politics, and Cultural Imagination in Indigenous Video: General Points and Kayapo Examples." *Media Worlds: Anthropology on New Terrain*, ed. Faye D. Ginsburg, Lila Abu-Lughod, and Brian Larkin, 75–89. Berkeley: University of California Press.

Turner, Victor. 1969. *The Ritual Process: Structure and Anti-structure*. Chicago: Aldine.

Vaid, Urvashi. 1995. *Virtual Equality: The Mainstreaming of Gay and Lesbian Liberation*. New York: Anchor.

Valentine, David. 2004. "The Categories Themselves." GLQ 10(2): 215–20.

———. 2007. *Imagining Transgender: An Ethnography of a Category*. Durham: Duke University Press.

van Gijsel, Marike. 2003. *Mujeres lesbianas en Managua*. Managua: Fundación Xochiquetzal.

Verdery, Katherine. 1991. *National Ideology under Socialism*. Berkeley: University of California Press.

Vilas, Carlos M. 1986. *The Sandinista Revolution: National Liberation and Social Transformation in Central America*. New York: Monthly Review.

———. 1989. *State, Class, and Ethnicity in Nicaragua: Capitalist Modernization and Revolutionary Change on the Atlantic Coast*, trans. Susan Norwood. Boulder, Colo.: Lynne Reinner.

———. 1992. "Family Affairs: Class, Lineage, and Politics in Contemporary Nicaragua." *Journal of Latin American Studies* 24(2): 309–41.

Vine, David. 2009. *Island of Shame: The Secret History of the U.S. Military Base on Diego Garcia*. Princeton: Princeton University Press.

Walker, Thomas W. 1991. *Revolution and Counterrevolution in Nicaragua*. Boulder, Colo.: Westview.

———. 1997. *Nicaragua without Illusions: Regime Transition and Structural Adjustment in the 1990s*. Lanham, Md.: Rowman and Littlefield.

———. 2000. "Nicaragua: Transition through Revolution." *Repression, Resistance, and Democratic Transition in Central America*, ed. Thomas W. Walker and Ariel C. Armory, 67–88. Wilmington, Del.: Scholarly Resources.

———. 2003. *Nicaragua: The Land of Sandino*, 4th ed. Boulder, Colo.: Westview.

Walker, Thomas W., and Ariel C. Armory, eds. 2000. *Repression, Resistance, and Democratic Transition in Central America*. Wilmington, Del.: Scholarly Resources.

Warner, Michael. 1993. *Fear of a Queer Planet: Queer Politics and Social Theory*. Minneapolis: University of Minnesota Press.

———. 1999. *The Trouble with Normal: Sex, Politics, and the Ethics of Queer Life*. New York: Free Press.

Warner, R. Stephen. 1995. "The Metropolitan Community Churches and the Gay Agenda: The Power of Pentecostalism and Essentialism." *Religion and Social Order* 5:81–108.

Warren, Kay B. 1997. "The Indigenous Role in Guatemalan Peace." *Cultural Survival Quarterly* 21(2): 24–27.

———. 1998. *Indigenous Movements and Their Critics: Pan-Maya Activism in Guatemala*. Princeton: Princeton University Press.

Weeks, Jeffrey. 1989. *Sex, Politics, and Society: The Regulation of Sexuality since 1800*. New York: Longman.

———. 1999. "The Sexual Citizen." *Love and Eroticism*, ed. Mike Featherstone, 35–52. London: Sage.

Weiner, James F. 1997. "Televisualist Anthropology: Representation, Aesthetics, Politics." *Current Anthropology* 38(2): 197–235.

Weismantel, Mary J. 2001. *Cholas and Pishtacos: Stories of Race and Sex in the Andes*. Chicago: University of Chicago Press.

Wekker, Gloria. 2006. *The Politics of Passion: Women's Sexual Culture in the Afro-Surinamese Diaspora*. New York: Columbia University Press.

Wessel, Lois. 1991. "Reproductive Rights in Nicaragua: From the Sandinistas to the Government of Violeta Chamorro." *Feminist Studies* 17(3): 537–45.

Weston, Kath. 1991. *Families We Choose: Lesbians, Gays, Kinship*. New York: Columbia University Press.

———. 1993. "Lesbian/Gay Studies in the House of Anthropology." *Annual Review of Anthropology* 22:339–67.

———. 1996. *Render Me, Gender Me: Lesbians Talk Sex, Class, Nation, Studmuffins . . .* New York: Columbia University Press.

Whisnant, David. 1995. *Rascally Signs in Sacred Places: The Politics of Culture in Nicaragua*. Durham: University of North Carolina Press.

Wieringa, Saskia, Evelyn Blackwood, and Abha Bhaiya, eds. 2007. *Women's Sexualities and Masculinities in a Globalizing Asia*. New York: Palgrave Macmillan.

Williams, Philip J. 1989. *The Catholic Church and Politics in Nicaragua and Costa Rica*. Pittsburgh: University of Pittsburgh Press.

Williams, Raymond. 1974. *Television: Technology and Cultural Form*. Hanover: Wesleyan University Press.

Wilson, Ara. 2004. *The Intimate Economies of Bangkok*. Berkeley: University of California Press.

Wright, Timothy. 2000. "Gay Organizations, NGOs, and the Globalization of Sexual Identity: The Case of Bolivia." *Journal of Latin American Anthropology* 5(2): 89–111.

Zamora, Daisy. 1992. *Riverbed of Memory*. San Francisco: City Lights.

Zimmerman, Lisa. 2000. *Sandinista: Carlos Fonseca and the Nicaraguan Revolution*. Durham: Duke University Press.

Žižek, Slavoj. 2005. "Against Human Rights." *New Left Review* 34:115–34.

INDEX

≑

Page numbers in italics refer to illustrations.

Betty la Fea (Ugly Betty) [television show], 9, 51

bien educada (well-mannered and well-educated), 61–63, 188n2. *See also* lesbian discussion groups

bisexual/s, 43, 68, 166, 174n8, 178n33. *See also* LGBTQ (lesbian, gay, bisexual, transgender, and queer); LGBTTIQQAA (lesbian, gay, bisexual, transgender, transvestite, intersex, queer, questioning, (queer) ally, and asexual)

Blackwood, Evelyn, 17

Blandón, Erick, 114, 190n6

Boas, Franz, 168

Bolaños, Enrique, 54, 56

La Boletina (magazine), 51, 130

Bolivia and Bolivarian Revolution, 29, 57, 163, 187n43, 192n29

Borge, Tomás, 35, 181n11. *See also* Frente Sandinista de Liberación Nacional (FSLN)

Bourdieu, Pierre, 88, 188n2

Boys Don't Cry (Los muchachos no lloran) [film], 70–74, 189nn10–11

Brazil, 125, 132, 163, 192n3

Butler, Judith, 11, 117, 161

Cabezas, Omar, 164–65

campo (country/rural locations) and *campesinos* (country/rural folk), 82–83, 85–87, 137–38

Carmelo (Aguirre, Carmen, La Caimana, Carlos), 33, 181n10

Carrillo, Héctor, 18

Catholic church, as moral influence, 9, 39, 53–54, 57–58, 59–60, 165

celebrity status, and mass media, 131, 193n7

Central Intelligence Agency (CIA), 37, 47

CEP-SIDA (Collective of Popular Educators Concerned with HIV/AIDS), 44. *See also* HIV/AIDS prevention and education; sexual health and behavior

Chamorro, Violeta Barrios, 3, 47, 49, 52, 54, 184nn28–29

characters, in television show, 132, 193n8

childhood sexual abuse, 54–56, 143–44, 185n37, 186nn40–41

choice, or sexual choice *(opción sexual)*, 66–70, 103–4

Christian fundamentalism *(fundamentalismo cristiano)*, 8–9, 48, 53, 53–54, 165. *See also* Catholic church

CIA (Central Intelligence Agency), 37, 47

civil society, in context of activism, 6–8, 174n9

clandestine or hidden activities, 65–66, 148–50, 155, 178n33

Clinton, Bill, 55, 185n37

cochonas (dykes): gender roles and, 72; as *machista*, 72; as sexual subject, 2, 19, 174n8, 179n36, 179n39; Somocismo era and, 32–33, 181n10; stereotypes in *telenovelas* and, 134, 145–47

cochones, cochón (fags, fag): *hombres hombres* with, 115, 136, 178n32, 179n38; overview of, 17, 177n30; as sexual subject, 2, 6, 174n8; Somocismo era and, 32–33, 181n10; stereotypes in *telenovelas* and, 134, 146–47. *See also maricón* (fag)

Colectivo Shomos (We Are Homos), 119–21, 174n11, 184n24, 191n21

Collective of Popular Educators Concerned with HIV/AIDS (CEP-SIDA), 44. *See also* HIV/AIDS prevention and education; sexual health and behavior

Collinson, Helen, 183n16

Comaroff, Jean, 171

communitarian politics, 11, 40–41, 166–67, 183nn19–20

concurso travesti (transvestite or cross-dressing contest), 111–12, 113, 114, 191nn13–14. *See also* LGBTTIQQAA (lesbian, gay, bisexual, transgender, transvestite, intersex, queer, questioning, (queer) ally, and asexual)

consciousness: consciousness-raising groups and, 62–63, 75, 89, 100, 188n8; for lesbians, 14, 61–63, 75, 89, 91; sexual identity development and, 75–84, 90–91, 189n17; *telenovela* and, 133, 138–39

Constitution of Nicaragua, 38, 48–50, 152, 186n41. *See also* government

Contras (Frente Democrática Nicaragüense) campaign by u.s., 37–38, 47, 182n14, 184n29

costeños (African and/or people of indigenous descent), 128, 192n2

country/rural locations *(campo)* and country/folk *(campesinos)*, 82–83, 85–87, 137–38

cross-dressing or transvestite contest *(concurso travesti)*, 111–12, *113*, 114, 191nn13–14. *See also* LGBTTIQQAA (lesbian, gay, bisexual, transgender, transvestite, intersex, queer, questioning, (queer) ally, and asexual)

Cuba, 28, 34, 45, 98, 182n15, 184n26, 192n3, 193n5

culture transformation: asylum case and, 161; overview of, 8, 14, 163; personal or private experience and, 52; postrevolutionary era and, 11, 45–46, 184n27; sexual rights activists and, 1–2; SFFP and, 101–3, *102*, 109–10, 190n11; *telenovela* and, 130, 132–33

danza, and *travestis*, 116

Darío, Rubén, 107, 190n8

Debord, Guy, 132, 194n18

de la Dehesa, Rafael, 125

derechos lesbianos (lesbian rights), 5–6, 19–20, 39–40, 90, 103–4, 173n5, 183n21. *See also* homosexual rights; human rights; sexual rights

desire: education of desire and, 21, 62, 85–87; gay men and, 17; lesbian identity in context of, 62, 67–70, 72, 76–77, 82–85; overview of, 13, 16–17; sexual scripts and, 18

dialogic relationship: print media and, 150, 152, 154–55; radio and, 98, 130, 147–49, 157; *telenovela* and, 133, 193n10

digital information and technology: overview of, 2–3; global discourse and, 166; mass media and, 9, 129, 131, 147–48, 155–56, 158–59, 194n16

discrimination: activism and, 51, 132; against gay men, 45–46, 98, 108, 135; against lesbians, 45–46, 63, 72, 74, 98, 108; against women, 26, 35, 40–41; Constitution and, 48–50, 152; employment options and, 23–24, 119, 189n15, 191n22; liberalism in context of, 105; overview of, 163–64; Sandinismo era and, 45–46; *telenovela* plotline and, 135, 146. *See also* antisodomy law (Article 204)

divorce and marriage, for lesbians, 104–5, 190n6

"drag" performances, by *travestis*, 93, 94, 111–16, *113*, *114*, 191nn13–14, 191nn13–15

dyke, popular term for *(marimacha)*, 179n36

dykes *(cochonas)*. *See* cochonas (dykes)

economics. *See* socioeconomics

education: mass media and, 129, 132, 193n9; pedagogical materials for public schools and, 53; women's access to, 29, 35, 36. *See also* HIV/AIDS prevention and education

education of desire, 21, 62, 85–87. *See also* desire

effeminate gay men, 23–24, 134–37, 191n21. *See also* gay men *(gays/homosexuales)*

egalitarianism (equality), 20, 36–37, 40

egalitarian model of sexuality: for gay men, 17–18, 136–37, 145–47, 178n33, 194n12; for lesbians, 20, 89, 146–47; sexual identity categories and, 167; in *telenovela*, 136–37, 145–47, 194n12

electoral politics, 27, 54–56, 185n37, 186nn40–41

Elias, Norbert, 88

employment, in context of gender presentation, 23–24, 119, 189n15, 191n22

equality (egalitarianism), 20, 36–37, 40. *See also* egalitarian model of sexuality

ethnographies of activists/advocates, 4, 168–71

facilitators, for lesbian discussion groups, 62–63, 64, 66–70, 76, 81, 88–91, 188n1

fag *(maricón)*, 17, 138

fags, fag *(cochones, cochón)*. *See* cochones, *cochón* (fags, fag)

femenina or *muy mujer* (very womanish), 19, 179n38

femininity (*femenina*): lesbians and, 73–74, 82–84, 139–41, 143, 177n30, 189n15; *travestis* in context of, 115–16; women and, 40, 47, 177n30, 183n19, 194n29. *See also* gender roles; masculinity; women

feminism: consciousness-raising groups and, 62–63, 89; identity politics and, 120, 192n26; outness of lesbians and, 120, 192n26; postrevolutionary era and, 47, 51, 55–56, 58, 58–59, 183nn19–20, 185n37, 187n46, 194n29; radio and, 50; Sandinismo era and, 40, 41, 183nn19–20; Somocismo and, 29–30. *See also* women and women's rights

Field, Les W., 14, 174n10, 180n1, 183n20

fiscal issues. *See* socioeconomics

fiscal terrorism, and sexual rights, 8–9, 175n13

fobias, 15, 56, 63, 71, 108, 166, 176nn25–26, 186n41. *See also* violence

focus group, for lesbian character's outness, 142–43

Fonseca, Carlos, 34, 181n11. *See also* Frente Sandinista de Liberación Nacional (FSLN)

foreign governments, as funding sources, 8, 48, 128, 132, 155–56, 192n1

Foucault, Michel, 10, 88

foundations, as funding sources, 8, 192n1

Frankfurt School, 194n18

Fraser, Nancy, 188n8

Freire, Paulo, 89, 133, 189n16

Frente Democrática Nicaragüense (U.S. Contras) campaign, 37–38, 47, 182n14, 184n29

Frente Sandinista de Liberación Nacional (FSLN), 34–41, 54–55, 58–59, 89, 181n11, 182n14, 183nn19–20. *See also* Sandinismo (Sandinista Revolution)

Friends (television show), 132

Friends [Female] Together (Amigas Juntas), 62, 74–77

FSLN (Frente Sandinista de Liberación Nacional), 34–41, 54–55, 58–59, 89, 181n11, 182n14, 183nn19–20. *See also* Sandinismo (Sandinista Revolution)

Fuera del Closet (Out of the Closet) [magazine], 12, 51, 64, 77, 98, 100, 190n4

Fundación Nimehuatzin, 51, 174n11

Fundación Xochiquetzal: overview of, 174n11; *Fuera del Closet* publication by, 12, 51, 64, 77, 98, 100, 190n4; lesbian discussion groups sponsorship by, 63–74, 99; poster for event and, 52; radio programs and, 149; Xochiquetzal as symbol for, 52, 77, 79

fundamentalismo cristiano (Christian fundamentalism), 8–9, 48, 53, 53–54, 165. *See also* Catholic church

funding sources: foreign governments as, 8, 48, 128, 132, 155–56, 192n1; foundations as, 8, 192n1; gay men and, 119–22; gendered power and, 118; individuals or groups as, 74, 99, 107; institutions as, 8, 48; Lesbian and Gay Pride and, 107, 109; lesbians and, 80, 120–21, 188n1, 188n2, 192n27; NGOS and, 8, 48, 119–20; organizations as, 99, 154, 190n5; SFFP and, 99; for *telenovela*, 128, 132, 192n1. *See also* socioeconomics

Gathering for Sexuality Free from Prejudice (Jornada por una Sexualidad Libre de Prejuicios), 52, 92–93, 98, 99, 106, 109, 120. *See also* Sexuality Free from Prejudice or Sexualidad Libre de Prejuicios (SFFP)

gay men (*gays/homosexuales*): activism and, 17–20; *activo* male partners and, 17, 178n32; asylum case in U.S. for gay man and, 160–62, 171; country/folk and, 137–38; desire and, 17; discrimination against, 98, 135; effeminate, 23–24; egalitarian model of sexuality for, 17–18, 136–37, 145–47, 178n33, 194n12; employment in context of gender presentation for, 119, 189n15, 191n22; funding sources and, 119–22; gender performance and, 136, 138; Mediterranean model of male sexuality and, 17–18, 178nn31–33; moral gay character in *telenovela* and, 137, 194n13;

normalization of, 135–36, 145–47; outness of, 119–22, 137–38; overview of,
15, 176n21; *pasivo* male partners and,
17, 178n32; queerness and, 135–36, 138,
146; rape of, 161; Sandinismo era and,
42–43, 45, 183n21; sexual rights for, 13;
as sexual subject, 137; *telenovela* characters and, 135–38, 145–47, 194n12,
194n13; as term of use, 2, 6, 174n8;
visibility and, 45, 122. *See also* lesbians
(lesbianas); LGBTQ (lesbian, gay, bisexual, transgender, and queer); LGBT-
TIQQAA (lesbian, gay, bisexual, transgender, transvestite, intersex, queer,
questioning, (queer) ally, and asexual);
men, and sexuality
GEDDS (Grupo Estratégico por los Derechos Humanos de la Diversidad
Sexual), 163–64, 166, 167
Geertz, Clifford, 7
gendering power, in context of *concurso
travesti*, 116–18
gender performance/s: in *telenovela*, 136,
138, 143, 145; *travestis* "drag" performances and, 93, 94, 111–16, 113, 114,
191nn13–14, 191nn13–15
gender rights, 39–40, 40–41, 50, 56,
75–76, 180n41, 183nn19–20, 183n21.
See also human rights; sexual rights
gender roles: gay men and, 17, 178n32;
lesbians and, 19, 67, 70–74, 82–85,
84–85, 189n15; machismo and, 5, 12,
17, 177n30; masculinity and, 19, 73–74,
177n30. *See also* femininity *(femenina)*;
men
global discourse: development schema
and, 155–56, 194n15; digital information and, 166; the global South and,
3, 13, 18–19, 108–9, 155–56, 167, 171,
176n21; interconnections and, 3, 156,
171; mass media, 150, 152, 153, 153,
155–56; sexual identity categories and,
16–17, 167. *See also* Latin America;
transnationalism; *and specific countries*
global North: *concurso travesti* discourse
in, 116; development schema by, 155–
56, 194n15; egalitarian model of sexu-

ality and, 17–18, 136, 146–47, 178n33;
global discourse and, 3, 150, 152, 153,
153, 155–56; the global South's inter-
connection with, 3, 156, 171; homosexuality in context of, 42–44, 183n22;
Mediterranean model of male sexuality and, 17–18, 178nn31–33; movements and, 13, 176n21; outness model
and association with, 122–23; sexual
identity categories in, 167; sexual
rights in, 15–16, 176n23, 177n27; terms
of use in, 108–9, 190n10. *See also*
global discourse; global South; United
States
global South, 3, 13, 18–19, 108–9, 155–56,
167, 171, 176n21. *See also* global North;
Latin America; *and specific countries*
González-Rivera, Victoria, 29–30, 43,
185n37
Gould, Deborah B., 124–25, 190n2
Gould, Jeffrey L., 30, 182n14
government: Constitution of Nicaragua
and, 38, 48–50, 152, 186n41; Ombudsperson's Office for the Defense of
Sexual Diversity Rights and, 164–65.
See also antisodomy law (Article 204);
political histories in context of sexual
rights; Sandinismo (Sandinista Revolution); Somoza era (Somocismo era);
and specific NGOS, *political groups, and
political leaders*
Gramsci, Antonio, 9–10
grassroots activism, and lesbian discussion
groups, 62, 74–77, 81–87, 189nn13–16
gringos/as, 7, 109, 110, 143, 168
groups or individuals, as funding sources,
74, 99, 107
Grupo Estratégico por los Derechos
Humanos de la Diversidad Sexual
(GEDDS), 163–64, 166, 167
Grupo Safo, the Iniciativa desde La Diversidad Sexual por los Derechos Humanos (Sexual Diversity Initiative for
Human Rights), 164
Grupo por la Visibilidad Lésbica (Lesbian
Visibility Group), 22, 130, 150–57, 151,
153

Guatemalan indigenous populations, 125, 182n15, 192n27

"El Guerrillero sin Nombre" (The Unknown Soldier or "Rambo") statue, 96, 96

Habermas, Jürgen, 194n18

Health and Sexuality (Salud y Sexualidad) [magazine], 9, 175n15

heterosexual *(heterosexismo)*, 12, 17, 75, 114, 166. *See also* men, and sexuality; women and women's rights

hidden or clandestine activities, 65–66, 148–50, 155, 178n33

HIV/AIDS prevention and education: CEP-SIDA initiative and, 44; Fundación Xochiquetzal and, 63, 98; lesbians and, 120, 192n5; NGOS and, 63, 98–99; outness in context of, 125; protest events and, 94, 96; Sandinismo era and, 44, 51, 184nn23–24; sex industry and, 119; Shomos and, 119–20. *See also* sexual health and behavior

hombres hombres (real men), 115, 136, 178n32, 179n38

hombruna (mannish or manly), 19, 82–84, 179n37

homo-lesbo-transfobia, 166

homophobia *(homofobia)*, 15, 56, 71, 108, 166, 176nn25–26, 186n41. *See also* violence

homosexuales/gays (gay men). *See* gay men *(gays/homosexuales)*

homosexuality, 35–36, 41–44, 137–38, 143–44, 178n33, 183n22. *See also* gay men *(gays/homosexuales)*; lesbians *(lesbianas)*

homosexual rights *(derechos homosexuales)*: gender bias in use of term, 24, 121–22, 192n28; Sandinismo era and, 35–36, 39–40, 41–46, 183n18, 183nn21–22, 184nn23–24, 184n27; SFFP and, 106; Somocismo and, 32–33, 35, 181n10. *See also* homosexuality; human rights; lesbian rights *(derechos lesbianos)*; sexual rights

Hoyt, Katherine, 186n41

Humanas ([Female] Humans), 22, 130, 150–57, *151, 153*

human rights: overview of, 6, 8, 10–12, 175nn17–18; activism in context of, 3, 4; antisodomy law and, 176n26; liberalism and, 3, 4, 10, 11–12, 25–26, 173n3; politics and, 11–12, 37, 47–49, 175n19, 182nn14–15; postrevolutionary era and, 47–49; Sandinismo era and, 37, 182nn14–15; SFFP and, 99, 101–3, *102*, 110–11; women's rights as, 170, 195n13. *See also* gender rights; homosexual rights *(derechos homosexuales)*; lesbian rights *(derechos lesbianos)*; sexual rights; women and women's rights

identity politics: desire in context of lesbians and, 67–70, 72, 76–77, 82–85; feminists and, 120, 192n26; Lesbian and Gay Pride and, 110; lesbians and, 14, 67–70, 72, 75–85, 87, 89–91, 120, 189n17, 192n26; Marxism and, 14, 87, 89; NGOS and, 119, 192n24; overview of, 3, 15; socioeconomics and, 14, 121

Iglesia Metropolitana Comunitaria (Metropolitan Community Church), 99, 190n5

"imagined community" link through mass media, 131, 192n6

imperialism, of U.S., 26–29, 37–38, 54, 180n3. *See also* anti-imperialism, and Sandino

incest, 9, 39, 56, 58, *58*

indigenous and/or African descent peoples *(costeños)*, 128, 192n2

indigenous populations, 43, 50–51, 125, 128, 182nn13–14, 182n15, 192n2, 192n27

individuals or groups, as funding sources, 74, 99, 107

institutions, as funding sources, 8, 48

internacionalistas, 7, 174n10. *See also* transnationalism

internal divisions, in Nicaragua, 34, 182n13

International Monetary Fund, 8, 52

Internet. *See* digital information and technology

intersex (*intersexual*), 166, 176n20. *See also* LGBTTIQQAA (lesbian, gay, bisexual, transgender, transvestite, intersex, queer, questioning, (queer) ally, and asexual)

intimate instruction, 87, 89, 91. *See also* lesbian discussion groups

Jackson, Jean E., 169

Jornada por una Sexualidad Libre de Prejuicios (Gathering for Sexuality Free from Prejudice), 52, 92–93, 98, 99, 106, 109, 120. *See also* Sexuality Free from Prejudice or Sexualidad Libre de Prejuicios (SFFP)

Kampwirth, Karen, 59, 187n46, 187n50, 194n29

Klimt, Gustav, 150, *154*

Kulick, Don, 195n7

La Caimana (Carmelo, Aguirre, Carmen, Carlos), 33, 181n10

Lancaster, Roger N., 18–19, 176n25, 177n30, 184n29

Latin America: global interconnectivity and, 171; lesbian identity accusations against feminists and, 120, 192n26; lesbians and terms of use in, 179n36; mass media influences in, 129, 192n3; Mediterranean model of male sexuality and, 178n31; sexuality in, 180n41; sexual rights activists/advocates in, 13. *See also* global discourse; the global South; *and specific countries*

Lesbian and Gay Pride (Orgullo Lésbico-Gay): antisodomy law opposition by, 108; events and, 97, 107–8, 111–12, *113*, 114, 191nn13–14; funding sources and, 107, 109; groups as supporters of, 107; homophobia and, 108; identity politics and, 110; Marxist values of praxis and, 1–2, 109; order of terms and, 108, 190n9; poetry readings and, 107, 190n8; pride and, 5, 45, 75, 77–79, 124–25; sexual minority politics and, 110–11; SFFP comparison with, 93–94,

97–98, 108–11; terms or vocabularies and, 108–9, 110; transvestite or cross-dressing contests and, 111–12, *113*, 114, 191nn13–14

lesbian discussion groups: overview of, 17, 20–21, 61–63, 90–91, 167, 188n1; attendance issues and, 64–66, 188n6; autological discourse and, 90, 189n17; *bien educada* and, 61–63, 188n2; consciousness for lesbians and, 14, 61–63, 75, 89, 91; consciousness-raising groups and, 62–63, 75, 89, *100*, 188n8; desire in context of identity and, 67–70, 72, 76–77, 82–85; education of desire and, 21, 62, 85–87; facilitators for, 62–63, 64, 66–70, 76, 81, 88–91, 188n1; femininity and, 73–74, 82–84, 189n15; funding sources and, 80, 188n1; gender rights and, 75–76; gender roles and, 67, 70–74, 82–85, 189n15; grassroots activism and, 62, 74–77; *hombruna* identity and, 82–84; identity politics in, 14, 75–84, 87, 89–91, 189n17; intimate instruction and, 87, 89, 91; *lesbiana* as construction and, 63–64; liberalism and, 17, 68–70, 81, 85, 87–90; Marxism and, 14, 87, 89; masculinity in context of public recognition and, 73–74; NGOs and, 63–74; pedagogical dynamics and, 66, 68–70, 74, 76, 79, 81, 84–85, 87–91, 189n16; pride and, 75, 77–79; rural grassroots activism and, 81–87, 189nn13–16; sexual choice and, 66–70; sexual identity development of individuals and, 75–84, 90–91, 189n17; sexual orientation and, 66–69; sexual subjects in country/rural locations and, 85–87; socioeconomics and, 62, 88, 188n2; solidarity practices and, 66; subaltern counterpublics and, 65–66, 188nn7–8; transnationalism and, 64, 73–74, 76, 81, 88

lesbian rights (*derechos lesbianos*), 5–6, 19–20, 39–40, 90, 103–4, 173n5, 183n21. *See also* homosexual rights; human rights; sexual rights lesbians *(lesbianas)*: clandestine activities and, 65–66; as construction, 63–64; country/rural locations or country/folk and, 82–83, 85–87; discrimination against, 63, 72, 74, 98; egalitarian model of sexuality for, 20, 89, 146–47; employment in context of gender presentation for, 189n15; femininity and, 73–74, 82–84, 139–41, 143, 177n30, 189n15; funding sources and, 120–21, 192n27; gender performance and, 143, 145; gender roles and, 19, 84–85; HIV/AIDS prevention and education and, 120, 192n25; identity politics and, 14, 67–70, 72, 75–85, 87, 89–91, 120, 189n17, 192n26; marriage and divorce in context of sexuality for, 104–5, 190n6; mass media portrayal of, 134, 194n11; normalization of, 141–43, 145–47; outness of, 120–23, 141–43, 192n26; overview of, 18–20, 179nn36–39, 180n41; print media publications and, 22, 130; in public sphere, 73–74; queerness and, 73, 140–41, 146; during Sandinismo, 104–5, 190nn6–7; scholarship on, 19, 180n41; sexual rights for, 13; as sexual subjects, 85–87, 143; stereotypical, 134, 143, 145–47; *telenovela* characters and, 134, 138–47, *144*; as term of use, 2, 19, 174n8; visibility and, 18, 22, 45, 73–74, 122–23. *See also* gay men *(gays/homosexuales)*; LGBTQ (lesbian, gay, bisexual, transgender, and queer); LGBTTIQQAA (lesbian, gay, bisexual, transgender, transvestite, intersex, queer, questioning, (queer) ally, and asexual)

Lesbian Visibility Group (Grupo por la Visibilidad Léésbica), 22, 130, 150–57, *151, 153*

lesbofobia, 63, 166

Lewinsky, Monica, 55, 185n37

LGBTQ (lesbian, gay, bisexual, transgender, and queer): overview of, 15, 166, 176n20, 195n7; terms of use and, 15, 108, 166, 174n8, 176n20, 190n10, 195n7; violence against, 15, 56, 71, 160–61, 176nn25–26, 186n41. *See*

also bisexual/s; gay men *(gays/homosexuales)*; lesbians *(lesbianas)*; violence

LGBTTIQQAA (lesbian, gay, bisexual, transgender, transvestite, intersex, queer, questioning, (queer) ally, and asexual), 15, 166, 176n20, 195n7. *See also* bisexual/s; gay men *(gays/homosexuales)*; lesbians *(lesbianas)*; violence

"liberal diaspora," 4, 173n3, 173n4

liberalism, 156; discrimination as antithetical to, 105; human rights and, 3, 4, 10, 11–12, 25–26, 173n3; lesbian discussion groups and, 17, 68–70, 81, 85, 87–90; "liberal diaspora" and, 4, 173n3; sexual choice and, 68, 104; sexual rights and, 11–12, 25–26; SFFP and, 104–6. *See also* egalitarian model of sexuality

loca (crazy, queen, queer), 17, 136, 138

locality, and mass media, 132, 144, 155–56, *155–56*, 193n8

long-sleeve *(mangas largas)* shirts as symbol of female masculinity, 19

lucha (struggle): continuum from revolution to, 4, 14; movement in context of, 12–14, 166, 176nn20–21; outness in context of, 21, 93, 122–27; sexual identity categories and, 17. *See also* sexual rights activists/advocates

machismo, 5, 12, 17, 177n30. *See also* masculinity; men

"macho" *(machista)*, 17, 33, 72, 177n30, 181n10

Manalansan, Martin F., IV, 18

mangas largas (long-sleeve) shirts as symbol of female masculinity, 19

mannish or manly *(hombruna)*, 19, 82–84, 179n37

mannish women *(masculinas)*, 19, 73–74, 177n30, 179n38. *See also* femininity *(femenina)*; gender roles; machismo; men

maricón (fag), 17, 138. *See also* cochones, cochón (fags, fag)

marimacha (popular term for dyke), 179n36

marriages and divorce, for lesbians, 104–5, 190n6

Marx, Karl and Marxism: overview of, 1–2; postrevolutionary era and, 9–10, 12; Sandinismo era and, 3, 28, 34–37, 40–43; SFFP and, 106

masculinas (mannish women), 19, 73–74, 177n30, 179n38. *See also* femininity *(femenina)*; gender roles; machismo; men

masculinity, and gender roles, 19, 73–74, 177n30

masking, 152–53

mass media: antisodomy law and, 151; celebrity status and, 131, 193n7; clandestine activities and, 148–50; digital technology and, 9, 129, 131, 147–48, 155–56, 158–59, 194n16; education and, 129, 132, 193n9; effeminate gay men and, 134; focus groups and the girl next door, 138–45, *140, 144*; global discourse and, 150, *152*, 153, *153*, 155–56; "imagined community" link through, 131, 192n6; lesbian characters and, 134, 194n11; locality and, 155–56; neoliberalism and, 155; outness and, 152–54; overview of, 21–22, 129–31, 156–59, 170, 192nn3–6, 194n18; print media and, 22, 130, 150–55, *152, 153*, 157–58, 193n6; radio and, 21–22, 50, 98, 99, 130, 147–50, 157–58; Sandinismo era and, 129–30, 193n5; sexual subjects and, 130–31; SFFP and, 98–99, 101–2; Somoza era and, 129–30, 193n5; sonoscapes and, 147, 149; U.S. films or television programs and, 9, 51, 129–30, 132, 193n5, 193n9; visibility and, 22, 130–31. *See also* dialogic relationship; public sphere; *Sexto Sentido (Sixth Sense)* [telenovela]

Mayorga, Silvio, 181n11. *See also* Frente Sandinista de Liberación Nacional (FSLN); FSLN (Frente Sandinista de Liberación Nacional)

Mediterranean model of male sexuality, 17–18, 178nn31–33

men, and sexuality, 17–18, 177n30, 178nn31–34, 180n41. *See also* gay men *(gays/homosexuales)*; homosexuality; machismo; masculinity

methodology and research, 6–7, 174n11

Metropolitan Community Church (Iglesia Metropolitana Comunitaria), 99, 190n5

Mexico, 26, 122, 125, 132, 137, 161, 163, 180n3, 192n3

Mogrovejo, Norma, 19, 122

Monicagate, 55, 185n37

Morales Henríquez, Viktor, 31–32

morals: religious influences on, 9, 39, 53–54, 57–58, 59–60, 165; sexual and moral impropriety in political histories and, 31–36, 55, 175n14, 181n7, 185n34, 185n37; sexual rights activism in context of, 8–9, 175nn14; of *telenovela* characters, 137, 143–44, 194n13

movement, in context of *lucha*, 12–14, 166, 176nn20–21

Movimiento Autónomo de Mujeres (Autonomous Women's Movement), 8, 49–50

Los muchachos no lloran (Boys Don't Cry) [film], 70–74, 189nn10–11

Murillo, Rosario, 55, 57–58

muy mujer or *femenina* (very womanish), 19, 179n38

Nameless Youth Program (*Programa Joven sin Nombre*) [radio program], 149–50

Narváez, Zoilamérica, 54–56, 185n37, 186nn40–41

nationalism, and Sandinismo era, 28, 34, 121

neoliberalism, 48, 52–54, 56, 155, 184n29. *See also* social conservatism

The New Daily (El Nuevo Diario), 9, 183n22

Newton, Ester, 118

NGOs (nongovernmental organizations): funding sources and, 8, 48, 119–20; gendering power in context of *concurso travesti* and, 118; lesbian discussion groups and, 63–74; outness and, 121–22, 123; overview of, 6, 8–9; postrevolutionary era activism and, 8–9, 48–52. *See also specific* NGOs

Nicaraguan Transgender Association (Asociación Nicaragüense de Transgénera), 164 nongovernmental organizations (NGOs). *See* NGOs (nongovernmental organizations)

normalization *(normalidad)*, 110, 135–36, 141–43, 145–47

North. *See* global discourse; global North; global South

El Nuevo Diario (The New Daily), 9, 183n22

Ombudsperson's Office for the Defense of Sexual Diversity Rights, 164–65

organizations, as funding sources, 99, 154, 190n5

Orgullo Lésbico-Gay (Lesbian and Gay Pride). *See* Lesbian and Gay Pride (Orgullo Lésbico-Gay)

orientación sexual (sexual orientation), 66–69

Ortega, Daniel, 9, 57, 57–60, 183n18, 185n34, 185n37, 186nn40–41, 187n43. *See also* Sandinismo (Sandinista Revolution)

outness *(declaración)*: under antisodomy law, 121–22; feminism and, 120, 192n26; of gay men, 119–22, 137–38; the global North model for, 122–23; groups and, 121–22; HIV/AIDS prevention and education in context of, 125, 192n29; of lesbians, 120–23, 141–43, 192n26; *lucha* in context of, 21, 93, 122–27; masking and, 152–53; NGOs and, 121–22, 123; overview of, 5, 15, 21, 93–94; print media, 152–54; Sandinismo era and, 44–45; *telenovela* and, 137–38, 141–43; visibility and, 122–23. *See also* public sphere; *and specific groups and organizations*

Out of the Closet (Fuera del Closet) [magazine], 12, 51, 64, 77, 98, 100, 190n4

Overcoming Together (Venceremos Juntas), 81–83, 86–87, 189n13

pasiva female partners, 19, 84. *See also* lesbians *(lesbianas)*

pasivo male partners, 17, 178n32. *See also* gay men *(gays/homosexuales)*

patrimony, and Sandino, 27, 27–29, 28, 34, 181n11

pedagogy: lesbian discussion groups dynamics and, 66, 68–70, 74, 76, 79, 81, 84–85, 87–91, 189n16; public school materials and, 53

personal or private experience, 3–4, 36, 52, 93, 126, 138, 171. *See also* consciousness

poetry and poetry readings, 107, 190n8

political histories in context of sexual rights: abortion controversy and, 39, 48, 53, 54, 57–59, 58, 187n48, 187n50; Alemán administration and, 52–54, 56, 186n41; Catholic church as moral influence and, 53–54, 57–58, 59–60; Chamorro administration and, 3, 47, 49, 52, 54, 184nn28–29; Christian fundamentalism and, 8–9, 48, 53; conservatives and liberals political power grabs and, 27; electoral politics and scandals in context of sexual abuse and, 54–56, 185n37, 186nn40–41; feminism and, 29–30, 40, 51, 55–56, 58, 58–59, 183nn19–20, 185n37, 187n46; FSLN and, 34–41, 54, 55, 58–59, 89, 181n11, 182n14, 183nn19–20; gender rights and, 39–41, 50, 56, 183nn19–21; homosexual rights and, 32–33, 35, 181n10; human rights and, 37, 47–49, 182nn14–15; internal divisions and, 34, 182n13; moral and sexual impropriety and, 8, 31–36, 175n14, 181n7, 185n34, 185n37; neoliberalism and, 48, 52–54, 56, 184n29; NGOs activism and, 8–9, 48–52; overview of, 20, 23–26, 60; pedagogical materials for public schools and, 53; re-"feminized" women and, 47, 194n29; Sandinista Renovation Movement and, 50, 185n34; Sandino's anti-imperialism and patrimony and, 27, 27–29, 28, 34, 181n11; sex industry and, 30–31, 35, 44, 181n6, 184n25; sexual abuse issues and, 54–56, 185n37, 186nn40–41; sexuality in modernity and, 9, 175n15; social conservatism and, 46–47, 57; Somoza era and, 29–36, 129–30, 181nn5–7, 181nn10–11, 181n11, 185n37, 193n5; therapeutic abortion provision and,

57–59, 187n50; U.S. imperialism and, 26–29, 37–38, 54, 180n3; violence and, 56, 186n41; women's rights and, 55–56; women's role in, 29–32; youth activism and, 50. *See also* antisodomy law (Article 204); Sandinismo (Sandinista Revolution); *and specific NGOs, political groups, and political leaders*

politics: electoral, 27, 54–56, 185n37, 186nn40–41; human rights and, 11–12, 37, 47–49, 175n19, 182nn14–15; personal or private experience interactions with, 36, 171; sexual rights activists/advocates in context of, 8–9, 171, 175nn14; sexual rights activists political models and, 4–5, 173n4; women as political subjects and, 39, 183n17; women's participation in, 29–32, 58, 183n16

postrevolutionary era: abortion controversy during, 48, 53, 54, 57–59, *58*, 187n48, 187n50; Alemán administration during, 52–54, 56, 186n41; antifeminist rhetoric and maternalist discourse during, 47, 194n29; anti-imperialism and, 56–57, 187n43; antisodomy law repeal during, 59–60, 187n50; Catholic church as moral influence during, 53–54, 57–58, 59–60; Chamorro administration during, 47, 49, 52, 54, 184nn28–29; Christian fundamentalism and, 53–54, 165; communitarian politics during, 11, 183nn19–20; Contras campaign during, 47, 182n14, 184n29; culture transformation and, 11, 45–46, 184n27; electoral politics and scandals in context of sexual abuse during, 9, 54–56, 185n37, 186nn40–41; feminism during, *51*, 55–56, *58*, 58–59, 183nn19–20, 185n37, 187n46; fiscal terrorism and, 175n13; gay men during, 45, 183n21; gender rights during, 50, 56, 183nn19–20, 183n21; the global North as viewed during, 183n22; HIV/AIDS prevention and education during, 51, 184nn23–24; homosexuality versus traditional values during, 183n22; homosexual

rights during, 183n18, 183nn21–22, 184nn23–24, 184n27; human rights during, 47–49, 182nn14–15; indigenous population treatment during, 182nn13–14; Marxism and, 9–10, 12; moral and sexual impropriety during, 55, 175n14, 185n34; neoliberalism during, 48, 52–54, 56, 184n29; NGO activism during, 8–9, 48–52; "out" sexual politics during, 44–45; party politics and, 56, 185n34, 186n41; pedagogical materials for public schools during, 53; political context for activism during, 175n14; re-"feminized" women during, 47, 194n29; Sandinismo era and, 56, 175n14, 182n13, 185n34, 186n41; sex industry during, 184n25; sexual rights during, 183n18; social conservatism in during, 46–47, 57; social theories and, 9–10; therapeutic abortion provision during, 57–59, *58*, 187n50; violence during, 56, 186n41; women and, 58, 183n16, 183nn16–20, 183n17, 183n19; women's rights during, 55–56, 183nn16–20; youth activism during, 50. *See also specific NGOs, political organizations and political leaders*

Povinelli, Elizabeth, 4, 69, 173n4, 189n17

power: development schema and, 155, 194n15; gendering, 116–18

praxis values, and Marxism, 1–2, 109

pride *(orgullo)*, 5, 45, 75, 77–79, 124–25. *See also* Lesbian and Gay Pride (Orgullo Lésbico-Gay)

print media, 22, 130, 150–55, *152*, *153*, 157–58, 193n6. *See also* mass media

private or personal experience, 3–4, 36, 52, 93, 126, 138, 171. *See also* consciousness

production, of *Sexto Sentido* television show, 131–32

Programa Joven sin Nombre (Nameless Youth Program) [radio program], 149–50

prostitution (sex industry), 30–31, 35, 44, 119, 181n6, 184n25

public sphere: *concurso travesti* and, 111–12, *113*, 114, 116–18, 191nn13–14; *danza* and, 116; "drag" performances

public sphere (*continued*)
by *travestis* and, 93, 94, 111–16, *113*, *114*,
191nn13–14, 191nn13–15; effeminate
gay men and, 23–24, 134–37, 191n21;
employment in context of gender presentation and, 119, 189n15, 191n22;
epistemic work of sexual rights activists and, 124–27, 192nn30–31; femininity in context of *travestis* and,
115–16; gendering power in context
of *concurso travesti* and, 116–18; lesbians and, 73–74; liberalism trope and,
126; overview of, 5, 21, 92–98, 167, 171,
190nn1–3; personal or private experience interactions with, 3, 93, 126, 171;
pride display during Sandinismo era
and, 45; socioeconomics of "drag" and,
111, 191n13; visibility and, 122–23. *See
also* mass media
Puntos de Encuentro (Common Ground),
50–51, 99, 128, 132–33, 149, 174n11,
193n10, 194n16. *See also Sexto Sentido
(Sixth Sense)* [telenovela]

(queer) ally, as term of use, 15, 166,
176n20, 195n7
queer/s and queerness: lesbians and, 73;
LGBTTIQQA and, 15, 166, 176n20,
195n7; queer theory and, 110; SFFP
and, 110; *telenovela* and, 135–36, 138,
140–41, 146; as term of use, 174n8; in
U.S., 15, 162. *See also* LGBTQ (lesbian,
gay, bisexual, transgender, and queer)
questioning, as term of use, 15, 166,
176n20, 195n7

radio, 21–22, 50, 98, 99, 130, 147–50, 153–
55, 157–58. *See also* mass media
"Rambo" (The Unknown Soldier or "El
Guerrillero sin Nombre") statue, 96,
96
Randall, Margaret, 183n16
rape, 9, 31–32, 34–35, 38–39, 56–58, 161,
185n37, 186n40
real men (*hombres hombres*), 115, 136,
178n32, 179n38
re-"feminized" women, 40, 47, 183n19,
194n29. *See also* femininity (*femenina*)

religion/s: Metropolitan Community
Church and, 99, 190n5; as moral influence, 8–9, 39, 48, *53*, 53–54, 57–58,
59–60, 165; Sandinismo era and, 34.
See also Catholic church
reproductive rights. *See* abortion controversy; women and women's rights
research and methodology, 6–7, 174n11
revolution, and continuum to sexual
rights, 4, 9–12, 14. *See also* postrevolutionary era; Sandinismo (Sandinista
Revolution)
rural grassroots activism, and lesbian discussion groups, 81–87, 189nn13–16. *See
also* grassroots activism, and lesbian
discussion groups

Saldaña-Portillo, María Josefina, 175n19
Salud y Sexualidad (Health and Sexuality)
[magazine], 9, 175n15
Sandinismo (Sandinista Revolution): abortion controversy during, 39; activism
in context of, 5–6; bisexual rights and,
43; Catholic church as moral influence
during, 39; Christian fundamentalism
and, 8–9; communitarian politics during, 40–41; Contras campaign during,
37–38, 47, 182n14, 184n29; equality or
egalitarianism and social projects during, 36–37, 40; feminism during, 40,
41; FSLN and, 34–41, 54–55, 58–59,
89, 181n11, 182n14, 183nn19–20; gay
men during, 42–43; gender rights during, 39–40, 40–41; the global North
as viewed during, 42–44; HIV/AIDS
prevention and education during, 44,
51, 184nn23–24; homosexuality versus traditional values during, 42–44;
homosexual rights during, 35–36,
39–40, 41–46; human rights during,
37, 182nn14–15; indigenous population
treatment during, 43; *lesbianas* during, 104–5, 190nn6–7; lesbian rights
during, 39–40, 103–4, 183n21; literacy
rates during, 35; marriages and divorces for lesbians during, 104–5, 190n6;
Marxism and, 3, 28, 34–37, 40–43;
mass media and, 129–30, 193n5; moral

and sexual impropriety of Somocismo and, 34–36; nationalism context for activism during, 34; nationalist motives during, 28, 34, 121; Ortega and, 9, 57, 57–60, 183n18, 185n34, 185n37, 186nn40–41, 187n43; outness and, 44–45; political context for activism during, 34, 42–43; popular support for project of, 34, 182n13; pride display during, 45; religious context for activism during, 34; sex industry during, 35, 44, 184n25; socioeconomics and, 7–8, 34, 40, 183n20; therapeutic abortion provision during, 38–39; thick experience and, 7; visibility and, 45; women and women's rights during, 35–36, 38–40, 120, 183nn16–20

Sandinista Renovation Movement, 50, 185n34

Sandino, Augusto César, 27, 27–29, 28, 34, 108, 181n11

Scott, Hilda, 33, 181n10

sex industry (prostitution), 30–31, 35, 44, 119, 181n6, 184n25

Sexto Sentido (Sixth Sense) [telenovela]: audiences and, 132, 193n8; celebrity status and, 131, 193n7; characters in, 132, 193n8; consciousness and, 133, 138–39; cultural transformation role of, 130, 132–33; culture transformation and, 130, 132–33; dialogic relationship between characters and viewers and, 133, 193n10; discrimination and, 132, 135, 146; effeminate gay men and, 134–37, 191n21; egalitarian model of sexuality in, 136–37, 145–47, 194n12; femininity of lesbian character in, 139–41, 143; funding sources for, 128, 132, 192n1; gay character in, 135–38, 145–47, 194n12, 194n13; gender performance of characters and, 136, 138, 143, 145; global discourse and, 156, 194n16; homosexuality as covert and, 137–38; lesbian character in, 134, 138–47, *144*; locality and, 132, 144, 155–56, 193n8; moral gay character in, 137, 194n13; morally risqué lesbian character and, 143–44, 194n13; normalization of

homosexuality and, 135–36, 141–43, 145–47; outness and, 137–38, 141–43; overview of, 128–29, 130, *146*, 155–58, 192n2; personal or private experience and, 138; production and, 131–32; queerness and, 135–36, 138, 140–41, 146; sexual scripts and, 145; sexual subjects and, 133, 137, 143, 146–47; socioeconomics and, 193n8; stereotypes and, 134, 145–47; visibility and, 145, 148; youth activism and, 129. *See also* mass media

sexual abuse, childhood, 54–56, 143–44, 185n37, 186nn40–41

sexual and moral impropriety, in political histories, 31–36, 55, 175n14, 181n7, 185n34, 185n37. *See also* morals

sexual asylum case, 160–62, 171

sexual choice or choice *(opción sexual)*, 66–70, 103–4

Sexual Diversity Initiative for Human Rights (Grupo Safo, the Iniciativa desde La Diversidad Sexual por los Derechos Humanos), 164

sexual health and behavior, 170–71, 196n14. *See also* abortion controversy; HIV/AIDS prevention and education

sexual identity categories, 16–17, 167

sexual identity development, of individuals, 75–84, 90–91, 189n17. *See also* consciousness

sexuality: in modernity, 9, 175n15; overview of, 16–18, 178nn31–35, 179n36–39, 180n41; scholarship on, 19, 180n41; sexual scripts and, 18, 145, 178n34

Sexuality Free from Prejudice or Sexualidad Libre de Prejuicios (SFFP): antisodomy law opposition by, 94, 97–98, 99, 106–7, 109; culture transformation and, 101–3, *102*, 109–10, 190n11; events and, 45–46, 49, 94, *95*, *96*, 96–99; funding for, 99; Gathering for Sexuality Free from Prejudice and, *52*, 92–93, 98, 99, 106, 109, 120; homosexual rights and, 106; human rights and, 99, 101–3, *102*, 110–11; Lesbian and Gay Pride comparison with, 93–94, 97–98, 108–11; liberalism and,

Sexuality Free from Prejudice (*continued*)
104–6; marriages and divorces for
lesbians and, 104–5, 190n6; Marxism
and, 106; mass media and, 98–99, 101–
2; normalization and, 110; organizational support for, 99, 190n5; overview
of, 11, 98, 109–10, 190n11; queer politics and, 110; radio shows and, 98, 99;
sexual choice and, 103–4; sexual minority politics and, 99, 100–101, 103,
109–10; sexual rights and, 103–4, 106,
190n7; solidarity practices and, 93,
190n2; transvestite or cross-dressing
contests and, 111–12, *113*, 114, 191nn13–
14; *travestis* and, 94, 114, 116–17; visibility and, 154. *See also* outness (*declaración*); public sphere
sexual minority politics, 45, 99, 100–101,
103, 109–10, 110–11, 126
sexual orientation (*orientación sexual*),
66–69
sexual rights, 15–17, 176n21. *See also* gender rights; homosexual rights (*derechos
homosexuales*); human rights; lesbian
rights (*derechos lesbianos*)
sexual rights activists/advocates: Christian
fundamentalism and, 8–9; civil society
in context of, 6–8, 174n9; continuum
from revolution to, 9–12; culture transformation and, 1–2; epistemic work
in, 124–27, 192nn30–31; *internacionalistas* and, 7, 42, 50, 174n10; moral
context for, 8–9, 175nn14; overview of,
1–4, 6, 174n7; political context for, 5,
8–9, 175nn14; as term of use, 6, 173n6;
terms of use by activists and, 6, 174n8;
thick experience and, 7. *See also lucha*
(struggle); sexual rights
sexual scripts, 18, 145, 178n34
sexual subject/s: *cochonas* as, 2, 19, 174n8,
179n36, 179n39; *cochones* as, 2, 6,
174n8; country/rural locations or coun-
try/folk and, 82–83, 85–87, 137–38;
mass media and, 130–31, 133, 137, 143,
146–47; normalization of, 137, 146–47
SFFP (Sexuality Free from Prejudice or
Sexualidad Libre de Prejuicios). *See*

outness (*declaración*); public sphere;
Sexuality Free from Prejudice or
Sexualidad Libre de Prejuicios (SFFP)
Shomos (We Are Homos), 119–21, 174n11,
184n24, 191n21
Sin Máscaras (Without Masks) [radio
show], 21–22, 130, 147–49, 153
soap opera (*telenovela*). *See Sexto Sentido
(Sixth Sense)* [telenovela]
social change. *See* culture transformation
social conservatism, 46–47, 57. *See also*
neoliberalism
social theory, 9–10, 175n16
socioeconomics: of "drag" performances,
111, 191n13; fiscal terrorism and, 8–9,
175n13; identity politics and, 14, 121;
lesbian discussion groups and, 62, 88,
188n2; Sandinismo and, 7–8, 14, 34,
40, 183n20
solidarity practices, 66, 93, 190n2
Somoza era (Somocismo era), 29–36,
129–30, 181nn5–7, 181nn10–11, 185n37,
193n5. *See also* political histories in
context of sexual rights; Sandinismo
(Sandinista Revolution)
sonoscapes, and radio programs, 147, 149
South, 3, 13, 18–19, 108–9, 155–56, 167,
171, 176n21. *See also* global discourse;
global North; Latin America; *and specific countries*
stereotypes, in mass media, 134, 145–47
subaltern counterpublics, 65–66, 188nn7–
8

telenovela (soap opera). *See Sexto Sentido
(Sixth Sense)* [telenovela]
television shows. *See specific television
shows*
Téllez, Dora María, 38, 44, 47, 179n39,
185n34
Thayer, Millie, 45
therapeutic abortion provision (Article
165), 39, 57–59, *58*, 187n50
Torovenado, 111, *113*
traditional values versus homosexuality,
42–44, 183n22
transfobia, 166

transgender *(transgénero)*, 15, 72, 166, 174n8, 176n20, 195n7. *See also* LGBTQ (lesbian, gay, bisexual, transgender, and queer)

transnationalism: *internacionalistas* and, 7, 174n10; lesbian discussion groups and, 64, 73–74, 76, 81, 88; "liberal diaspora" and, 4, 173n3, 173n4. *See also* global discourse

transsexual, as term of use, 166, 174n8

transvestite or cross-dressing contest *(concurso travesti)*, 111–12, *113*, 114, 191nn13–14

travestis (biological men who wear women's clothing): *concurso travesti* and, 111–12, *113*, 114, 191nn13–14; *danza* and, 116; "drag" performances by, 93, 94, 111–16, *113*, *114*, 191nn13–14, 191nn13–15; femininity and, 115–16; gendering power and, 116–18; LGBT-TIQQA and, 15, 166, 176n20, 195n7; as term of use, 174n8, 176n20; *transfobia* and, 166

Ugly Betty (Betty la Fea) [television show], 9, 51

Unified National Opposition (UNO) Party, 47, 184n28

United Nations Decade for Women, 170, 195n13

United States: CIA and, 37, 47; clandestine sexual activities in, 178n33; development schema and, 155, 194n15; effeminate gay men in mass media and, 134, 194n11; feminist consciousness-raising groups in, 62–63, 89; global interconnectivity and, 171; imperialism of, 26–29, 37–38, 54, 129–30, 180n3, 193n5; lesbians in, 134, 192n26, 194n11; mass media programs from, 9, 51, 129–30, 132, 193n5, 193n9; queerness in, 15, 162; sexual asylum case in, 160–62, 171; transgender in, 72; violence in, 15, 71. *See also* global North

U.S. Agency for International Development (USAID), 52, 128, 132, 155–56, 192n1

U.S. Contras (Frente Democrática Nicaragüense) campaign, 37–38, 47, 182n14, 184n29

The Unknown Soldier ("El Guerrillero sin Nombre" or "Rambo") statue, 96, *96*

UNO (Unified National Opposition) Party, 47, 184n28

Valentine, David, 168

Venceremos Juntas (Overcoming Together), 81–83, 86–87, 189n13

violence: childhood sexual abuse and, 54–56, 143–44, 185n37, 186nn40–41; incest and, 9, 39, 56, 58; against LGBTQ people, 15, 56, 71, 160–61, 163–64, 176nn25–26, 186n41; rape and, 9, 31–32, 34–35, 38–39, 56–58, 161, 185n37, 186n40; visibility in context of, 162

visibility *(visibilidad)*: gay men and, 45, 122; lesbians and, 18, 22, 45, 73–74, 122–23; mass media and, 22, 130–31, 145, 148, 150, 152–55; outness and, 122–23; violence in context of, 162

Walker, William, 27

Warren, Kay B., 13, 115, 125, 169, 192n3

We Are Homos (Colectivo Shomos), 119–21, 174n11, 184n24, 191n21

well-mannered and well-educated *(bien educada)*, 61–63, 188n2. *See also* lesbian discussion groups

womanish, very *(femena* or *muy mujer)*, 19, 179n38

women and women's rights: discrimination against, 26, 29–32, 35, 40–41; education access for, 29, 35, 36; femininity and, 40, 47, 177n30, 183n19, 194n29; human rights and, 170, 195n13; moral and sexual impropriety in politics and, 8, 31–36, 175n14, 181n7, 185n34, 185n37; political participation by, 29–32, 58, 183n16; as political subjects, 39, 183n17; postrevolutionary era and, 40, 47, 55–56, 58, 183nn16–20, 194n29; rape of, 9, 31–32, 34–35, 38–39, 56–58, 185n37, 186n40; as

women and women's rights (*continued*)
re-"feminized," 40, 47, 183n19, 194n29;
during Sandinismo era, 35–36, 38–40,
120, 183nn16–20; Somocismo era and,
29–32; therapeutic abortion provision
and, 39, 57–59, *58*, 187n50. *See also*
abortion controversy; feminism; lesbians (*lesbianas*)

Women's Network against Violence, 6
World Bank, 8, 52
Wright, Timothy, 192n29

Xochiquetzal (Aztec goddess), 52, 77, 79.
See also Fundación Xochiquetzal

youth activism, 50, 129, 149–50